THE
FLY
FISHER'S
READER

LEONARD M. WRIGHT JR., ed.

A FIRESIDE BOOK
PUBLISHED BY SIMON & SCHUSTER INC.
New York London Toronto Sydney Tokyo Singapore

F

SIMON AND SCHUSTER/FIRESIDE
SIMON & SCHUSTER BUILDING
ROCKEFELLER CENTER
1230 AVENUE OF THE AMERICAS
NEW YORK, NEW YORK 10020

SIMON AND SCHUSTER, FIRESIDE AND COLOPHON ARE
REGISTERED TRADEMARKS OF SIMON & SCHUSTER INC.

DESIGNED BY DIANE STEVENSON/SNAP·HAUS GRAPHICS
MANUFACTURED IN THE UNITED STATES OF AMERICA

10 9 8 7 6 5 4 3 2 1
10 9 8 7 6 5 4 3 2 1 (PBK.)

Library of Congress Cataloging-in-Publication Data

The Fly fisher's reader: an unabashedly biased sampling of Angling's
finest literature / [edited by] Leonard Wright.
p.   cm.
A collection of reprints of articles and stories originally published from
1881 to 1989.
"A Fireside book."
Includes bibliographical references.
1. Fly fishing.   2. Fishes.   I. Wright, Leonard M.
SH456.F585   1990
799.1'2-dc20   89-28695
                                                                CIP

ISBN 0-671-70174-6
      0-671-68206-7 (PBK.)

"Frequent Fliers" by Bill Barich. *California Magazine*, April 1989.
Copyright © 1989 by Bill Barich. Reprinted by permission of the author.

"The Priest's Omnibus" by T. C. Kingsmill Moore. From *A Man May
Fish*. Copyright © 1960 by T. C. Kingsmill Moore. Reprinted by permission of Colin Smythe, Gerrads Cross, Bucks, England.

CONTENTS

Preface

Contents

Contents

Contents

PREFACE

To limit a collection of stories and articles to those about fishing with an artificial fly may appear, at first glance, to be cutting a very thin slice out of sporting literature. On closer examination, however, I think you'll find the opposite to be true. Fishing has produced a library that dwarfs that of any other sport, and the fly-fishing sections of these shelves contain the vast majority of quality books.

This volume's Contents points up this embarrassment of riches. Some of the most famous books and authors are not represented here. These omissions are in no way meant as a judgment of, or slight to, any authors. It's just that there are so many top-flight ones that they couldn't all be crammed into a single book.

Similarly, some of the best-known, best-loved fishing pieces don't appear here either. The reason for this is that they have already been anthologized—some of them several times. A book of reruns can be a treasure. But reruns of reruns would be redundant.

A great many books on fishing, including some sampled here, are devoted to teaching the reader how to catch more fish. That is not the aim of this collection. However, it would be hard, indeed, to read selections from Gordon, Hewitt, La Branche, Skues, or Fox, to name just a few, without picking up a pointer or two.

The purpose of this book, like that of most anthologies, is to give you a taste of some of the finest works in the field. It gives you a sampling of a wide variety of books—many of which you may then want to read in their entirety.

Another advantage of an anthology is that you don't have to wade through an entire volume to reach the surprise ending or the juiciest passages. You can read as little, or as much, as you like at a sitting without being left dan-gling. The pieces in this book range from a few hundred words to several thousand in length. Again, the Contents tells you the amount of reading you're taking on, and I've added short blurbs to each title to tell you the type of fish story you'll be getting into.

I hope you'll meet some new authors through this book. I'm certain you'll experience some new types of fly-fishing. You couldn't possibly have visited all the areas or all the fisheries you'll read about here. And, unless you've caught six-foot alligators on streamer flies, you'll be casting to some brand-new species as well.

I have resisted the temptation to group these pieces by category. You won't find all the humorous or all the dry-fly stories huddled together under one heading. I feel that wouldn't be fair to the reader who starts in trustingly at page one and trudges straight on through. He'd get over-surfeited on hors d'oeuvres at the beginning and bloated on desserts toward the end. I have tried to serve up the courses so that each one acts as a sorbet to the next.

Some world-class authors are represented here, so there must be a lot of superb writing on the following pages. However, since there's little critical agreement on what "great writing" really is, I haven't used that as a yardstick in making my selections.

My choices are not only personal favorites, but they all also meet the following requirements. The stories, the fishing, the facts or ideas they contain are especially interesting. And they are all written in a clear, vivid, usually memorable, style. I don't know whether or not that makes them great writing. But I'm convinced it makes them great reading. And that's what a book really should be, isn't it?

FREQUENT FLIERS

Bill Barich

*The wizened old anglers at California's
Hot Creek Ranch fish by their wits, not by
the rules.*

A couple of years ago, just after the trout-fishing season opened, I took a trip to Hot Creek, a famous dry-fly stream, with my friend Paul Deeds, who grows plums and prunes on a forty-acre spread in Sonoma County. Deeds is a high-strung fellow, and he was worried that we might run into bad weather and die in one of those unexpected spring blizzards that sometimes whip through the mountains, but I convinced him he was being overly sensitive, too cautious, a little cowardly and foolish—in short, everything a serious angler shouldn't be.

From San Francisco, we followed a route through Yosemite. An icy wind was blowing, and it began to snow while we were driving over Tioga Pass. As the flakes hit our windshield, Deeds laughed bitterly, his gift of prophecy confirmed. "I hope you brought your mittens," he said, repeating himself a few times for effect. Here was country humor at its finest.

The highway led us past the town of Mammoth Lakes, and when Deeds saw a sign for Hot Creek Ranch, we turned onto a trunk road and soon came to a sweeping meadow. The creek cut through the meadow, snaking about in wide curves and oxbows. It wasn't a very broad stream, no more than twenty-five feet across at any point. Nine rustic A-frames were set along it, looking out on black mountain peaks dusted with fresh snow.

The ranch manager had a big house set back from the meadow and we found him on his lawn, tinkering with a motorcycle he uses to patrol the property for trespassers. He wiped the oil from his fingers, had us register and assigned us to one of the cabins. It had a nice front porch looking out at the mountains, and it came with a library of old magazines and paperback romances. Even before we'd carried in our groceries, Deeds was at the kitchen table sorting through his tackle. He had some beautiful caddis flies, and he handled them delicately, with the touch of an artist.

By early evening, the wind had quit, and we walked to the creek to fish. We wore sneakers instead of hip boots because wading isn't permitted at the ranch. The idea is to protect the weed beds; they provide cover for brown and rainbow trout as well as supply them with oxygen.

We crossed a footbridge and stopped by a quiet pool at the base of the chalky bluff. Deeds tied up an elkhair caddis to his leader and made a cast upstream, in the classic tradition of dry-fly fishing. The caddis settled lightly on the surface, the way a newly hatched insect might do, and drifted back toward him in a smooth, straight path, riding high on its bristly wings. As the fly approached, no bigger than a speck of dust, Deeds gathered up slack line in his free hand, and then made another cast, letting the leader unfurl in an elegant loop. It had the quality of skywriting, leaving behind a wisp of itself, an image on the retina that slowly dispersed.

I moved to a spot where the creek was narrower, about twenty yards away. For a moment I stood still and watched for bugs, but none were hatching—it was too cold. Trout stay deep under such conditions, and you have to tease them into hitting wet flies or nymphs fished below the surface, but the ranch only allows the use of dries. (These rules can be a pain, but they make for quality fishing.) I

1 4
—

tied on a caddis imitation of my own and started casting blind, but I had no faith and could have been tossing a stone into a well, hoping to hit a target at the bottom. I could feel the snow on the mountains, an arctic chill, and had to do a jig every few minutes to keep my toes from freezing. Soon I was dreaming of bonefish and margaritas and the Florida Keys.

While I was dreaming, I heard a noise and turned to find an extremely old angler puffing back to his cabin. He must have been in his eighties and was using his rod almost like a cane. As he trudged along, he cursed the meadow, the creek, the wind—pretty much anything he could think of. He was a retired banker from Santa Barbara, and he told me he'd gotten caught in a hailstorm that morning. This was the worst weather he'd seen in twenty years of visiting the ranch, he said. All you could do was to crawl into bed and wait for tomorrow. "Or the day after that," he added, before going on.

Deeds is a country person and wakes at dawn. Give him a kitchen to root through, and he'll bang pots, slice potatoes, crack eggs and whistle a medley of Bo Diddley tunes. By the time I got up, he had a huge omelet cooking, along with a frying pan of home-cured bacon. "They say food like that's bad for you, but I don't believe it," he said contentedly, lighting a panatela after we'd eaten. Yes, we were back in a prescientific world, where truth is an aspect of desire.

Outside, the sun was shining on the meadow, and bugs were hatching everywhere—caddis and mayflies rising in clouds. Trout were feeding actively, dimpling the water with their lips; sometimes a big fish would leap from the creek to snatch an insect from the sky. It was a feat of aerobics that made you fumble for your gear. In just three casts, Deeds had a fourteen-inch rainbow and held it up for me to appreciate before letting it go. I tried a tiny gray sedge, size twenty, and a trout attacked it with a vicious slash. For a second or two, the fish was hooked, but then it dipped, swirled and spit out the fly, receding into memory.

A half hour later, I was still in the same place, stupidly casting the same fly to the same trout, in violation of a basic law of angling. If you disturb the water, you're supposed to move on, because you've spooked the fish. Yet even Deeds, who's an expert and covers every part of the stream, wasn't having any luck. His first trout was his only trout. When I joined him farther along the creek, he was sitting on the ground with his hat off, studying a riffle.

"There," he said, pointing to a spot in front of him, and on cue a fat-bellied rainbow jumped to swallow a bug. Deeds smiled. "Makes you want a shotgun, doesn't it?"

Around noon, tired from our efforts, we returned to our cabin. About five other anglers fell in with us, and I noticed they were all gents of a certain age—well into their seventies. "I feel like a goddam kid in this bunch," whispered Deeds, who's pushing fifty. Obviously, the physical ease of fishing Hot Creek had attracted them. There were no boulders to climb over, no fast water to negotiate. We traded pleasantries with them and were surprised to hear that they'd each caught several fish.

"They must have a secret," I said to Deeds.

"Sure, they do. It's called lying."

When the wind came up again late that afternoon, nearly carrying off Deeds's rod in a gust, he insisted there had to be a more sheltered stream somewhere in Inyo County. What about the Owens River? On a Forest Service map, it looked to be just seven miles away, so off we went into a brilliantly clear alpine light. The road we traveled was dirt, or some weird amalgam of dirt, flint, old tin cans and rusty sawblades, and we had to proceed at a crawl to keep from shredding the tires. In ten minutes we'd gone a mile and had wandered into a landscape dominated by the stinking odor of rotten eggs—the sulphury fumes of a hot spring.

There are hot springs all through the Sierra, particularly in areas of geological unrest. Some are no larger or deeper than a bucket, while others are as spacious as a kidney-shaped pool. You find them in rocky outcrops, in lava beds and pine forests, in small-town backyards adja-

cent to chiropractic offices. This one was in a little park—
an oasis in the midst of dust and lizards and sun-baked
earth. Our map showed that it was a part of upper Hot
Creek, but the water in it hardly moved and the soil
around it had a crusty, alkaline look. A dozen people were
soaking in it, floating on their backs, eyes closed, like
mummies.

Everyone believes that Californians strip naked at the
first opportunity, but it's not always true. The floaters had
on bathing suits, so we went back to the cabin and got
ours. We had to climb down a long wooden staircase to
reach the hot spring. Oh, but the water was soothing! It
crept between our bones and seemed to massage every
weary tissue in our bodies, and in no time at all we'd
melted into it, reduced to a blissful, quasi-piscine state.

Last morning at Hot Creek. Deeds was already out fishing when I got up. Against the toaster, he'd propped a note:
"Ate bacon, left eggs. Hope you didn't want bacon." I ate
the eggs, drank some bitter black coffee and walked from
the cabin to the meadow. The grass was dewy, and the
stream was the color of slate, but there were no clouds anywhere, just a ribbon of blue sky. As I crossed the footbridge, a pair of cinnamon teal swam out from beneath it,
turning their beaks this way and that.

By eight o'clock, the temperature was in the low seventies. Insects of every kind were on the wing, skittering
along the surface of the creek. They created a spectacle of
mindless energy, born into the light, oblivious of the fish
that lay waiting for them. It was like watching the myth of
Narcissus enacted by thousands of bugs. Rainbows rose to
suck them in, flashing silvery scales. When trout are on
the feed, they make a loud, slurping sound, as if they were
eating a bowl of soup, and an angler who's trying but failing to fool them becomes nervous and upset, casting badly,
swearing, then casting badly again.

One of my bad casts so disgusted me I threw down my
rod. But my line kept drifting, swinging out below me in
an arc, and my fly got soggy and heavy and sank into the
weeds. Now it was a dry fly performing in the manner of a

wet, underwater—no rule against that at the ranch!—and I was curious to see what would happen. A minute later, the line began to twitch. A trout had struck at the submerged fly and had managed to hook itself. The fish was a fine brown, and I reeled it in and released it. On my next cast, I deliberately let the fly sink at the end of its drift; again a trout swam up to take it. Eager to share my discovery, I went looking for Deeds. He'd mastered the trick on his own, though, after seeing the banker from Santa Barbara haul in three rainbows in rapid succession.

"You get that old," said Deeds, "and I guess you don't care much about the technicalities anymore."

All afternoon and evening, we caught and released good trout, and we were very hungry at dusk, ready to cook some steaks on the porch barbecue. Deeds fiddled with our radio, hoping to get a station that broadcast something other than reports on grain prices and hog futures. On a clear night in the Sierra, you can pull in programs from every western state, and we listened to a minor-league ball game from Albuquerque before switching to a Merle Haggard concert.

In the morning we loaded the car and swept the cabin clean. On any stream, if the fishing goes well, there comes a moment when you reach a plateau of satisfaction. You sit on a bank to rest, lean your back against a tree and feel liberated from the many concerns of your daily life. For a brief time, you get a chance to simply exist, on a par with the birds and weeds and grasses, and it's this moment, more than any other, that you take home with you, along with the uneaten carrots and potatoes, and the leaders still in their packages.

THE PRIEST'S OMNIBUS

T. C. Kingsmill Moore

*High adventures with fresh-run sea trout
on an unsung river in Donegal.*

W henever anything in our house has to be turned, squeezed, bent or extracted, a cry goes up for "The Priest's Omnibus," and some part of that paragon of tools will do the trick. This chapter tells how I came to possess it.

It had been planned not as a fishing holiday, but as one which would give my wife a rest and the children a trouble-free beach. However, the map showed a river adjacent and so a rod found its way into the car. The hotel proprietor, a German, was not encouraging. Yes, he had the fishing rights on the river, and he had heard that there were white trout and even salmon, but his guests never brought anything back but "Things so," and he indicated a three-ounce fish with dramatic finger and thumb.

The map showed that the river divided just above a bridge some two miles from the sea. Reaches below a junction are generally good, and the contours indicated a flat stretch where I might find deep pools. Next day I set out for the bridge. There was a pool sure enough, fairly deep and wide, but with banks encumbered by bushes and too much sheltered from the wind. It produced three fish, all of them under the pound. Half a mile further down, the river plunged into a close tunnel of trees, but in the interval there had been two short pools, rather too rapid, and another ending in a narrow slow-flowing tail constricted by a shingle spit. The short pools each gave a fish. The shingle tail was very calm, very exposed and very slow. I attacked it with a single fly, kneeling and fishing up as carefully as if I was nymphing on the Itchen. It yielded eight fish. With thirteen in all, from half a pound to two pounds, I returned to be greeted by a perfectly hysterical proprietor and that night all the hotel ate white trout for dinner. Clouds of incense floated around me, but I was not at ease. The proprietor evidently expected a repeat performance—any amount of repeat performances—unaware that I had been fortunate enough to catch the river at the right point of a falling flood. Next day I tried the same stretch again, and got only eight white trout, but a small salmon on top of them helped to preserve my reputation.

In Ireland whenever a salmon is hooked the countryside seems to sprout population, and while I was playing the fish the parapet of the bridge was a row of watching faces. When it was landed all of them disappeared except one, who waited while I carried up my prize. From past experience I suspected that he would be the local poacher, the very man I wanted. Poachers, whatever their methods (and in Ireland we have a nice variety), must know the places where fish lie and, being on the whole an easy-going and broad-minded lot, are not averse to giving some help to a reasonable angler. A reasonable angler is one who is willing to pay for his information.

The conversation opened along well-known lines, congratulatory comments on his part, deprecation on mine. Then I made a monstrous error. I asked a direct question as to where were the best pools. He shrank into himself like an alarmed sea anemone and disclaimed all acquaintance with fish. Only after prolonged fencing did we find a way out. His grandfather, he said, had been a famous fisherman and apparently a very garrulous old gentleman. The grandson had a retentive memory. In the form of stories heard from his grandfather he gave me all the information I wanted, and a suitable recognition of his ancestor's prowess was not refused.

In case any reader may find himself near this river (it is the Eany in South Donegal) I may mention the two best pools to which my acquaintance introduced me. The first, on the main river, is easy of access, being directly below the next bridge above the junction. In favourable conditions it is good for two or three decent sea trout. The second, on the smaller river about half a mile above the junction, is approached deviously along a cart track, through a farm yard, and between two pig sties. For its size it is about the best sea trout pool I have met. About fifty yards long, hour-glass in shape, it has all the ugliness which characterizes the first class pool. Sea trout, when they leave the sea, prefer a lake to a river and if they cannot get to a lake, they choose a pool which is the nearest thing to a canal. Feeding little in fresh water, they have no need for a brisk stream to bring food past their noses, but they do require to conserve their energy for spawning. A fringe of water lilies along the edge is a sure sign of a good pool, for water lilies do not like a strong current any more than sea trout.

Conditions were now worsening. The river was low, the weather bright, and the wind fitful. Trout could still be caught, but they were smaller and fewer. Delicate casting, fine tackle and small bright flies were needed. Freeman's Fancy and the Gold and Magenta Bumble were the best. The proprietor eyed me with disfavour. He felt I was not really trying. When my conscience, which had slumbered while the fishing was good, woke up to remind me that this was meant to be a family holiday, and I deserted the river for a couple of days, he looked as if he would like to put me out of the hotel.

There came a night when the rain crashed against the window with a noise sufficient to waken even as heavy a sleeper as myself, and in the morning pools were everywhere. The places which had served me well up to this would have their banks under water, but I had walked a large part of the smaller river with this contingency in mind, and had picked out some spots which were likely to hold fish in flood. White trout do not make runs as lengthy as salmon and will take a breather in the quieter parts of streams before moving on to the deep pools where they are going to settle down.

The hour-glass pool had become a lake, but, a little further down, the river ran between high clay banks in a steady flow which slackened at a turn and bore towards my side. Under the slacker water there was, I knew, a big rock which in normal times stood up well above the surface but was now invisible. A wall of gorse ran along the bank, and only at one place was there a loophole from which I could fish. As my fly swept behind the rock, there came a boil but no tightening. My next cast had the same result. Evidently the fly was coming across too quickly. He might take at the third cast, but if he did not, my chance was gone. A white trout hardly ever rises more than three times. Something had to be done to slow up the traverse of the fly.

Under the far bank the water moved noticeably slower. If the fly could be drifted down in that quieter patch till it was opposite the fish, there was a chance of bringing it more gently across. The far bank was a clay cliff bare of vegetation, and this gave me an idea. Off came the dropper. I cast my tail fly hard at the vertical clay, shooting three or four yards as I did so. Gut and six feet of line smacked against the bank and slithered down into the water, bunched, but not tangled. Now it was a question of "mending" to prevent the centre current getting a hold, and "feeding up" to allow the fly to drift down. The height of my own bank made both tactics easy and all went well. The cast straightened out, the fly took the proper course till it was level with the fish, and a final exaggerated mend allowed it to come slowly over his nose. This time there was more than a boil, and it was unmistakably a heavy fish. He made straight off downstream and round the bend, the line bearing on a clump of willow-bay half submerged by the flood. Islanded in the gorse, I had no chance to follow, and he seemed set for a return to the sea.

At last the reel drum moved more slowly, and I was able

to brake. Something queer had happened. The pull was still strong, but there was a deadness about it, a lack of direct contact. In a moment the mystery was solved, for the fish exploded into the air almost at my feet. He had turned in his tracks, leaving forty-five yards of drowned line in a big loop down-stream, and could do pretty well what he liked. This was no salmon. He was everywhere—a swirl under the far bank, a gleam up-stream, and then crash, crash, crash, as he leaped into the air over and over again so rapidly that it looked as if he were bouncing off the water. There was no possibility of control till those loose yards had been recovered on to the reel, and even then I could not stop his fury. His own efforts and not any pressure from me at last exhausted him, and the rest was routine, save for the final difficulty, known to every fisherman, of landing a big fish with a short net from a high bank. It was done at last, and he lay before me a white trout of just over five pounds.

"The best trout ever I saw caught. Man, but he could lep!" My friend had emerged from the gorse, his caution temporarily abandoned in his enthusiasm. I got a couple more while the flood was high, and the next three days restored the proprietor to enthusiasm. By this my fishing was organized. The compass gave me the orientation of all the pools, and while still at the hotel, I could tell which of them the wind would be striking in a favourable way, and how the sun would be shining on the water, always an important consideration. As the best pools are widely separate, a car was necessary to get from one to the other, and a certain amount of time was taken up in jointing and disjointing the rod—(for I will never carry a rod sticking out of a window), but soon I became expert in doing this in the minimum of time. It is not necessary to detach line or cast, only to pull out enough line to allow the separated joints to be laid side by side, the cast wrapped round the bundle, and the whole put on the back seat.

The river ran down again, and with fishing at a discount we went for a drive, crossing the bridge below the junction. The water whispered over the ford only an inch or two deep; the smaller branch looked as if it were stagnant. A

23

moorhen crept out of the sedges to enjoy the sun, flirted
her white petticoats salaciously and departed with a sharp
"Eeyek." Distant shots reminded me that yesterday had
been the twelfth.

Our drive took us in a half circle, crossing the larger
branch by a bridge some miles up-stream. I stopped to
make a small adjustment to the car, while my wife looked
over the parapet. She began to gesticulate, and I ran over.
The river was a muddy torrent. There had been no rain on
our route, but I knew what had happened. Those distant
shots had been thunder, and in the steep valley of the Blue
Stacks, where the river begins, the clouds had burst. With
haste we might get to the junction pool before the flood.

We made it easily. Everything was as before. The moorhen repeated her turn. Silence and heat enveloped us.
Then in the distance, we heard a mutter which swelled to a
grumble and then to a roar as the flood burst round the
bend. It came in a steep-fronted wave, thick with debris,
carrying with it the pitiful carcass of a late-born lamb. The
bushes bent beneath its attack, the smaller river, invaded
by the water from the main branch, flowed backwards in a
rapid stream, and over the ford there was now more than
three feet of water. Still the river rose. There could be no
fishing today, but tomorrow! Alas, by tomorrow the flood
had gone. The downpour had been short and local. The
river dropped as rapidly as it had risen.

The last day of our holiday came. The afternoon would
be taken up with packing and preparations, but there had
been rain in the night and so I was out early to get a few
trout before lunch. Wind and water were perfect. Three
came from the shingle tail, two from the bridge, and five
from the hour-glass pool, so with about a stone of fish on
my back I left the river for the last time. On the way back
to the car I met a young priest, rod in hand, who asked me
how I had done. I showed him. "Well," he said, "I fished
this river as a lad, and now I'm back on holiday from
America, and I've had three days on it, but I never saw a
bag of fish like that. How did you get them?" The cast was
still on my rod, the magenta and claret bumbles as drop-
pers. Examining them, he asked whether they were not too

small, and what had become of their wings. "Try them yourself," I said and gave him three or four.

Next day as I was pulling away from a Donegal garage where I had refuelled for my drive to Dublin my wife said, "Stop, there's a man running after the car and waving." I stopped and my acquaintance of yesterday came up panting. "Wait," he said, "I must get you a bottle of whisky." "But why?" I said. "Those flies of yours—I never had such a day!" I declined the whisky but he insisted I must take something as a memento. "Listen, I have a gadget—it does everything—it's American—you can't get it in this country. It's in my car." He ran back to where his car was parked, and returned with the tool. And that is the story of the Priest's Omnibus.

Except for the priest, I did not meet another angler, which struck me as peculiar, so I determined to ask my friend the reason. By now we were on the best of terms. Ever since the capture of the big trout he had begun to expand, often turning up to watch me fish. I suspected at first that he wanted to head me off from places where scales and trampling betrayed the use of a net, and this may have been so, but he certainly showed a keen interest in up-stream fishing and the use of small flies, both of which were new to him. He explained the absence of other fishermen as occasioned by the belief that the river fished well only during a few hours of falling flood. Anglers from a distance found it difficult to hit off the right time, and local anglers, not having motor cars, fished only the pool nearest to them while the flood was still high and big flies were effective. When the flood ran down these flies were useless (he did not add that other methods of capture, difficult to employ in a flood, in low water became easier and more profitable than angling). As for the guests at the hotel, they were accustomed to brown trout, and fished rapid water where no self-respecting white trout would lie. I had been lucky enough to tap his local knowledge. I had a car, and methods which extended the period in which trout could be caught. To his explanations I should add that the weather had on the whole been favourable, and that the run of fish was later and rather better than usual.

BASS CONVERT

Nick Lyons

A world-class "trout junkie" confesses to a growing addiction to a bigger, perhaps gamier, fish.

Though I have been publicly judged a "trout junkie," I recently acquired an addiction that may prove harder to kick: bass madness, of the smallmouth variety.

Now one can do a thing for a long time without becoming an addict; and I did not begin to fish for smallmouths last night. But some time during my misspent teens I lost my heart to those "rose moles all a-stipple upon trout that swim," and bass, perch, pickerel, pike, bluegills, crappie, and carp and every other fish I'd caught in fresh water has played a slow second to them ever since. Until last year—when the accumulation of twenty years of random bass fishing, whenever there were no trout, suddenly came to a fever pitch.

The first smallmouths I caught were in a feeder creek that emptied into a reservoir I fished for trout in early April. I was thirteen, and had come up from the city by train, alone, and had fished ten hours without so much as a tap. Then, in rapid succession, on night crawlers, I caught three hard-battling fish, about fourteen or fifteen inches apiece, in the creek. I'd never seen such fish before and, in my city bred ignorance, called them "green trout"—though they fought harder for their size than any trout I've ever taken. A rather gruff warden advised me what they were, and became much more genial when the fish, released from my stringer, miraculously managed to swim feebly away. The bass season started in three months.

I also caught good smallmouths in the Ten Mile River, near Wingdale, New York, in the late summer and early fall, again while fishing for trout. Mort Seaman and I would cast the lethal little C.P. Swing across and slightly upstream, let it swing down with the current, jerk and jiggle it a few times, letting it flutter there, fall back, dart up again, and then retrieve. There'd be a sharp twitch— usually while the spinner fluttered—and then a tug, and the line would quickly angle to the surface and the fish was up and out and shaking.

"Got one?"

"Bass"—with a certain disgruntled, sinking of the voice. "Only a bass."

Though they fought hard, they were always a disappointment: I was fishing, I figured, not for bigger or stronger game but for fairer. Imperceptibly, I was becoming not only a trout addict but, worse, a trout snob.

The only times I deliberately fished for smallmouths were on trips to the Thousand Islands near Alexandria Bay with Mort and his father. We usually went in October, when the trout season was over. For anyone, like me, glued to the grey city but loving woods and particularly waters passionately, those trips were a special joy. We'd fish with a well-weathered, knowledgeable old guide, and I can still see him standing at the prow with baseball cap, grey chino pants and shirt, his hand on the steering rod, squinting into the spray as the long grey boat swept across the choppy waters of the St. Lawrence, its prow dipping and rising as he steered a sure course toward a passage between two islands. Sometimes we'd fish our largest shiners for northern pike in the thin green weeds along some island's shore. It was savage to see those four-inch shiners come back with four or five teeth gashes along their sides, but even the six-pounders seemed sluggish: the guide didn't like pike and, though they were larger, neither did we. Nor, particularly, did we like drifting certain channels for largemouth, which also ran larger. We'd come for smallmouths and that's what we wanted most.

There was a special hole called, as I remember, Dick's Dock, and every time we approached it during the years we went to the St. Lawrence, my heart would begin to pound and flutter with abandon. The spot had gotten its name from an abandoned wooden dock that served as the principal marker for a dropoff thirty yards from shore. The guide would bring the boat in close to shore and then, working the anchor along the bottom, he would move us out on a line with a lighthouse on the opposite hill until the anchor suddenly fell free and dropped twenty-five feet. In October, when the winds blew chill and the trees had turned flaming orange and red, the smallmouths would school up just below the ledge off Dick's Dock. We always had good luck there, every time we tried it—even, years later, when Mort and I went back alone.

We'd take a live shiner from the bait well, hook it firmly through the lips, and cast it over, using two or three heavy split shot for weight. You didn't have to do much more than wait, and now and then lift up lightly to make sure you weren't hooked on the bottom. Sometimes the bass would take when you lifted.

Thump. Thump. Thump. You could feel the bass taking with steady tugs, deep in forty-five feet of water, and then you counted six or seven, gave the fish several feet of line, and struck hard. You didn't have to do much to induce the bite, but hooking them was something of a problem. You either had the touch or you didn't. You couldn't explain it to someone else. Mort's father got plenty of strikes but he caught far fewer fish than Mort or myself: We'd been born to it.

If it was a good fish, you could not turn it, did not dare to, but heard the line pull out against the drag on your spinning reel even as you reeled. Then the fish would begin to angle up toward the surface, thirty, maybe forty feet from the boat, and the guide would say, "He's a big 'un, all right. Don' try'n turn him now. Let him jump four, maybe five times. Keep that line taut!"

And up the fish would go bright green and leaping fiercely, with sky hooks hanging and twisting and then falling back with a crash. Two more jumps. Then another. And then you'd settle into the happy work of edging him always closer, closer to the boat and the guide's ridiculously large but helpful boat net.

Sometimes the fish would run to four or five pounds. Mostly they'd be two or three but never weak-willed.

Mort and I even had a special handshake that represented that special *thump, thump, thump;* we'd use it when we met, even, eventually, in mixed company, and we still use it today, twenty-five years later. It is an emblem.

We enjoyed those long brisk days on the St. Lawrence, those memorable meals at a Canadian farmhouse—with endless platters of chicken and steak followed by home-made blueberry pie topped with fresh strawberry ice-cream. And we enjoyed and later often talked about the fine fishing we'd had. But after a trip or two by ourselves, we never went back. Not in all those years. Mort found the lure of the salt and the size and gameness of stripers, bluefish, bonefish, and tarpon too alluring. Who could blame him? And I lost my heart to the long rod, a box of feathers, and the elusive trout. Who, I thought, could blame *me?* I was having more fun than ever—and isn't that what we all go out for, anyway?

Then, last August, I visited some close friends in Maine —not particularly to fish, though, as always, I had a fly rod tucked in with my baggage, just in case. They arranged for me to spend three days at Ed Musson's deer camp on a little island in Great Pond, near Aurora, and for three days all thought of trout vanished. To be sure, I asked about trout first, but Ricky, Ed's young son, said the lake got too warm and you could only catch trout in the spring; but he'd caught a four pound smallmouth on a frog just the other day and I might possibly get some on my fly rod in the evenings or early mornings when they came in near the lily pads. If I had a mind to.

I did.

I'd never caught a smallmouth on a popper, though I'd taken bluegills that way. It was worth a try.

I'd never been to Maine and I looked long before I began to fish. This was a different world. The water was auburn with tannic acid seepage from the woods. Somewhere across the flat little lake, a loon cried long and shrill. From the back of the island, you could see neither house nor telephone pole, only a broad marsh and pine and hemlock and oak. The place was lousy with black flies. Were you to take those away, I'd as well be on Great Pond for a week as any hallowed trout stream. It was still and magical and wild.

I discovered that first afternoon that there is a different, slower rhythm required for bass-bugging than for dry-fly fishing; the added weight of the bug jerked the line and leader awkwardly. The first adjustment I made proved a sound one: I reduced the length and also the tippet size of my leader, from over ten feet and 4X to eight feet and 1X. The difference immediately changed the zig-zag verticles I'd been throwing; it also proved no deterrent to the bass. I've since gone to seven feet and 0X, which gives me even better control. The bass don't seem to mind.

I also cut two feet from the end of my double-taper, which further improved my casting. Now, using the #5 weight glass rod I'd brought along, I began to cast comfortably, waiting that extra second for the slower bug to straighten the line behind me, then pushing the line forward with more deliberation.

One's first bass on a popping bug is a memorable shock.

I'd begun my serious fishing on Great Pond about seven o'clock, after spending the afternoon on shore, fussing with my equipment. I kept the rowboat casting distance from the edge of the lily pads and let it drift slowly down their length, casting in and retrieving with short upward jerks of the rod that made the bug ploop enticingly. Sometimes I dipped the oar to turn the boat slightly but the lake was placid and my movement never more than a touch. I knew I was too early. Ricky had said the fish didn't come in until the sun went down, and he looked like a young man who knew what-of he spoke. I didn't get my first strike, a short, until after eight-o'clock. Suddenly the water boiled behind

the bug, I struck back ferociously, and nearly put the #2
hook in my right eye.

The size of the swirl set my heart to thumping. This was
a brand of surface fishing for larger stakes than I'd realized. I cast another twenty, thirty times, probing the open
pockets in the pads, twitching the bug, letting it rest, jig-
gling it, popping it loudly—trying to find the proper rec-
ipe. I was not there at the right season, but with some hard
work I hoped to pick up a fish or two.

Ploop. Ploop. Rest

Slam. The water exploded.

The fish took in an awesome swirl, jumped once, twice,
then sounded. With my heavy leader I turned it before it
reached the pads, then followed it with the rod as it angled
past the bow of the boat and out into deep water. In a few
more minutes I had it in the net, my first smallmouth on a
fly: a chunky, hemlock-green hellion that, pound for pound,
as Ilenshall insisted, outfought any other fish I'd ever had
on.

For all the fight it had put up, and its dramatic rise, I
was surprised the fish wasn't larger. Well, larger ones
would come someday when I was better at this new game,
and if they acted like this one had...well, this thing might
be worth pursuing.

When I left Great Pond three days later, I wondered precisely what had produced such a memorable experience for
me. Surely the surroundings were part of it all; smallmouths, like trout, thrive best, and are best fished for, in
wild, unpolluted water. This lake was ideal. Though it was
too shallow in the summer for trout and landlocks, it was
ideal bass-bugging water, and no more than a handful of
people fished it. When I fished in against the pads, I could
see only the pines and hemlocks along the shore, the slate-
grey boulders, the lighter shades of green as the water
grew shallow over wood and rock, and I heard only the
tuba-croaks of bullfrogs and that shrill, haunting call of
loons. Except for the nasty black flies, which I forgot once I
started to fish, and the fact that this was not moving
water, one could want nothing fairer. The world of the lake

was as mysterious and charged with life as a stream. And I enjoyed the curious mixture of lazy, languid, intensely quiet floating and casting, and the bold drum of expectation. I was all eye and ear. I watched the little bug grow alive on the surface, heard it gurgle and ploop—watched and felt and heard those chunky smallmouths explode upon it.

I took several more—not many, not every time, morning and evening, I went out: but enough. None was over two-and-a-half pounds, but each filled me.

I was hooked.

Then all that winter I readied my gear, buying hair-bugs, cork poppers, large balsawood poppers; bass-bug-tapered lines and leaders; even another rod, a #6 weight, to give me a bit more leverage. Though many oldtime bass fishermen recommend a #7 or #8, I managed everything I wanted to do with the #6, and enjoyed its lightness more.

Every year does not bring a trip to Maine, but I happily settled for an extended stay in the Catskills. There were trout streams—old friends—I wanted to revisit, creeks I wanted to explore. "Was there any smallmouth fishing?" I asked a number of fellow trout addicts. Several didn't know and didn't care. "Bass? Are you sinking *that* low, Lyons?" One said the lower Schoharie was worth exploring, another that the lower Esopus had some good bass. The Ashokan might be worth a try.

I tried—and it was a delight. Slowly, as the summer wore on, I found myself preferring the reservoir more and more. There were not many, but I enjoyed wading the shores, casting a long line, waiting expectantly. Each night, as I wended my way back through the skeletal trees in the dark, I carried home new lessons and new respect for this great game fish.

Where had I been?

How had I missed them all these years?

And would the passion flag or hold?

In September, a voluble doctor I knew invited me out on the reservoir in his new boat. I leaped at the chance. I'd never fished the Ashokan except from the shore; perhaps

I'd take one like the monster I'd seen leaping, too far out, several nights in a row.

The day was windy and sharply chill; grey-black clouds rushed unpleasantly across the sky. We set out, me rowing, the good doctor ensconced in the back seat comfortably, trolling a Rapala the size of most trout I catch.

"That way. Toward the island!" he shouted against the wind.

The wind and the choppy waves kept carrying me further off course—right, then left. The sky grew darker.

"That way! Over *there!"*

"I'm trying."

"Don't you know how to row?"

I leaned forward, then pulled back with all due muscle. "I know how to row."

"It's no good out here at all," he said, shaking his head vigorously. He'd fished the lake precisely once before with his new spinning rod and his new aluminum boat. He'd always summered at the shore and fished for blues.

A fat red welt began to form on my left palm. Working against the heavy waves, my shoulders ached.

"No. No-no-no. Where are you going? *Oooops.* Had one then. I'm sure of it. They'll hit like that and let go, won't they? You're the expert. Maybe you should circle around." I began to circle. "No. Better head over to the island. The island is where they are. That way. That's where they are."

I settled into my work. I was glad to be out, as I always am and my hour—the witching hour—would come.

"There's one. Ah-ha! Got him. I got one! See?"

I saw. A rock bass smaller than the Rapala.

Ten minutes later: "There's a good one. See!"

I saw. A thirteen incher—ill-fated. It came straight in. Right to the top guide. Then it found itself on the bottom of the boat, with me disengaging the fifty-seven hooks. It was no use. It couldn't be turned back; that rapid trip it had just taken, the perfect plethora of hooks would, as the sage Mr. Woody Allen says, have caused "cardiac arrest in a yak."

"Ha. See how good this Rapala is? Great little lure, isn't

it? Fifty times as good as that little thing you've got on. Why aren't you catching any? Ha. You're the expert."

I rowed some more. Rain began and swelled and pelted the hell out of us. The bottom of the boat filled with bilge. The doctor kept talking. "That's three, right? Three already. Some little lure, this Rapala. Why haven't you caught any?"

I dropped the oars and made two hasty casts into the heavy wind, my first of the day. I hadn't been aware that I was in the Bassin' Man's Olympics. The casts went about ten feet.

"Not much you can do with that rod, is there?"

I put the long rod down carefully and took up my oars again. I was soaked and freezing and the rain came in with greater and greater rushes.

Suddenly the doctor bellowed like a moose: "WHERE ARE YOU GOING? YOU'LL BREAK MY LINE!"

Behind the boat, his line stretched out high and far.

3 4

———

"You've hooked me onto something," he protested, shaking his head. "Back up. Back up. BACK UP QUICK!"

I obediently backed a few feet. "You sure it's hung up?"

"DAMMIT. What *else?*" He was livid. He did not want to lose his Rapala.

What else was soon apparent. A gigantic—I mean, absurdly huge, fat, and bronze-green—smallmouth, on what must have been atomic power, raised itself a foot up out of the water, sloshed and fumbled, felt the fifty-seven hooks, thrashed with a swirl larger than a garbage can thrown in, and took the Rapala away with it to munch for dinner.

The doctor sat stone silent for a moment.

Then he slammed his rod down on the water.

Then he shook his head.

An hour later and the rains had stopped and it was dark and we were drifting close to the spot where he beached the boat. The water was glassy below the swirling mist. I could barely make out the bug chugging, plooping along the surface. But I could hear it. The doctor had not said a word in an hour. He had not hooked another fish. I had taken one two-pounder and released it. In a moment another swirled at my bug, took it, lurched away, and soon found itself—in the faint reflection of the moon—having a single hook extracted from its jaw.

"Got one!" shouted the doctor.

"Great!" I said, genuinely pleased.

"Feels big!"

"Be careful with it. Don't pull too hard."

"Something's wrong."

As he reeled, the boat edged slowly toward the shore, on which the gigantic Rapala was safely hooked.

It is a new spring and the lure is still there, quite untroubled by my last day out last fall. Trout remain a delight to me, and always will. But I'll never unhook my brain from the abrupt, electric crash when a solid two-pound smallmouth takes my popper at dusk, bending my rod—and heart. I doubt, really, whether I'll fish with the good doctor again—bass snob that I am—but I'll see that reservoir this year. And instead of mooching some dry flies from Dave Whitlock this winter, I commissioned him to make me up some sinking hair-frogs, to expand my day a bit beyond dawn and dusk. I have this dream, see, about taking big ones during the day, on Hi-D line and frogs, fished very, very deep.

Perhaps there's a message in that.

THE IRON BLUE

John Waller Hills

Why do trout commit suicide for a tiny fly that hatches out when the weather's at its nastiest?

Little blew dun. **Made of the Down of a Mouse for body and head, dubt with sad Ash-colour'd Silk, wing of the sad coloured feather of a Shepstone quill.**

The Angler's Vade Mecum.
By JAMES CHETHAM. 1681.
Earliest dressing of the iron blue.

It was as cold a May day as I remember. The sky was a dirty grey, a wild gusty wind blew from the north, and the young green of the trees seemed to have lost all freshness and brilliance. The Test ran swift and full, but even its clear water looked dark, dull and forbidding.

Not a fish showed till two o'clock. The morning passed without a sign of life, and the weather if anything grew worse. I ate my sandwiches walking, to keep warm. At last a fish did actually rise, but it must have been due entirely to light-heartedness, for there was nothing to rise at. However, he took a blue upright ribbed with gold wire and proved on landing to be nearly 2 lb. in weight. An unenterprising animal: but I was cheered to get him. Time was running, and it was something to save a blank, for assuredly no day ever looked more like a blank. After landing him, I began to walk upstream. Only one other rod was out, he was far below me, and there were four empty beats above mine. Better move towards home, thought I: perhaps things may be more prosperous above: anyhow nothing is lost thereby, there is good fishing all the way. So up I walked slowly, watching the water like a hawk. Three o'clock came, the gale was more violent than ever, and colder. Even my optimism began to desert me. And then, unexpectedly, things began to happen.

I forget what it was that first attracted my attention, probably the splash of a fish, for the water was whipped into such waves that flies and even rises were hard to see. At all events, I suddenly realised that the river, as if by magic, was speckled with iron blues. Blown sideways by the gusts, hurried downstream by the wild wind, children of the storm that they are, on they came, their narrow purple wings looking too delicate to live out the gale, ever more and more of them, till every square foot of the surface carried them. And, equally suddenly, trout began rising, good trout, and rising strongly and well, as they always do in a downstream wind.

All this takes longer to tell than it did to experience. I crept up to a rising fish, knelt down, and began lengthening my line. Oh that wind! It was not even dead in my face, it was right into my shoulder, the hardest of all against which to throw. But the first cast that went near my fish he took, and rushed madly downstream, my reel screaming. I had to take him a long way before I got him out, a beauty of 2 lb. 1 oz. That was better. A brace.

I walked quickly back to where I had hooked him, and looked up. Then I saw that provided I made no mess of it, I might do great things. Just above me was a pool, very deep, with a swift turbulent stream coming in at right angles at the head and a quicker run also at right angles below. You know the sort of pool: full of swirls, eddies, and cross currents, inhabited by large and experienced trout, who roam about, now rising in the backwater, now in the current, then moving into almost still water, and eating half a dozen nearly stationary flies. On a calm day, you can catch them, if you see or guess which way they are turning, and drop your fly almost on their nose, putting it right into their mouths. But to do this you must cast very accurately, you must be at the top of your form. Moreover, you must cast very often: for owing to the different currents running in all directions, your fly will only float an inch or two without drag: and before it drags you must whip it off and cast again: for cunning trout must never see drag, never, never. All this constant casting is very tiring, even when all is in your favour, on a calm day. It is much more so with a wind against you, for accurate placing is infinitely harder, and you have to take three or four throws to do what you should do in one.

So difficult did it seem that I halted a moment, in quick indecision. Should I tackle this water, holding big trout, but horribly difficult in a head wind, or should I move on to the even-flowing beat above? The question was settled for me. A fish rose just where the quick run left the pool, on the very lip, and if ever I saw a fish between 3 and 4 pounds it was he. No fisherman could possibly leave such a prize. After several bad shots, I got the fly in front of him; he rose confidently, I struck, but too quickly, and missed him. I waited, cursing myself: but after a minute, yes, there he was rising again, rising again regularly. I had not pricked him. I nipped off my blue upright and knotted on a winged iron blue. This floated beautifully over him. He rose again, and this time he was hooked. He made one bolt up into the pool, jumped, then turned and rushed down the racing stream below. I ran back into the meadow to keep the line taut, but he came so fast that it got slack. I reeled furiously, felt the fish, off he careered again, but my line brushed against something, underwater weed no doubt; only a touch, but it was enough, he was off. What a tragedy.

It was no use lamenting. Mechanically I took off the iron blue, and tied on a blue upright again. I walked back to where I had hooked him. Fly was thicker than ever, chiefly iron blue, but also large winter duns, small dark olives and medium olives, a wonderful sight, only to be seen on a chalk stream. Something moved far over the river. The throw, being across the wind, was easier, but I laid the fly down too hard and it sank. He took it all the same. I pulled, and felt fast as a rock. He also dashed downstream, but I could keep the line tight. I ran down and got below him on a short line, and we fought out a desperate battle over 100 yards of water. A lovely trout, 3 lb. 7 oz., a picture to look at.

But I wasted no time admiring him. Several were rising in the swirly water, and would undoubtedly take if I could get a fly to them. It was hard work to do this, and tiring too, in that bitter wind: for with roaming fish you may put the fly off their tail instead of before their nose, many casts are needed even on a calm day, and even more on such a storm-swept water. I failed at three fish running, owing to drag and wind, thoroughly rousting their suspicions, but doing nothing more. Then I got one, well over the pound and a half limit.

By that time, all the fish in that particular pool had been either caught, risen, or frightened. It was possible, no doubt, to get another, or more than one: but that involved giving the pool a rest, and time was running. So I reeled in, and walked quickly up to the beat above. Here the broad shining Test ran straight, with a swift, even current, and the problem would be easier. The fish, too, had had a mighty meal undisturbed, and at the same time had not had time to eat too much, and grow dainty and suspicious. But what was even better, the wind had fallen perceptibly. The fly still floated down steadily, less thick certainly, but in quite sufficient quantity.

The first trout I spotted was rising close under my bank. A left-handed cast, straight into the wind he was, and many were the throws I made before my fly, an iron blue this time, went right. He was lying above some tall dead grasses, and the shot had to be accurate, or the line bounced off the grass, and the fly blew wide. But at last he had it, and when struck bolted across the river, my rod bending double. I worked him down, and had my net off the sling to net him, when all unexpectedly the fly came away. My next fish also escaped. When hooked, he rushed

across the river in a succession of jumps, falling back into
the water with a smash, and at the last leap he threw the
hook. Both were heavy fish. Such things will happen. Next
I wasted precious minutes over a fish which when landed
proved to be just undersized, and I began to get anxious.
The fly was growing scarcer, and the day was drawing in.
After such a hatch, was I to return with only four trout? I
walked slowly up, scanning the water. At last, there he is,
right under the opposite bank, and a beauty too, for I can
see him. In some ways, the cross-stream cast is the easiest,
for if you are cunning and throw six inches short, the trout
never sees your gut and will turn his head out to take your
fly. And so it happened. I waited till he had turned back,
and gave a good pull. It was long before this gallant fish
yielded, but he did so at last. He weighed only 1 ounce
under 3 pounds. And just as I got him out another fish put
up his head in midstream, and he too was caught. I looked
at my watch. It was six o'clock and all was over. I had
bagged six fish, and under their comfortable weight I
trudged happily homewards.

4 0
—

Now what, I said to myself, were the particular features
of that admirable day? First of all, the hatch of fly. It is
nearly forty years since I caught my first trout on the Test,
and it is the fashion to say that the fly then was much
more plentiful than now. This was undoubtedly true even
five years ago: whether it is true now I feel doubtful. Certainly mayfly is very thick again, and not only mayfly, for
I am sure that the small fly is increasing too. Indeed, I
have rarely seen a greater hatch. True, it did not last long,
about three hours: but during the time it was on the river
was covered. They are very wonderful things, these big
hatches, one of the great events of nature. Oh, the Test is
not decadent, I said to myself, it is still the greatest of
trout streams. Next the weather. Most writers upon chalk
streams tell us about sun and flowers and summer
meadows. The iron blue loves none of these. He delights in
rough and bitter winds, grey skies, and cold air. He rejoices
in our hard northern spring. And the more he is buffeted,
the more happily he rides out the storm. Lastly, when the
iron blue is on, trout prefer it to any other fly. On this day

there had been quantities of insects, amongst them that favourite food, the winter dun; yet I saw nothing eaten except the iron blue.

Thus ended the day, a day of hard work, and of failure mingled with success. What more can the fisherman desire? And what sport can compare with fishing?

PAULSON,
PAULSON,
EVERYWHERE

Robert Traver

A young district attorney—always on the lookout for trout hot spots—finds there is no justice.

For many years I was district attorney of this bailiwick, and during that time I naturally had much to do with game wardens and, of course, with overzealous citizens who collided with the hunting and fishing laws. Indeed, I discovered some of my best fishing spots through these uneasy encounters; and while the following yarn is scarcely a fishing story, in any sporting sense, it *is* about trout and about some of the trout waters I found while plying my D.A. trade.

Up my way old township politicians never die; they merely look that way. Instead they become justices of the peace. It is a special Valhalla that townships reserve for their political cripples and has the following invariable rules of admission: The justice of the peace must be over seventy; he must be deaf; he must be entirely ignorant of any law but never admit it; and, during the course of each trial, he must chew—and violently expel the juice of—at least one (1) full package of Peerless tobacco. It is preferable that he speak practically no English, and that with an accent, but in emergencies an occasional exception is permitted to slip by. Sometimes I preferred the former.

I could write a lament as thick as this book about the grotesque experiences I have had trying justice court cases out before some of these rural legal giants. It is a depressing thought. Instead I shall tell you about the trial of Ole Paulson before Justice of the Peace Ole Paulson.

Ole Paulson of Nestoria township was charged with catching forty-seven brook trout out of season with a net. Ole Paulson was in rather a bad way because it is never legal to take or possess forty-seven brook trout in one day; to fish for them in any manner out of season; or ever to take brook trout with a net, in or out of season. Ole Paulson promptly pleaded not guilty and the case was set for trial before His Honor, Justice of the Peace Ole Paulson, also of Nestoria. I drove up there to try the case rather than send one of my assistants, not because I panted to sit at the feet of Justice Paulson, Heaven knows, but largely because I was dying to find out precisely where a man could ever *find* forty-seven brook trout in one place, regardless of how he took them. It was also a riotously beautiful September day, and afforded the D.A. a chance to escape from that personal prison he inhabits called his office.

"Vell, hayloo, Yonny!" His Honor greeted me as I entered his crowded courtroom, a high-ceilinged, plaster-falling, permanently gloomy establishment from which he ordinarily dispensed insurance of all kinds, assorted tourist supplies, game and fish licenses, live bait, not to mention various and sundry bottled goods and rubber accessories. "Ve vas yoost satting here vaiting for yew!"

"Was you, Your Honor?" I cackled gleefully, warming up disgracefully to this local political sachem, pumping his limp hand, inquiring about his rheumatism—or was it his flaring ulcers?—respectfully solicitous over his interminable replies, making all the fuss and bother over him that both he and the villagers demanded whenever the District Attorney came to town to attend court. It was understood that we two initiates into the subtle mysteries of the law had to put on a show for the groundlings.... The courtroom was crowded, every adult male in the community having somehow gathered enough energy to forsake the village tavern for a few hours and move across the street for the trial.

I turned to the People's star witness, the eager young game warden who had arrested the defendant. "Is the jury chosen yet?" I asked him in a stage whisper that must have been audible to a farmer doing his fall plowing in the next township. There could be no sneaky professional secrets in Judge Paulson's court—the penalty was swift and sure defeat.

"Yes," the game warden answered, "I struck the jury this morning. The list of jurors was prepared by Deputy Sheriff Paulson here. The six jurors are all here now."

It had not escaped my notice that I seemed to be getting fairly well hemmed in by Paulsons, but it was a trifle late to get into that now. I'd have to trust to the Lord and a fast outfield. I turned to Justice Paulson and said: "Very well, Your Honor, the People are ready to proceed with the trial."

"Okay den," His Honor said, rapping his desk with a gavel ingeniously contrived from a hammer wrapped in an old sock. He pointed to six empty chairs against a far wall. "Yantlemen of da yury," he announced, "yew vill now go sat over dare." Six assorted local characters scrambled for their seats, relaxed with a sigh, and were duly sworn by Justice Paulson. Allowing the jurors to sit for the oath was only one of his minor judicial innovations.

Justice Paulson, exhausted by administering the oath, opened a fresh package of Peerless and stowed away an enormous chew in his cheek. There was a prolonged judicial pause while he slowly worked up this charge. He spat a preliminary stream against a tall brass cuspidor. *"Spa-n-n-n-g!"* rang this beacon, clanging and quivering like an oriental summons to evening prayer. "Okay," His Honor said in a Peerless-muffled voice.

"The People will call Conservation Officer Clark," I announced, and the eager young game warden arose, was sworn, took the stand—and told how he had come upon the defendant, Ole Paulson, lifting the net from Nestoria creek just below the second beaver dam in Section 9. "I caught him red-handed," he added.

"Do you have the trout and the net?" I asked the young warden, slyly noting the latitude and longitude of this fabulous spot.

"Oh, yes," he answered. "The net is in my car outside—and the trout are temporarily in the icebox in the tavern across the street. Is it okay if I go over and get them now?"

I turned to His Honor. "Your Honor, the People request a five-minute recess," I said.

Judge Paulson, moon-faced and entirely mute now from his expanding chew of Peerless, whanged another ringer, banged his homemade gavel on his desk and, thus unpouched, managed to make his ruling. "Yentlemen, Ay declare fi'-minoot intermissin so dat dis hare young conversation feller kin go gat his fish." He turned to a purple and bladdery bystander. "Sharley," he said, "go along vit him over an' unlock da tavern."

I gnawed restlessly on an Italian cigar while Charlie, the tavern owner and my sole witness, went across the street to fetch the evidence. The jury sat and stared at me in stolid silence. His Honor replenished his chew, like a starved Italian hand-stoking spaghetti. *"Whing!"* went the judge, every minute on the minute. A passing dog barked. The bark possessed a curious Swedish accent, not "woof" but *"weuf"!* I wondered idly whether "Sharley" and my man had got locked in a pinochle match when lo! they were back, the flushed tavern keeper appreciatively licking his moist chops over the unexpected alcoholic dividend he had been able to spear. The jury watched him closely, to a man corroded with envy. The young officer placed the confiscated net and a dishpan full of beautiful frozen brook trout on the judge's desk and resumed the witness chair.

"Officer, you may state whether or not this is the net you found the defendant lifting from Nestoria creek on the day in question?" I asked, pointing.

"It is," the officer testified.

Pointing at the fish: "And were all these fish the brook trout you removed from the net?"

"They were."

"Were the fish then living?"

"About half. But they were nearly done in. None would have survived.

"How many are there in the pan?"

"Forty-seven."

I introduced the exhibits into evidence and turned to Judge Paulson. "The People rest," I said.

"Plink!" acknowledged Judge Paulson, turning to the defendant. "Da defandant vill now race his right han' an' tell da yury *hiss* side of da story." It was not a request.

Ole Paulson was sworn and testified that it was indeed he who had been caught lifting the writhing net; that he had merely been patrolling the creek looking for beaver signs for the next trapping season when he had come across the illegal net; that the net was not his and was not set by him; and that he was just lifting the net to free the unfortunate trout and destroy the net when, small world, the conservation officer had come along and arrested him for his humanitarian pains. "Dat's all dare vere to it!" he concluded.

I badgered and toyed with the witness for several minutes, but it was an unseasonably hot September day and I could see that the fans were anxious to get back across the street to their hot pinochle games and cool beer, so I cut my cross-examination short. In my brief jury argument I pointed out the absurdity of the defendant's story that he was out prowling a trout stream in mid-September looking for beaver signs for a trapping season that opened the following March. I also briefly gave my standard argument that every time a game violator did things like this he was really no different from a thief stealing the people's tax money—that the fish and game belonged to *all* the people....The members of the jury blinked impassively over such strange political heresy.

"S-splank!" went Judge Paulson, scoring another bull's-

eye. Had any man moved carelessly into the crossfire he would have risked inundation and possible drowning.

The defendant's argument was even briefer than mine. "Yantleman of da yury," he said, rising and pointing scornfully at the fish net. "Who da hecks ever caught a gude Svede using vun of dem gol-dang homemade Finlander nets? *Ay tank you!*" He sat down.

"B-blink!" went the Judge, banishing the jury to the back room to consider their verdict.

The jury was thirstier than I thought. "Ve find da defandant *note gueelty!*" the foreman gleefully announced, two minutes later.

"Whang!" rang the cuspidor, accepting and celebrating the verdict.

After the crowd had surged tavernward, remarkably without casualty, I glanced over the six-man jury list, moved by sheer morbid curiosity. This was the list:

> Ragnar Paulson
> Swan Paulson
> Luther Paulson
> Eskil Paulson
> Incher Paulson
> Magnus Carl Magnuson

I turned to Deputy Sheriff Paulson. "How," I asked sternly, "how did this ringer Magnuson ever get on this jury list?"

Deputy Paulson shrugged. "Ve yust samply ran out of Paulsons," he apologized. "Anyway, Magnuson dare vere my son's brudder-in-law. My son vere da defandant, yew know!"

"Spang!" gonged His Honor, like a benediction. "Dat vere true, Yonny," he said. "My nephew dare—da deputy sheriff—he nefer tell a lie!"

I lurched foggily across the street and banged on the bar. "Drinks fer da house!" I ordered, suddenly going native. "Giff all da Paulsons in da place vatever dey vant!"

THE MAYFLIES

Romilly Fedden

Creative — though questionable — tactics for elevating trout that seem glued to the bottom.

For me no pipe has tasted half so sweet since that morning of early June when Jean Pierre and I went fishing. On such a day you smoke it only as far as you must tread the dusty high-road; like to the faithful who loose their shoes from off their feet when entering holy ground, so you knock out the dottle on the last kilometre-stone and then turn off into Pan's sun-splashed temple.

We followed the green glooms of the winding trail, all tremulous with wildflowers, past clumps of foxglove bells, where fat bees crawled and buzzed contentedly, and then we reached the shadow-haunted pool. Here in the late gloaming the fauns and dryads keep their tryst, but earlier come the slow-moving cattle to the watering, led by a goddess of untutored grace, white-coiffed, sedate with shining, dreamy eyes.

All this is true, for when you pass that way you'll find the pool's brink splashed to purple mire where cows have stood with gleaming sides and misty breath, the water dripping from their cool, moist nozzles; and at the pool's end, where the path sweeps round under the thick nut-branches, you'll come upon the print of small, hooved feet. The foolish might suppose this the spoor of Widow

Chouan's goats, but they abide, at least, a *lieue* away and would not stray so far; besides, these marks were never made by Breton goat, they show a hoof more arched and classic.

At this spot is a tinkling runnel screened by great bracken fronds and heather. Beyond the ground breaks steeply away, and you emerge on open rock-strewn country. Here and there you will see a homestead with its orchard, but for the most part uncultivated land; all this the peasants call "the happy valley."

We count words pleasant or unpleasing by past significance, by their bearing on our personal remembrance. I wish that I could change this name, for some of us cannot forget another "happy valley" in far Picardy, where things that once were men lay huddled stark and black-faced under a brazen and a cloudless sky. But here we would blot out all infamy, hark back to living days of June, before the world went mad. Therefore we will call this Breton vale "the golden valley." And truly, for in the spring it is a symphony of gold and variant green. Then summer comes, and finds it clad in gold and black. (No, not the black of printer's-ink, but that which the painter uses in thin transparent glaze to harmonise a gaudy colour or to restrain a glaring light.) In autumn this landscape turns to gold and rose, for at that time great piles of apples lie in the orchards, the hillside is aflame with sun-tanned whin and heather, brambles and red berries. With the coming of the evening light the stalks of dead asphodels gleam like coral, and oak-leaves are as molten gold.

Within this valley are two streams separated by a long strip of rough pastureland; they join some few miles further down at the mill of Kastennec. We reached the first and smaller stream to find it alive with Mayfly. A big hatch of fly on such a brook is a sight which must be seen to be fully realised.

The larvæ for the past two years have spent a drab existence within the riverbed, but now, with the warmth of a second summer season, they work to the surface, and emerge in the *sub-imago,* or first winged state known as the *green drake*. But it is only the female who changes her clothes openly upon the river's brim, unlacing her caddis corsets, and arranging her "transformation" for all the world to see. The male, on the other hand, is something of a poltroon; moreover, he hates to get his feet wet, so crawls up the nearest reed-stem on to the bank, and then he hatches, after which he seldom ventures over the water, but hurries off inland as fast as he can flutter. There, with swift and unerring instinct, the lady seeks him out, willy-nilly he must become the father of her children. In point of fact, this is the serio-comedy of "Man and Superman" as played in Mayfly land. So is Mr. Bernard Shaw vindicated even in the insect world.

After the brief honeymoon is passed, the lady returns to the river-side. (We hear no more of her luckless spouse.) She is now known as the *grey drake,* a buxom dame with all the airs and assurance of a wedded woman; further, she is about to become a mother. A few minutes more will see her hovering above the river, dropping her eggs in one by one. She has, indeed, a most prodigious family! Yet have they many enemies, and roving sticklebacks will thin their ranks during the two years that they must remain in the soft gravel nursery. The old drake is now growing weary, her birth-flights slow. Lower and lower she falls, till at length she sinks inanimate upon the water. It is then that, with wings outstretched, she floats away down-stream as the *spent-gnat*. This final phase provides food of the fish; but it is while undergoing the earlier, *sub-imago* change that the female is most freely taken by the trout, while swallows and birds of all kinds devour the Mayfly in their hundreds.

Here on our little brook fat green drakes were fluttering everywhere, crawling up the reed-stems, hovering above the alder-bushes, and floating gaily down the sun-capped ripple where the fish were rising furiously. Alas! these trout are only small ones; this golden, shallow brook holds but fingerlings, eight to the pound. They would be fun with an 00 midge on finest drawn point; but now we were out for bigger game, and a great *Marquis* on stout gut amongst these small fry seemed coarse and out of place. We caught ten and returned nine, and then I moved on across the pastures and reached the larger stream. Here all was quiet, not a fish broke surface, and curiously enough, though such a short distance away, not a single Mayfly floated on this water. High overhead a swarm of *undertakers* soared and dipped continuously in their weird "dance of death." Apparently their carnival was over, and we arrived too late. Yet what a stream it was, with those long oily runs between the starry white-flowered weeds, and those green slow-moving depths under the willow-trees. Just the water to hold big fish. The only thing to be done was to sit down and wait patiently for those big fish to rise. The grass was soft and fragrant. Now and again a dabchick would move amongst the masses of white water-ranunculus, or a skimming swallow dint the river's surface to form a widening circle, bearing a short-lived hope. Once a pearl-throated ouzel splashed in the shadows, but never once a trout.

The stream some distance higher up is fast-flowing, with shallow goils and amber stickles. In turn were these all carefully fished with a spent gnat, and no result. Eventually I returned to sit again and watch in the shade of the same willow-tree. The dabchicks still bobbed up and down amidst the weed to tantalise by poignant hint, breaking the monotony of silence. The day was very hot, the midges tiresome. Jean Pierre had got my landing-net. He knew perfectly well that I should need it if I hooked one of these problematical trout of which I had heard so much. He evidently preferred to catch fingerlings. By now he must have murdered some dozens at least, and not a quarter-pounder among the lot. I was perspiring, tired, and very cross. I could not then appreciate the fact that there are worse places in which to while away the hours of such a day than the green shade of that deep-grassed river-bank; but Nature was sympathetic; despite the gnats and heat I fell asleep.

Some half-hour later, blinking through the sunlight, I marked the coming of Jean Pierre. Apparently he was heading a triumphal procession. My landing-net was held on high, and behind him marched Mariic and Suzanne, carrying various cardboard boxes and an improvised butterfly-net. Jean Pierre was hot, damp, and smiling. His pockets bulged, and as we watched, from out his person a few Mayflies escaped to hover in halo round his head. Then he explained. It had taken some time to go to the farm and procure boxes and an extra net, even longer to catch a sufficient quantity of bait. True, the big fish were not moving, there was no hatch of fly; why, then we must create a hatch of fly, after that our fish would rise and feed on them.

My old friend is wise in the ways of all creatures which move beneath the waters, and yet this theory of his seemed oversanguine. I confess I was somewhat sceptical as I followed him up to the head of that long, deep reach to sit with Mariic and Suzanne while he commenced operations.

First Jean Pierre took a tin of Mayflies from his pocket, emptying them into the butterfly-net, which was then twisted over and soused in the river. Jean Pierre and Nature do not commence their tactics on the surface, so this first batch of fly must travel down as submerged as possible. The net was now lowered till it rested on the gravel-bed, its open mouth against the stream; from time to time it turned for a moment to allow the current to carry off a few of the insects. Lying full-length on the bank and looking down through the clear water, one could see the flies quite plainly, but not their wings, which were so sodden and flattened as to be practically invisible. In fact, each full-fledged drake was made to play, very creditably, the rôle of hatching nymph. Batches of fly continued to enter the net and follow each other in increasing numbers, borne along in the slowly moving current. At length I imagined I saw a faint grey flash from the depths some distance below. Then came the suggestion of a swirl in the shadow of the willow-trees. Jean Pierre had seen it, too, for the next lot of fly were allowed to float upon the surface. As the vanguard of that argosy bobbed into the shade of the first willow it was seized by a rising trout. I sprang for my rod, but Jean Pierre waved me back. Things must be done decently and in order. Three fish at least must be steadily feeding before we could think of commencing to fish for them.

Then a trout rose almost under our feet, just sipping the fly from the scarcely ruffled surface. At the edge of a weed-bed a great fish came up with a boil and another fly vanished. A third trout was assiduously sucking away a few yards below, and there were informative oily swirls some distance down the far bank.

It was then that Jean Pierre laid hold of the landing-net, then that Suzanne was allowed to grasp the last and largest cardboard box. Her instructions were terse, ruthless, and complete. Only one half-inch must the lid be raised. As each fly crawled out must his head be firmly pinched, his not too agile person cast upon the waters. Equably, one by one, must these victims reach the voracious trout while we attacked some hundred yards below.

What need to recount the crowded hour which followed? All of us, some time or other, must have known the joys of a Mayfly carnival. Moreover, the interest of that day lay not so much in the actual catching of the fish as in the way they were induced to feed, in spite of their sulky humour.

The account of Jean Pierre's miraculous hatch of fly may sound incredible, yet it can be vouched for by one who actually saw the feat performed; and I believe, given a sufficient quantity of Mayflies to allure the fish, that a similar artificial rise could be created on any of our southern chalk streams. If we carry the theory of these tactics a little further there will come a day when we shall have our hatch of Duns and Spinners to time and order, so shall we bring about our own damnation and ruin the delightful uncertainty of the game.

The bag that day was not excessive, yet we took four and a half brace within that length of river, the best fish being just under two pounds. Of course, we failed to land the really big one, but then (as many fishers know), that always seems to happen. His loss must ever remain a poignant memory. His weight we dare not estimate aloud. At times Jean Pierre and I still speak of him in whispers, my old friend's arms stretched wide. He was a great fish, and put up a royal fight. Through all its length and strife our good luck held uncannily, cutting for us a pathway through the weeds, guiding the line through countless snags of sunken root and bramble. Only when the battle was really won, the great fish lying in all his glorious spotted length, dead-beat upon the surface, only then did fate play us false. That moment stands clear-cut. The whole scene focussed in a small Mayfly, rosy with sunlight, securely imbedded in a great open jaw. I see the lowering landing-net, Jean Pierre's strong arm stretched out; above, the arched rod strung by the tense line, the taut gut, frayed by the snags and perilously whitened at its finer end, the sun-touched fly confident, secure. Then fate laughed. The cast snapped. Slowly the great fish rolled over and sank like a phantom in the depths.

A DAY ON THE NAR

Edward R. Hewitt

*From the man who taught two genera-
tions of American trouters with hard-core
"how-to" pieces, a rare idyll of a day a-
stream.*

My old friend Sir Neville Jodrell had often told me that no matter what anyone said, the most delightful rural fishing in England was in Norfolk, the flat, low-lying county facing the North Sea. He had asked me to Stanhoe many times, but something always seemed to prevent the visit. At last the chance came and I was on the train for King's Lynn. My bags and rods were in the rack opposite, and it all seemed very pleasant until a distinguished-looking, grumpy old gentleman entered the compartment at the last moment, and sat down opposite. The train had no sooner got into motion than he roared out, "Don't you know, sir, that you cannot have your luggage above my head? Sir, you must remove it at once."

He had evidently noticed that I was an American, and this seemed like a red rag to a bull. The bags were easily placed above my own head, and I settled down to read, looking now and then at the lovely Cambridgeshire scenery, and listening to him snort every little while.

At last we arrived at King's Lynn, with Sir Neville on the platform waiting to greet me. The old gentleman bowed to him most cordially and he introduced me as his old friend, paying a visit. The old gentleman was all suavity at once, when he knew that I belonged to the gentleman class, and had not taken a first class compartment by mistake. As we drove along in the antiquated car, Sir Neville told me that old Birkbeck had the lower part of the Nar fishing, was considered one of the best trout fishermen in England, and had been trying for years to join the group which had Lord Leicester's good fishing on the Nar at Castle Acre.

"It would never do, you know, to have him, although he is a fine fisherman; he is only a banker after all!"

This was my first introduction to the feelings of the old gentry of Norfolk, the most clannish county in England. Sir Neville's father had been connected with the Norwich Cathedral, and the family had been gentry in the county since the Conquest. Of course it would never do to let in a banker on good fishing for gentry only!

A twenty-mile drive brought us to Stanhoe, which was a Georgian type of house, built by Sir Robert Walpole to live in while his large house, Holcomb Hall, was being constructed.

Lady Jodrell was as charming as ever at dinner, and afterward, over the coffee and port in the study, Sir Neville jumped up and cried out: "We have found the pass, we have found the pass."

I thought the port had gone to his head, but I asked "What pass? I have never heard of it."

"Don't you know that there has always been a tradition in the family that we had a pass signed by Edward, the Black Prince, to allow Sir Paul Jodrell and thirty archers to pass over to England after the battle of Crecy? I could never find it, and behold, the other day in looking over an old book, it fell out. It must have been there for a least two hundred and fifty years."

He opened the desk, and handed over a small piece of yellowed parchment, with the wax seal of the Black Prince on it and the pass in archaic English. It seemed not out of place in the hands of the descendant of that captain of the archers. Taken to the British Museum, they stated that this was the only pass of this kind known. Sir Neville wrote me later, that he had decided that it should be carefully preserved, and had sent it to the Manchester Museum together with some other Jodrell relics, and you will see it there when you visit the museum.

These old Georgian houses are famous for their cellars for maturing port. They knew just how to build them in those days. A firm of wine merchants in London had offered Sir Neville to fill his cellar with port and he could take anything he liked any time, keeping a record of what he used, if he would allow them to store in the cellar. I did not look, but the port we had was certainly stored at the right temperature and for the right length of time.

The next day was fine, and we got off early. I had not realized the great chances I had taken the night before in the drive from Lynn in the old car. It was wandering all over the road, as the steering gear had half a turn of looseness in the wheel and the knuckles and cross rods were so loose that they rattled. Sir Neville, brought up with horses, had never become accustomed to cars, although he thought he was a wonderful driver, as in truth he was. No one else could have avoided an accident for a half-hour. Everyone in Norfolk knew him, and gave him all the road, so we finally reached the mill on the Nar in safety, at the top of the Nar water.

Nearly all the streams in England have these old brick water mills, where the local flour is ground. They form part of the countryside.

The Nar is a small stream of beautiful, clear, chalk water, about ten or fifteen feet wide, running through water meadows, from the mill down. These so-called water meadows were made by the monks of the Middle Ages so that the gates could be closed and the meadows flooded. They had found that in this way they could secure an earlier crop of grass, and also a fine second crop, by again flooding after the first was cut. In our times, all these works have gone to decay, but in some places they still greatly improve the fishing.

Below the mill was a large, circular pool of clear, deep water with a big bed of weeds at one side. I looked in and

could see no fish, but the miller said there were plenty
there, and large ones, so I got below and tried a dry fly.
Nothing happened, and I was about to give up, when a
small butterfly flew across, close to the bunch of weeds.
The whole water just exploded. At least four large trout
tried for the butterfly at once. When it had quieted down, I
tried again, with a larger dry fly, and finally succeeded in
taking one fish about twelve inches long, but never saw
the big ones again. If I had known the "Neversink skater"
then, I think there would have been a different story to
tell.

When it became evident that we would get no more at
the mill, we returned to the car, and drove down a mile or
so to the village of Castle Acre. As we went along Sir Neville told me a little of the history of the place. The rise of
ground near the stream had been the site of a prehistoric
fort of the ancient Britons. When the Romans took the
country they built a fort and camp there, and used this as a
rallying center for the legions when there was an attack by
the Northmen on the coast. During the last war, the general staff considered that this would be the best place for a
gathering of troops for repelling a German landing, and it
was made the center for this purpose. So little have mili-
tary dispositions changed in two thousand years. During
the Middle Ages, there was a castle built from the remains
of the Roman fort, and gate towers standing today are
probably Roman. A large abbey sprang up with its great
church, and this thriving religious center prospered until
Henry the Eighth placed his mark of destruction upon the
place.

We unloaded our tackle and lunch from the car, and carried them down through the ruins of the abbey to the part
overlooking the stream, and rigged up for a good fish before lunch.

The stream was full of trout, from eight to twelve inches
long, but, as with all English streams I have fished, they
were wary and extremely hard to catch, at least for an
American. However, every little while one could be found
feeding close to the bank and if the right fly were placed
delicately enough at just the proper place, a rise would

often take place. It was delightful sport, and I managed to get about six or eight fish before lunch, wondering all the time if there were not some old, big fellows under the shelving banks, which could be coaxed out if one only knew how. Anyway, I saw none of them and tramped back to the old abbey ruins, when I heard Sir Neville's whistle. As we sat eating the delicious lunch, with two kinds of wine topped off with a fine old port, Sir Neville told me more of the history of the valley. It appears that in the reign of Queen Elizabeth, Lord Coke, who was her Lord Chief Justice, was buying up the land for his great estate. The Queen became jealous at the amount of property he seemed able to acquire and sending for him, remarked: "It doth not please me that thou shouldst acquire so large an estate, and I bid thee cease."

"I obey Your Majesty's commands but crave just one favor, that I be permitted to purchase just three more acres."

"Thy wish is granted; go purchase thy three acres, but see to it that thou dost not disobey my commands."

Lord Coke returned to Norfolk and at once purchased the lands of the Monasteries of Castle Acre, West Acre and East Acre, twenty thousand acres in all. When the Queen heard of this, she took it as a grand joke on herself and allowed him to keep these lands, which form the Leicester estate of today, descended directly from Lord Coke.

Two hours is a short time for such a lunch, but too soon it came time for the afternoon fishing before tea at the Inn, with its old theatre for strolling Shakespearean players. Sir Neville had told me of a large trout which lived in a pool above the Abbey; a certain old washerwoman, famous for cuddling trout, had been unable to catch it, although she had removed all the other fish from this pool. When I got to the point where I could see the water around the bend, I watched carefully for any sign of the big trout. Yes, there was a ring close to the overhanging left bank—there it was again; that fish was feeding regularly. It must be the big trout. I approached carefully within casting distance and could see, every few rises, the big back fin come out as he sucked in the drifting flies. This was not a hard cast, but a single mistake would be sure to put him down. A one-cast fish for a certainty. Well, the tackle was all right, and here was my chance. Several false casts and a full one up the opposite side of the stream showed that the fly would set up well, and the leader make the proper curl. It was now or never, so here goes. Just as the cast was straightening out a puff of wind blew the fly to the bank and it settled on a flat blade of grass, flush with the water, and rested there. It looked as if the trout had not been alarmed, because he came up for another natural fly. When it was about time for him to rise again, I pulled the fly gently from the grass, and it came floating right over where he had risen. The telltale ring appeared and the fly sank. A lift of the rod, and I felt the fish, at the same moment he sensed the fly and turned and rushed downstream past me, almost hitting my waders. Long experience is a good companion for such a situation, and I just fed him loose line from the reel and ran downstream, as I knew he would not go far. Sure enough, there he was, resting behind a bunch of weeds but not fast in them. Getting below him again, and tightening the line, I made him run up a little in the channel, and then turn and rush again downstream. In those English chalk waters, as long as a trout is working down you have a good chance to keep him out of the weeds so that he will not get foul of them, but if he starts up, he will bore into them and then your chances are small of ever landing your fish. Two rushes tired this fellow out, and he came to a clear pool where I could handle him. In those days, I carried a net, and had no difficulty in getting this under him. A wonderful trout, golden yellow, deep and fat, about three and a half pounds. A big one for so small a stream. I had had my fun and was ready for tea when Sir Neville whistled. He wanted to know if there had been any sport. I told him I would show him when we reached the inn. Tea was already on the table when we took off our things, and I laid out the big fish. Sir Neville was delighted and kept looking at him for some time. Finally he said: "Do you want this fish?"

"Good gracious, no, do anything you like with him. He has done all he can for me already."

"Well, I was just thinking that my Labor opponent lives in this village, and it might make a better feeling if I sent him a big fish."

The trout was wrapped up, and Sir Neville wrote a card, and the boy went off with it. I thought that this was the last I would ever hear of that fish, but no! When Sir Neville died, five years ago, Lady Jodrell sent me a clipping from the Lynn paper giving an account of his life and how beloved and respected he was by all classes in the county. Among his characteristic good deeds was that he had caught the big trout from the pool at Castle Acre on the Nar, and generously sent it to his political opponent. A reputation-making trout, my big fish!

THE LONGEST
SILENCE

Thomas McGuane

*A top novelist takes you to the Florida
Keys for the most-prized, and elusive, fish
on the flats.*

hat is emphatic in angling is made so by
the long silences—the unproductive pe-
riods. For the ardent fisherman, progress
is toward the kinds of fishing that are
never productive in the sense of the blood
riots of the hunting-and-fishing periodicals. Their illusions
of continuous action evoke for him, finally, a condition of
utter, mortuary boredom. Such an angler will always be
inclined to find the gunnysack artists of the heavy kill
rather cretinoid, their stringerloads of gaping fish appalling.

No form of fishing offers such elaborate silences as fly-
fishing for permit. The most successful permit fly-fisherman in the world has very few catches to describe to you.
Yet there is considerable agreement that taking a permit
on a fly is the extreme experience of the sport. Even the
guides allow enthusiasm to shine through their cool, professional personas. I once asked one who specialized in permit if he liked fishing for them. "Yes, I do," he said
reservedly, "but about the third time the customer asks,

'Is they good to eat?' I begin losing interest."

The recognition factor is low when you catch a permit. If you wake up your neighbor in the middle of the night to tell him of your success, shaking him by the lapels of his Dr. Dentons and shouting to be heard over his million-BTU air conditioner, he may well ask you what a permit is, and you will tell him it is like a pompano, and rolling over, he will tell you he cherishes pompano like he had it at Joe's Stone Crab in Miami Beach, with key lime pie afterward. If you have one mounted, you'll always be explaining what it is to people who thought you were talking about your fishing license in the first place. In the end you take the fish off the conspicuous wall and put it upstairs, where you can see it when Mom sends you to your room. It's private.

I came to it through bonefishing. The two fish share the same marine habitat, the negotiation of which in a skiff can be somewhat hazardous. It takes getting used to, to run wide open at 30 knots over a close bottom, with sponges, sea fans, crawfish traps, conchs, and starfish racing under the hull with awful clarity. The backcountry of the Florida Keys is full of hummocks, narrow, winding waterways and channels that open with complete arbitrariness to basins, and, on every side, the flats that preoccupy the fisherman. The process of learning to fish this region is one of learning the particularities of each of these flats. The channel flats with crunchy staghorn-coral bottoms, the bare sand flats, and the turtle-grass flats are all of varying utility to the fisherman, and depending upon tide, these values are in a constant condition of change. The principal boat wreckers are the yellow cap-rock flats and the more mysterious coral heads. I was personally plagued by a picture of one of these enormities coming through the hull of my skiff and catching me on the point of the jaw. I had the usual Coast Guard safety equipment, not excluding floating cushions emblazoned FROST-FREE KEY WEST and a futile plastic whistle. I added a navy flare gun. As I learned the country, guides would run by me in their big skiffs and 100-horse engines. I knew they never hit coral

heads and had, besides, CB radios with which they might
call for help. I dwelled on that and sent for radio catalogues.

One day when I was running to Content Pass on the
edge of the Gulf of Mexico, I ran aground wide open in the
backcountry. Unable for the moment to examine the lower
unit of my engine, I got out of the boat, waiting for the tide
to float it, and strolled around in four inches of water. It
was an absolutely windless day. The mangrove islands
stood elliptically in their perfect reflections. The birds
were everywhere—terns, gulls, wintering ducks, skim-
mers, all the wading birds, and, crying down from their
tall shafts of air, more ospreys than I had ever seen. The
gloomy bonanza of the Overseas Highway with its idiot
billboard montages seemed very far away.

On the western edge of that flat I saw my first permit,
tailing in two feet of water. I had heard all about permit
but had been convinced I'd never see one. So, looking at
what was plainly a permit, I did not know what it was.
That evening, talking to my friend Woody Sexton, a permit
expert, I reconstructed the fish and had it identified for
me. I grew retroactively excited, and Woody apprised me of
some of the difficulties associated with catching one of
them on a fly. A prompt, immobilizing humility came over
me forthwith.

After that, over a long period of time, I saw a good
number of them. Always, full of hope, I would cast. The
fly was anathema to them. One look and they were gone.
I cast to a few hundred. It seemed futile, all wrong, like
trying to bait a tiger with watermelons. The fish would
see the fly, light out or ignore it, sometimes flare at it,
but never, never touch it. I went to my tying vise and
made flies that looked like whatever you could name,
flies that were praiseworthy from anything but a practical point of view. The permit weren't interested, and I no
longer even caught bonefish. I went back to my old fly, a
rather ordinary bucktail, and was relieved to be catching
bonefish again. I thought I had lost what there was of
my touch.

•   •   •

One Sunday morning I decided to conduct services in the skiff, taking the usual battery of rods for the permit pursuit. More and more the fish had become a simple abstraction, even though they had made one ghostly midwater appearance, poised silver as moons near my skiff, and had departed without movement, like a light going out. But I wondered if I had actually seen them. I must have. The outline and movement remained in my head—the dark fins, the pale gold of the ventral surface, and the steep, oversized scimitar tails. I dreamed about them.

This fell during the first set of April's spring tides—exaggerated tides associated with the full moon. I had haunted a long, elbow-shaped flat on the Atlantic side of the keys, and by Sunday there was a large movement of tide and reciprocal tide. A 20-knot wind complicated my still unsophisticated poling, and I went down the upper end of the flat yawing from one edge to the other and at times raging as the boat tried to swap ends against my will. I looked around, furtively concerned with whether I could be seen by any of the professionals. At the corner of the flat I turned downwind and proceeded less than 40 yards when I spotted, on the southern perimeter of the flat, a large stingray making a strenuous mud. When I looked closely it seemed there was something else swimming in the disturbance. I poled toward it for a better look. The other fish was a very large permit. The ray had evidently stirred up a crab and was trying to cover it to prevent the permit from getting it. The permit, meanwhile, was whirling around the ray, nipping its fins to make it move off the crab.

Now my problem was to set the skiff up above the fish, get rid of the push pole, drift down, and make a cast. I quietly poled upwind, wondering why I had not been spotted. I was losing my breath with excitement; the little expanse of skin beneath my sternum throbbed like a frog's throat. I acquired a fantastic lack of coordination. Turning in the wind, I beat the boat with the push pole, like a gong. I conducted what a friend has described as a Chinese fire drill. After five minutes of the direst possible clownage I got into position and could still see the permit's fins break-

ing the surface of the ray's mud. I laid the push pole down,
picked up my fly rod, and, to my intense irritation, saw
that the ray had given up and was swimming, not seeing
me, straight to the skiff. The closing rate was ruinous. I
couldn't get a cast off in time to do anything. About 20 feet
from the boat the ray sensed my presence and veered 15
feet off my starboard gunwale, leaving the permit swimming close to the ray but on my side. As soon as I could see
the permit perfectly, it started to flush, but instead just
crossed to the opposite side of the ray. Taking the only
chance offered me, I cast over the ray, hoping my line
would not spook it and, in turn, the permit. The fly fell
with lucky, agonizing perfection, three feet in front of the
permit on its exact line of travel. There was no hesitation;
the fish darted forward and took—the one-in-a-thousand
shot. I lifted the rod, feeling the rigid bulk of the still un-
alarmed fish, and set the hook. He shimmered away, my
loose line jumping off the deck. And then the rod suddenly
doubled and my leader broke. A loop of line had tightened
itself around the handle of the reel.

I was ready for the rubber room. I had been encouraged
to feel it might be five years before I hooked another. I
tried to see all that was good in other kinds of fishing. I
thought of various life-enhancing things I could do at
home. I could turn to the ennobling volumes of world literature on my shelves. I might do some oils, slap out a
gouache or two. But I could not distract myself from the
mental image of my lovingly assembled fly rushing from
my hands on the lip of a big permit.

I had to work out a routine that would not depend on
such exceptional events for success. One technique, finally,
almost guaranteed me shots at permit, and that was to
stake out my skiff on the narrow channel flats that are
covered with a crunchy layer of blue-green staghorn coral.
Permit visit these in succession, according to tide and a
hierarchy of flat values known mainly to them but intuited
by certain strenuous fishermen. I liked to be on these flats
at the early incoming tide—the young flood, as it is called
—and fish to the middle incoming or, often, to the slack

high. The key was to be able to stand for six hours and watch an acre of bottom for any sign of life at all. The body would give out in the following sequence: arches, back, hips. Various dehydration problems developed. I carried ice and drank quinine water until my ears rang. Pushups and deep knee bends on the casting deck helped. And, like anyone else who uses this method, I became an active fantasizer. The time was punctuated by the appearances of oceanic wildlife, fish and turtles that frequented the area as well as many that did not. With any luck at all the permit came, sometimes in a squadron and in a hurry, sometimes alone with their tails in the air, rooting along the hard edge of the flat. The cast would be made, the line and leader would straighten and the fly fall. On a normal day the fly only made the permit uncomfortable, and it would turn and gravely depart. On another the fly so horrified the fish that it turned tail and bolted. On very few days it sprinted at the fly, stopped a few inches short, ran in a circle when the fly was gently worked, returned and flared at it, flashed at it, saw the boat and flushed.

On very hot days when the cumulus clouds stacked in a circle around the horizon, a silky sheen of light lay on the water, so that the vision had to be forced through until the head ached. Patience was strained from the first, and water seemed to stream from the skin. At such times I was counting on an early sighting of fish to keep my attention. And when this did not happen I succumbed to an inviting delusion. I imagined the best place to fish was somewhere very far away, and it would be necessary to run the country.

I reeled up my line and put the rod in its holder. I took the push pole out of the bottom and secured it in its chocks on the gunwale. Then I let the wind carry me off the flat. I started the engine and put it in forward, suffering exquisitely a moment more, then ran the throttle as far as it would go. The bow lifted, then lowered on plane, the stern came up, and the engine whined satisfactorily. Already the perspiration was drying, and I felt cool and slaked by the spray. Once on top, standing and steering, running wide open, I projected on my mind what was remembered of a suitable chart to get to this imaginary place where the fish were thick enough to walk on. I looked up and was reproved by the vapor trail of a Navy Phantom interceptor. I ran up the channels, under the bridge, using all the cheap tricks I thought I could get away with, short-cutting flats when I thought I had enough water, looking back to see if I made a mud trail, running the banks to get around basins because the coral heads wouldn't grow along a bank, running tight to the keys in a foot and a half of water when I was trying to beat the wind, and finally shutting down on some bank or flat or along some tidal pass not unlike the one I just ran from. It was still as hot as it could be, and I still could not see. The sweat was running onto my Polaroids, and I was hungry and thinking I'd call it a day. When I got home I rather abashedly noted that I had burned a lot of fuel and hadn't made a cast.

6 8

The engine hadn't been running right for a week, and I was afraid of getting stranded or having to sleep out on some buggy flat or, worse, being swept to Galveston on an offshore wind. I tore the engine down and found the main bearing seal shot and in need of replacement. I drove to Big Pine to get parts and arrived about the time the guides, who center there, were coming in for the day. I walked to the dock, where the big skiffs with their excessive engines were nosed to the breakwater. Guides mopped decks and needled each other. Customers, happy and not, debarked with armloads of tackle, sun hats, oil, thermoses, and picnic baskets. A few of these sporty dogs were plastered. One fragile lady, owlish with sunburn, tottered from the casting deck of a guide's skiff and drew herself up on the dock. "Do you know what the whole trouble was?" she inquired of her companion, perhaps her husband, a man very much younger than herself.

"No, what?" he said. She smiled and pitied him.

"Well, *think* about it." The two put their belongings into the trunk of some kind of minicar and drove off too fast down the Overseas Highway. Four hours would put them in Miami.

It seemed to have been a good day. A number of men

went up the dock with fish to be mounted. One man went
by with a bonefish that might have gone 10 pounds. Woody
Sexton was on the dock. I wanted to ask how he had done
but knew that ground rules forbid the asking of this question around the boats. It embarrasses guides who have had
bad days, on the one hand, and on the other, it risks passing good fishing information promiscuously. Meanwhile, as
we talked, the mopping and needling continued along the
dock. The larger hostilities are reserved for the fishing
grounds themselves, where various complex snubbings
may be performed from the semi-anonymity of the powerful skiffs. The air can be electric with accounts of who cut
off who, who ran the bank on who, and so on. The antago-
nism among the skiff guides, the offshore guides, the pompano fishermen, the crawfishermen, the shrimpers,
produces tales of shootings, of disputes settled with gaffs,
of barbed wire strung in guts and channels to wreck prop
and drive shafts. Some of the tales are true. Woody and I
made a plan to fish when he got a day off. I found my
engine parts and went home.

69

I worked out two or three bonefish patterns for the inside bank of Loggerhead Key. The best of these was a turn-
off point where the bonefish which were contouring the
bank hit a small ridge and turned up onto the flat itself.
By positioning myself at this turning point, I would be able
to get casts off to passing fish and be able to see a good
piece of the bank, down light, until noon.

One day I went out and staked the boat during the mid-
dle-incoming water of another set of new moon tides. I
caught one bonefish early in the tide, a lively fish that
went 100 yards on his first run and doggedly resisted me
for a length of time that was all out of proportion to his
weight. I released him after giving him a short revival ses-
sion and then just sat and looked at the water. I could see
Woody fishing with a customer, working the outside of the
bank for tarpon.

It was a queer day to begin with. The vital light flashed
on and off around the scudding clouds, and there were
slight foam lines on the water from the wind. The basin

that shelved off from my bank was active with diving birds, particularly great brown pelicans, whose wings sounded like luffing sails and who ate with submerged heads while blackheaded gulls tried to rob them. The birds were drawn to the basin by a school of mullet that was making an immense mud slick hundreds of yards across. In the sun the slick glowed a quarter of a mile to the south. I didn't pay it much attention until it began by collective will or chemical sensors to move onto my bank. Inexorably, the huge disturbance progressed and flowed toward me. In the thinner water the mullet school was compressed, and the individual fish became easier targets for predators. Big oceanic barracuda were with them and began slashing and streaking through the school like bolts of lightning. Simultaneously, silver sheets of mullet, sometimes an acre in extent, burst out of the water and rained down again. In time my skiff was in the middle of it, and I could see the opaque water was inch by inch alive.

Some moments later, not far astern of me, perhaps 70 feet, a large blacktip shark swam up onto the bank and began traveling with grave sweeps of its tail through the fish, not as yet making a move for them. Mullet and smaller fish nevertheless showered out in front of the shark as it coursed through. Behind the shark I could see another fish flashing unclearly. I supposed it was a jack crevalle, a pelagic fish, strong for its size, that often follows sharks. I decided to cast. The distance was all I could manage. I got off one of my better shots, which nevertheless fell slightly behind target. I was surprised to see the fish drop back to the fly, turn and elevate high in the water, then take. It was a permit.

I set the hook sharply, and the fish started down the flat. Remembering my last episode, I kept the loose, racing line well away from the reel handle for the instant the fish took to consume it. Then the fish was on the reel. I lowered the rod tip and cinched the hook, and the fish began to accelerate, staying on top of the flat, so that I could see its wildly extending wake. Everything was holding together: the hookup was good, the knots were good. At 150 yards the fish stopped, and I got back line. I kept at it and got the fish within 80 yards of the boat. Then suddenly it made a wild, undirected run, not permitlike at all, and I could see that the blacktip shark was chasing it. The blacktip struck and missed the permit three or four times, making explosions in the water that sickened me. I released the drag, untied the boat, and started the engine. Woody was poling toward me at the sound of my engine. His mystified client dragged a line astern.

There was hardly enough water to move in. The prop was half buried, and at full throttle I could not get up on plane. The explosions continued, and I could only guess whether or not I was still connected to the fish. I ran toward the fish, a vast loop of line trailing, saw the shark once, and ran over him. I threw the engine into neutral and waited to see what had happened and tried to regain line. Once more I was tight to the permit. Then the shark reappeared. He hit the permit once, killed it, and ate the fish, worrying it like a dog and bloodying the water.

Then an instant later I had the shark on my line and running. I fought him with irrational care: I now planned to gaff the blacktip and retrieve my permit piece by piece. When the inevitable cutoff came I dropped the rod in the boat and, empty-handed, wondered what I had done to deserve this.

I heard Woody's skiff and looked around. He swung about and coasted alongside. I told him it was a permit, as he had guessed from my starting up on the flat. Woody began to say something when, at that not unceremonial moment, his client broke in to say that it was hooking them that was the main thing. We stared at him until he added, "Or is it?"

Often afterward we went over the affair and talked about what might have been done differently, as we had with the first permit. One friend carries a carbine on clips under the gunwale to take care of sharks. But I felt that with a gun in the skiff during the excitement of a running fish, I would plug myself or deep-six the boat. Woody knew better than to assure me there would be other chances. Knowing that there might very well not be was one of our conversational assumptions.

. . .

One morning we went to look for tarpon. Woody had had a bad night of it. He had awakened in the darkness of his room about three in the morning and watched the shadowy figure of a huge land crab walk across his chest. Endlessly it crept to the wall and then up it. Carefully silhouetting the monster, Woody blasted it with a karate chop. At breakfast he was nursing a bruise on the side of his hand. We were, at 6 a.m., having grits and eggs at the Chat and Chew restaurant. A trucker who claimed to have driven from Loxahatchee in three hours flat was yelling for "oss tie." And when the girl asked if he really wanted iced tea this early in the morning he replied, "Dash rat. Oss tie." My breakfast came and I stared at it listlessly. I couldn't wake up in the heat. I was half dreaming and imagined the land crab performing some morbid cadenza on my pile of grits.

We laid out the rods in the skiff. The wind was coming out of the east, that is, over one's casting hand from the point we planned to fish, and it was blowing fairly stiff. But the light was good, and that was more important. We headed out of Big Pine, getting into the calm water along Ramrod Key. We ran in behind Pye Key, through the hole behind Little Money, and out to Southeast Point. The sun was already huge, out of hand, like Shakespeare's "glistening Phaethon." I had whitened my nose and mouth with zinc oxide, and felt, handling the mysterious rods and flies, like a shaman. I still had to rig the leader of my own rod; and as Woody jockeyed the skiff with the pole, I put my leader together. I retained enough of my trout-fishing sensibilities to continue to be intrigued by tarpon leaders with their array of arcane knots: the butt of the leader is nail knotted to the line, blood knotted to monofilament of lighter test; the shock tippet that protects the leader from the rough jaws of tarpon is tied to the leader with a combination Albright Special and Bimini Bend; the shock tippet is attached to the fly either by a perfection loop, a clinch, or a Homer Rhodes Loop; and to choose one is to make a moral choice. You are made to understand that it would not be impossible to fight about it or, at the very least, quibble darkly.

We set up on a tarpon pass point. We had sand spots around us that would help us pick out the dark shapes of traveling tarpon. And we expected tarpon on the falling water, from left to right. I got up on the bow with 50 feet of line coiled on the deck. I was barefoot so I could feel if I stepped on a loop. I made a couple of practice casts—harsh, indecorous, tarpon-style, the opposite of the otherwise appealing dry-fly caper—and scanned for fish.

The first we saw were, from my point of view, spotted from too great a distance. That is, there was a long period of time before they actually broke the circle of my casting range, during which time I could go, quite secretly but completely, to pieces. The sensation for me, in the face of these advancing forms, was as of a gradual ossification of the joints. Moviegoers will recall the early appearances of Frankenstein's monster, his ambulatory motions accompanied by great rigidity of the limbs, almost as though he could stand a good oiling. I was hard put to see how I would manage anything beyond a perfunctory flapping of the rod. I once laughed at Woody's stories of customers who sat down and held their feet slightly aloft, treading the air or wobbling their hands from the wrists. I giggled at the story of a Boston chiropractor who fell over on his back and barked like a seal.

"Let them come in now," Woody said.

"I want to nail one, Woody."

"You will. Let them come."

The fish, six of them, were surging toward us in a wedge. They ran from 80 to 110 pounds. "All right, the lead fish, get on him," Woody said. I managed the throw. The fly fell in front of the fish. I let them overtake it before starting my retrieve. The lead fish, big, pulled up behind the fly, trailed, and then made the shoveling, open-jawed uplift of a strike that is not forgotten. When he turned down I set the hook, and he started his run. The critical stage, that of getting rid of loose line piled around one's feet, ensued. You imagine that if you are standing on a coil, you will go to the moon when that coil must follow its predecessors out of the rod. This one went off without a hitch, and it was only my certainty that someone had done it before that kept me from deciding that we had made a big mistake.

The sudden pressure of the line and the direction of its resistance apparently confused the tarpon, and it raced in close-coupled arcs around the boat. Then, when it had seen the boat, felt the line, and isolated a single point of resistance, it cleared out at a perfectly insane rate of acceleration that made water run three feet up my line as it sliced through. The jumps—wild, greyhounding, end over end, rattling—were all crazily blurred as they happened, while I pictured my reel exploding like a racing clutch and filling me with shrapnel.

This fish, the first of six that day, broke off. So did the others, destroying various aspects of my tackle. Of the performances, it is not simple to generalize. The closest thing to a tarpon in the material world is the Steinway piano. The tarpon, of course, is a game fish that runs to extreme sizes, while the Steinway piano is merely an enormous musical instrument, largely wooden and manipulated by a series of keys. However, the tarpon when hooked and running reminds the angler of a piano sliding down a precipitous incline and while jumping makes cavities and explosions in the water not unlike a series of pianos falling from a great height. If the reader, then, can speculate in terms of pianos that herd and pursue mullet and are themselves shaped like exaggerated herrings, he will be a very long way toward seeing what kind of thing a tarpon is. Those who appreciate nature as we find her may rest in the knowledge that no amount of modification can substitute the manmade piano for the real thing—the tarpon. Where was I?

As the sun moved through the day the blind side continually changed, forcing us to adjust position until, by afternoon, we were watching to the north. Somehow, looking up light, Woody saw four permit coming right in toward us, head-on. I cast my tarpon fly at them, out of my accustomed long-shot routine, and was surprised when one fish moved forward of the pack and followed up the fly rather aggressively. About then they all sensed the skiff and swerved to cross the bow about 30 feet out. They were down close to the bottom now, slightly spooked. I picked up, changed direction, and cast a fairly long interception. When the fly lit, well out ahead, two fish elevated from the group, sprinted forward, and the inside fish took the fly in plain view.

The certainty, the positiveness of the take in the face of an ungodly number of refusals and the long, unproductive time put in, produced immediate tension and pessimism. I waited for something to go haywire.

I hooked the fish quickly and threw slack. It was only slightly startled and returned to the pack, which by this time had veered away from the shallow flat edge and swung back toward deep water. The critical time of loose line passed slowly. Woody unstaked the skiff and was poised to see which way the runs would take us. When the permit was tight to the reel I cinched him once, and he began running. The deep water kept the fish from making the long, sustained sprints permit make on the flats. This fight was a series of assured jabs at various clean angles from the skiff. We followed, alternately gaining and losing line. Then, in some way, at the end of this blurred episode, the permit was flashing beside the boat, looking nearly circular, and the only visual contradiction to his perfect poise was the intersecting leader seemingly inscribed from the tip of my arcing rod to the precise corner of his jaw.

Then we learned that there was no net in the boat. The fish would have to be tailed. I forgave Woody in advance for the permit's escape. Woody was kneeling in the skiff, my line disappearing over his shoulder, the permit no longer in my sight, Woody leaning deep from the gunwale. Then, unbelievably, his arm was up, the black symmetry of tail above his fist, the permit perpendicular to the earth, then horizontal on the floorboards. A pile of loose fly line was strewn in curves that wandered around the bottom of the boat to a gray-and-orange fly that was secured in the permit's mouth. I sat down numb and soaring.

I don't know what this kind of thing indicates beyond the necessary, ecstatic resignation to the moment. With the beginning over and, possibly, nothing learned, I was persuaded that once was not enough.

YUGOSLAVIA

Negley Farson

*The enchantments of trout fishing in Slo-
venia by one of America's finest—though
least-known—angler/authors.*

In that mountainous corner where Austria, Italy,
and Yugoslavia meet, the Yugoslavs were quietly
making a sportsman's paradise. This was chiefly
because of the ski-huts they were building in the
Dinaric Alps. Even in midsummer you could climb
along snow-faces for days. You could lose yourself in the
snow-fog, as I have done, feel that this time, for a certainty, your number was up—then have a break in the
mist and see three chamois staring at you from a land-
mark of red rocks. From these snows come streams, then
rivers, which hold some of the finest trout in all Europe.
And while it may seem a strange statement, the finest
consistent trout fishing I have ever had was in the
mountains of Slovenia.

To illustrate what I mean by consistent I will say that
one dusk I took twelve trout out of the Savitca, every one
of them over a pound, of which the largest weighed a kilo.
The next night I took eleven, all over a pound. The next
night I took ten, all over a pound. The number dwindles
because I was fishing a restricted spot; I was poaching the
Regent's river. This will be no news to him, because he
found that out, and refused to give me an interview as a
consequence. What he doesn't know is that, after he had

come up to his little hunting-lodge in the mountains, and discovered me, I still poached his river at nights at least once a week.

Whether he or I shall ever see that river again is a thing that interests me greatly.

These rivers came down from a tableland of tumbled mountains many of whose northern faces were covered with perpetual snow. You could climb with the spring in that part of the world, for when the snows melted away in the lower clearings and the first crocus pushed up through unmelted snow pockets, the forest was still dark winter. When the beech leaves were glinting along the lake shore their buds were still closed tight a few thousand feet higher up. The banks of the lower streams became blue with gentians; the big, bell-like gentian and the little one of the brighter hue. The alpine valleys became a carpet of wildflowers, and soon, as you climbed, you came on primulas, pink, mauve, and yellow among the higher rocks. Then a climb to reach an edelweiss became a breathless risk.

In these mountains, where a man had been killed, the peasants painted and put up a little memorial ikon to a rock or tree. If Hans was painted upside down, you knew he had fallen from a cliff. If he was painted lying prone on the ground, with another man standing with an axe or a saw in his hand, then you knew a tree had fallen upon him while they were logging. They were painted with a primitive earnest skill. So were the peasant paintings of the Saints on the white walls of all the little churches. St. Christopher was the favourite, shown carrying Christ across the water on his shoulder. The three inns upon the lake were owned by a Holy Order. Mine was called the St. James. Next to it was a little church called the Holy Ghost. And here at a certain Sunday every spring the peasants came to hold a service for the Mayfly.

I never knew the reason. But for two years I watched them gather there, all of them carrying umbrellas, all praying on the Day of the Mayfly.

It was a pastoral land, where the valley filled with the tinkle of cow and goat and sheep bells at sunset...as the

7 8
—

boys brought them down. Then, one night, you heard the rattle of carts going by; the peasants were taking all their cattle up into the higher alpine meadows.

Up there there were seven lakes; one pink, one aquamarine blue, one royal blue, one green. And in the wilderness of rocks that lay around them there was another memorial, not quite so sympathetic. It was to three Russian soldiers who had escaped from the Germans. They lay in the grave which they had been made to dig before the Germans shot them. The Yugoslav Alpine Club had put up a plaque to them. You could climb Triglav, and look down into Italy. And in these high passes I have seen Slovenians climb back, escaping from Mussolini, that sawdust Caesar.

There were wild strawberries on the sunny slopes.

I have never seen such beautiful trout. In the swift, icy, bouldered Savitca their backs were a pale mauve. Their spots were vivid scarlet. In the lake itself I once caught one trout, weighing over a kilo, which was darker but which must have had a million scarlet spots. He was so beautiful that I wanted to put him back. But he had almost killed himself before he would let me take him. Then there was a golden grayling, which, with its deep sides, rose sharply in the swift runs and almost broke your line before he would let you land him. The *esche* was much more prized in the Balkans than any trout. With his small mouth you would not think him capable of such a fight.

The swift Savitca splayed out into the lake over a shelf of round rocks. It swung against the far bank in its last rush. Standing on the bouldered other side you cast into the swift stream pouring down the far bank. When a fish struck he almost pulled your arm down. He was like a fighter who leaps from his chair and fights from the tap of the gong. In such water there is no time for either fish or man to sulk. In the early spring they are in the river. When the water loses its pace a bit they move out into the lake. Then, when the lake warms, they move up into the river again. But now, in the hot July suns, the snows are melting furiously in the upper mountains; the Savitca is liquid ice. And you dare not fish it without waders—or else your legs will swell.

The *Fischer* had told me that there were 10-pound trout in this lake. I had never believed him. Then one day when I was wading out to cast over the edge of this bouldered shelf a great black shape shot past me. It was after a trout of at least a kilo. The trout took refuge under the branches of a tree that had caught, swept down, upon the pebbled tableland. I watched the drama. I could almost see the little trout gasping for breath; it had been so frightened. The big cannibal trout lay at the door of the tree, waiting for it. As slowly as I could I removed my leader and tried to put a little Devon on my line. It might break my rod, but it would have been worth it. Flash—the long, black, cannibal trout had seen my movement—and he was gone.

This *Fischer* was the curse of this mountain paradise. He—and the Authority; a fox-terrier little bureaucrat, wearing a green hat with an enormous chamois brush.

"You must pay 150 dinars State tax," said the Authority.

That is about 15 shillings, not much more than a trout licence in Somerset, but—

"You must pay 10 dinars every day that you fish."

"To whom?"

"To the State."

Well, a shilling a day was not much, but—

"You must give up all the trout. You may buy them back for 45 dinars a kilo."

"From whom?"

"From the State."

"But they are my trout."

"They belong to the State. All the trout belong to the State. If you do not want to buy them the State will not charge you for them. The State will keep them."

"Well, what next?"

"You must have a *'Fischer.'*"

"Oh, come now!" I remonstrated. "Surely, you don't mean that I have to take a man with me when I wade up these streams?"

The Authority nodded.

Unofficially, he was a charming person. I liked his little green hunting-suit, and the metal edelweiss attached to the stern of his green *Jäger* hat.

"But I'm not a spy!" I protested. "Surely, I do not have to be watched all the time?"

"It is an Ordinance," said the Authority.

I attempted to defy it. The first day, I went off in a boat by myself on the lake. I rowed to a remote elbow of it. I rose a 1½-lb. trout. And I lost it.

"Schade!" came a voice from the bushes on the bank. "What a pity!"

A man stood there eyeing me. He was not dressed in that soft Jäger green, yet I knew that his brown velvet suit was an official uniform of some sort. He did not wear a chamois brush, nor did he carry a shot-gun on a sling.

"I," he said, "am the *Fischer.*"

"How do you do?" I said.

"Grüss Gott," he smiled benignly.

"You must," he announced, "have a *Fischer.*"

I now saw that on his back, instead of a rifle or a shot-gun, was slung a little green barrel. It was like a monstrous green cigar with both ends clipped. I also saw that, argue as I might, I must have a *Fischer.*

I put on my waders and we went up a stream. It is much easier to write that than it is to do it, for the *Fischer* made me climb a mountain first. Then we dropped down through the pines into a gorge of grey rock, with a mountain stream racing through it. There were deep bottle-green pools, but most of the stream was waterfall, rapids, or long slides down the steep shelves of rock.

These the *Fischer* approached in a crouching position, stalking carefully among the beds of blue gentians and anemones. *"Da!"* His finger pointed to some swirls of air-clear water. Lying behind a rock I saw a trout. Its back was so light in colour that it seemed almost transparent. Again and again I tried, until the fly finally landed just above the rock, sucked round it in the eddy, and the trout took it.

He was about three-quarters of a pound, apple-green, dappled with scarlet little spots. The *Fischer* took him

carefully, opened the trap door and slid him into the atten-
uated barrel.

That night when we came down from the mountain I had
six of these beauties, splashing about in the little green
barrel. Another day I got sixteen, three of which were well
over a pound each. One day I got only three; but they were
all over a pound and one was over a kilo. All these fish
were taken back to the hotel where the *Fischer* put them
into a little stream-fed pool, where they swam about happily until they were taken out and eaten.

This was all very well. I loved this contented country
where I watched the crops grow and ripen, and then saw
the wheat harvested with only sickles or scythes. Where,
as I occasionally walked across to one particular corner of
the lake I watched the villagers twisting their own ropes
out of a particular kind of grass they grew for it, where the
cobbler made all their shoes, and the women spun and
wove, and where the upper loft of each house was a store-
house for its crops, whilst a good half of its lower floor was
the stable. Its fire-house, housing its little token fire-fight-
ing pump, had the statue of what appeared to be a Roman
centurion on its wooden bell tower, pouring a bucket of
water over a symbolic blaze. These people were about as
self-contained as any community I had met.

And that was the way I wanted to be; I did not want that
Fischer always at my elbow. The chief obstacle against il-
licit fishing was that, even if I did catch them without him,
I could not bring them back to the hotel. For there I would
be caught. The obvious answer to this was to cook them
myself, out in the woods. And this my wife and I and my
boy did for many and many a day that first summer. We
did it so well—I might add in anticipation—that when we
came down there the next spring, and I, smiling, shook
hands with the little Authority again, he threw up his
hands and said, in effect, that once I had paid him the
initial 150 dinars State tax—I could do damn well what I
liked. I was too much trouble.

We bought a cheap frying-pan at a town about thirty
miles down below. Then, with this in my rucksack (and a

pound of butter), my wife, my boy, and I set off on an apparently innocent row up the lake. The *Fischer* was always hanging around somewhere at first, watching me to see if I took out a rod. I could not conceal a trout rod; but it was easy to stick the little four-piece Bristol bait-casting rod up the sleeve of my old tweed coat. So that my first lawbreaking was done with Devons. The Devon with the little red bead at its tail was a horrible killer when cast off the mouth of the Savitca. Usually, it only needed half an hour to get us four or five one- or two-pound trout. Then we would row down the lake to a long rocky peninsula, build a fire, and fry the trout, cut up into chunks, in sizzling butter.

I looked up once to find the *Fischer* standing over my shoulder when I had a frying-pan full of them. *"Nu! Nu! Nu! Herr* Farson!" was his admonition. And he shook his finger at me, wagging his head. The next morning the Authority drove up in his pony-trap, quite prepared to be nasty about things. But he had a beautiful little German weapon hung on a strap over his shoulder; a sixteen-bore shotgun, with a small-calibre rifle beneath its web—and I was so enchanted about this that he forgave me for everything. Over a couple of litres of the resin-like white wine that was grown somewhere in that region he extolled the virtues of his sporting gun: "You see—I am equipped for either birds or deer...or perhaps...who knows?...it might be a chamois."

"But of course!" I said; "why not?" Why not a chamois?

So I broke the gun and peered through its beautifully kept barrels, admired the clean rifling, threw it up to my shoulder. And the Authority suggested we might have another litre, and clapped his hands. While the *Fischer* stood by, near the kitchen, gnashing his teeth like the wolf in Red Riding Hood.

Then the *Fischer* came down on us one night when an Austrian Count, his Countess, my wife, my boy, and I were having a glorious picnic on a rock—with the flames of our fire lighting up the boughs of the pine trees behind us— and pounced on a man whom he took to be me, but who was, to the dismay of the *Fischer,* a Captain of the Imperial Guards in Belgrade, Prince Paul's principal A.D.C. He was fishing with a piece of cheese.

I then tried, although it was not very successful, taking out just a couple of leaders and a small length of line in my pocket—and snatching out trout from the pools of a mountain stream high up behind the village. I would just cut a thin sapling and fish with that. In the still upper pools, lying on my stomach, I would let a dry fly land lightly. Or I would let a wet fly drip with the swift water behind the lee of some rock. I found it fascinating. I always felt that, this way, I would catch the fish of all fish some day; for I saw some enormous big trout lying at the bottom of these lonely pools. But, it seemed, only the little fools would take. Still, enough of them would fill the frying-pan.

There were only certain occasions when the *Fischer* ever showed any real admiration, even love, for me. These were when I caught a grayling. I got my first one below an old weir, where the full force of the water poured over, crashed against an opposite wall of rock, then shunted off into a rapid. I was fishing in the froth of bubbles and foam, so that when the grayling took my fly—it was a very worn little Blue Upright—I did not know what I had got.

But, without even seeing it the *Fischer* knew. *"Esche! Esche! Esche!"* he kept shouting, jumping up and down behind me on the bank.

Now my German is limited, so the *Fischer* and I always talked a peculiarly bastard lingo which was about one-third German and two-thirds Russian. For this part of the world had belonged to Austria before the last war; the *Fischer* had been a soldier in the Austrian army; and, so as many Austrians did, he had spent three years in a Russian prison camp in Siberia. So that when we brought that grayling home, I trying to tell him what its name was in English—"Gray-link!" said the *Fischer*—the proprietress of the Hotel Holy Ghost called my wife to help disentangle the excited *Fischer* and me from our language while she weighed the fish. It weighed exactly 1¼ kilos! Not a bad "gray-link" for any part of the world.

· · ·

Life was not all just one round of fun in that part of the
world, not for me. I had gone down there that first summer, dead broke—£500 overdrawn at the bank, in fact—
because I had just had a silly row with the new owner of a
newspaper on which I had worked for eleven happy years. I
had to make a new life. I had a book to write that, I knew
(or at least I hoped), would be my shot in the locker. And
that book had to be written. I never put on my trousers in
the morning—except for two or three breaks of four days
each when we were climbing between the ski-huts along
the snows of the Italian frontier—until I had written ten
pages. That was an unbroken vow. Meanwhile, my wife,
my boy, and I lived on four shillings a day each. We had
come down from England, 2nd and 3rd Class, without even
sleepers. And it was after the day's work was done, usually
around lunch time, that I would climb or fish.

But it was in the evening after dinner, when I should
have been resting, that I found it the most fascinating time
to fish. There was a bridge below the hotel, on the far side
of which stood an ancient little whitewashed Catholic
church. On its wall, too, facing the water, was a peasant
painting of St. Christopher carrying Christ on his
shoulder, wading knee deep through painted water as miraculously clear as the real water which flowed beneath
his feet.

Here every evening was a rise of trout such as I would
not have believed possible. You could stand on the bridge
in the still spring nights and hear splash after splash after
splash.... And if you waded out from the bushes at the foot
of the ancient church, not caring if the water did come over
your waders, you had fishing such as you might dream of
in heaven. It was here that I used the unnamed fly tied by
the Captain in the English Army of Occupation at Co-
logne. It was a whitish, hackled arrangement, with a grey
body; and I fished it until there was little of it left except
the bare hook. Its effectiveness increased with its bedraggled condition. Night after night I clumped back to the
hotel, almost stupefied by my good luck—the miracle of
that fly. And I would slide a bagful of beautiful fish out on

the verandah table. In that dim porch light, with the reflection from the green vines, the beauty of those fish had
something haunting about it. We loved to touch them, turn
them over, pick them up, admire them. The silent shake of
the old Austrian count's grey head had something reverent
about it. Here was the Adoration of the Fish.

I state this solemnly. I have never had quite that hushed
feeling about the trout anywhere else. And we all felt it.
Then one night there was a terrific strike, my rod bent in
the dark; it bent, it bent, it bent.... For you could not allow
the fish to run into the rapids immediately below. And
then it straightened out. The line came back empty. The
fly was gone. I climbed up the bank by the church with
that feeling that I was not meant to catch any more fish
below the feet of St. Christopher painted on its walls.

I never did.

JOTTINGS OF A FLY-FISHER

Theodore Gordon

Wise observations on the vagaries of trout and salmon by the father of American dry-fly fishing.

I had one great day in June, 1901, and the sport was especially welcome, coming after a disappointment. Starting after midday, I reached the stream I was about to fish late in the afternoon with rain falling in torrents. I put on my waders during a lull, and found the water not only very high, but so much discolored that fishing was out of the question, at least with any prospect of success. There was no train to return that evening, or I would certainly have gone home. The rain ceased early in the evening, but I went disconsolately to bed and dropped off to sleep with the roar of the swollen stream sounding in my ears. The next day was Saturday, and when I went to breakfast, I was told that the water had cleared considerably. I soon found this to be the case; it was clear enough for fly, though still very high. The sky was overcast and it remained cloudy all day, constantly threatening rain; in fact, I believe that a few drops did fall from time to time.

Under these circumstances I was not long in getting under way. For some time I could do nothing. I could not reach the casts I knew, so as to fish them properly. At last I was encouraged by capturing a small trout of about a quarter of a pound. Proceeding downward I came to a place where the stream was greatly expanded over a wide rocky bed. Far out in the middle, near several large stones under water, was a kind of pool of fairly deep water, yet with a heavy current through it, while directly below was a large and dangerous rapid. We knew the place above the rapid of old as the haunt of large trout. With great difficulty I succeeded in wading out far enough to fish this place properly, by casting a long line, although the water was within an inch or so of the tops of my stockings. I was fishing with only one fly, a kind of nondescript, tied by myself, with a light yellow body of wool on a No. 10 hook. At about the third cast, when the line was well extended and the fly over the lower end of the hole or depression, and just where the water probably began to shallow a trifle, I detected a very modest rise. I struck, and instantly an immense fish leaped from the water. The leap was diagonally across, not directly away from me, and really the trout appeared a perfect monster in this position, the curve of its broad back and wide spotted side, with the splendid propeller, a tail that to my excited eyes appeared as big as a palm-leaf fan, the fish cleared the water by many inches, and a desperate rush for liberty followed. I thought just then that I could not move (I changed my mind afterward), and had only thirty yards of line on my reel. Before I could curb this charge, only three or four turns were left me on the spool (you must remember that I had hooked the fish at the end of a long cast); in fact, I don't think that I really stopped the trout at all; he turned of his own will when he struck shallow water. I put on all the pull I dared, under which the fish gradually dropped back into the deepest part of the pool. I had recovered many yards of line when suddenly the trout rose toward the surface, a great swirl appeared, and then my reel screamed again. Before I could say Jack Robinson or even John, the fish had rushed down the stream and was in the heavy swift water at the head of the rapid. Nothing could stop him then; any attempt to butt him would have torn out the small hook, or caused a break in my fine cast. The line was quickly exhausted and I followed in water which for some yards was up to my waist. No thought of getting my wading stockings full then. The coarse rocks were cruel and the footing exceedingly bad, but I stumbled on, my legs like towers of lead. I was about winded when the fish took it into his head to stop in the rapid, probably behind some stone, but it appeared to be right in the middle of the rushing current. The check was but momentary, but it enabled me to get opposite the fish, and as he checked his wild career once more before reaching the shallows at the bottom, I managed better and felt that I had my good fellow in hand. I think that we were both pretty well played out by this time, and after many short rushes I stranded the fish where there was so little water that he fell over on his side. On getting him in hand I was greatly disappointed to find that instead of a five-pounder he was two pounds less.

Had this fish been lost, say, in running the rapid, he would have been remembered as that four- or five-pound trout that got away. Nevertheless, he was a noble trout and made a great fight.

8 9

The water was cold and the fish very active that day. It is not the rule for brown trout to leap, but many of those caught did so more than once. I took a two-pound trout that did not, but most of the fish were of large size. The basket consisted of twenty-four trout; twenty of these I carried home next day, and they nearly filled the big creel, capable of containing twenty pounds of fish. This was a wonderful day's sport; in some respects the best of my life.

The large stream, high cold water, unusual average size and activity of the fish, combined with the depression and disappointment of the day before, all seemed to enhance the sport and make of this a record day indeed. In a petty brook such fishing is not possible, as even if you take a large fish he has not room to show his powers and is apt to sulk. The heavy water and peculiar place in which the largest fish was hooked made the sport rather like salmon fishing in miniature.

We forget most of the disagreeable or unpleasant incidents attending our sport, but we never forget the big fish we have lost. When a boy of thirteen years I saved all my pocket money for a considerable period to purchase a fly rod; it was too good a rod for a boy without experience and was soon broken. I remember the sad affair very well, as a large fish played an important part in the event.

At the end of a thicket on Bonny Brook (this, by the way, was a favorite breeding place for a single pair of woodcock) was quite a deep pool, with hollow grassy banks, forming a fine retreat for trout. A common snake fence divided the thicket from a meadow, and by standing on one of the lower rails I could cast my worm in the pool. I did so on this occasion and the swift current carried the bait under the hollow bank; I was not conscious of a bite, but on trying to withdraw the line found it was held fast. Forgetting my delicate tackle, a vigorous pull was given, the rod bent double and a large trout was drawn to the surface. Becoming wildly excited, I endeavored to haul the fish out on the narrow margin between the fence and the pool; the trout was actually drawn half out of the water; when the rod broke in two places, the trout disappeared and before I could gain control of the line, freed himself from the hook. I could have lifted up my voice and wept; my feelings can hardly be realized. My legs were weak, and a sensation of utter goneness and woe possessed me. To break my beautiful new rod was a frightful misfortune, but to lose that trout was calamity indeed. I had never seen such a trout; it was at least twelve inches long and may have weighed three-quarters of a pound. The big friend who accompanied me soon came up; he was older than I, and for some years I could not forgive him his efforts to make a joke of my loss, and to tease me about it. In my excited grief I had foolishly appealed to him for sympathy. The woes of childhood and youth are not always shortlived.

Trout were numerous in all cold brooks in those days, but even in the large streams a pound specimen was a large fish. I remember seeing but one two-pound trout during my boyhood; this seems rather remarkable, as I was familiar with some of the big limestone streams in Pennsylvania. They were deep and rich in food for trout; a peculiar moss which was common in them was filled with larvæ, snails, shrimps, etc. Many flies appeared on the water and the evening rise of trout was something to be remembered. Very little fishing was done after the early part of the season, which began then on "All Fools' Day."

According to my recollection the trout were in good condition, and on one opening day I made a basket of thirty-eight good fish during a snowstorm; the temperature could not have been low, as the snow melted as fast as it fell.

Glancing over a book called "Sixty-three Years' Angling" recently reminded me of a fine old salmon fisher, now gone to his rest, as the views of the author and my friend agreed and in some respects were uncommon. They believed that the salmon takes the fly in anger, because he is tantalized and annoyed by it. The author of the work goes so far as to say that the pattern of fly used for salmon is not of the slightest consequence. "Why the salmon takes the fly" has been the subject of much discussion and argument for many years, and all that we can do is to form our own opinions from such reliable evidence as we have before us. After learning from books how to tie trout flies, I became ambitious and devoted much of my leisure to the more complicated insects, or rather lures, used for salmon.

It is very difficult to obtain the requisite materials in this country, but those necessary to tie a few of the standard patterns were imported, and after working for three hours on a single Jock-Scot, I succeeded in turning out quite a pretty fly. In an account of the fishing season in the river Eden, in North Britain, a new fly was mentioned as having proved very killing that year, one salmon of forty-nine and a half pounds and another of forty-three pounds having been taken with it. The formula of the fly was given and I copied it. It proved to be a very harmonious creation of blue and silver, orange and black, golden pheasant toppings, etc., and I gave one or two to each of my salmon-fishing friends. One of these gentlemen was on the Restigouche in June of that year fishing the club waters on the invitation of a friend.

On a bright, hot day many rods were at work, but the fish were not inclined to rise, and none were taken until one of the guides, an Indian, I think, in looking over my friend's stock of flies, noticed the Eden fly I had given him. He attached it to the leader and casting over the same water five large salmon were risen and hooked. The best fish weighed thirty-eight pounds. Were those salmon made angry by the Eden fly and not by the Jock-Scots, silver-doctors, Durham-rangers, black-doses and other flies presented to them? My friend was the only one among many who had any sport on that day. By the way, the form of the Pennell hook, a plain tapered shank with gut loop (not an eyed hook), was disliked by all the guides at that time. The hook was rather slender, and Mr. Pennell has since brought out a much heavier hook, with a returned eye for salmon flies.

It is unfortunate that so few fishermen keep a record of their sport, with the attending circumstances, as much interesting and often valuable information is lost forever. Experience is the great teacher, and if that of many could be brought together, we would know far more than we do of many things bearing upon our art. The man who keeps everything he learns locked up in his own breast will know far less than he who compares notes with his fellows. My reason for writing these random notes and recollections is that they may remind other men of their interesting experiences, and perhaps induce them to write also.

There are a great many amateur flytiers in this country, but they have no medium of communication. In the course of years many new materials are discovered, and if one is a fair observer one picks up a little practical information about entomology.

I am surprised that more ladies do not take an interest in fly-fishing. It is well within their powers, and those accustomed to exercise soon become enthusiastic. Eight years ago a young lady was my fishing companion quite frequently, and although we had to tramp four or five miles to reach the best part of the river, she never became too tired to enjoy the sport. She wore a Tam O'Shanter, sweater, short jacket and skirts, with stout shoes and leggings, and waded, as I did, without waterproofs, which are only a nuisance in warm weather. The constant exercise prevents one from taking cold, care being taken not to lie about long enough at lunch time to become chilled, though there is little chance of that when the summer sun is high in the heavens.

This girl soon learned to cast a fly quite well, in spite of the fact that her rod was a poor one (a split bamboo nine feet in length and weighing four and a half ounces is just the thing for a lady). She saw portions of a most beautiful trout stream never before visited by a woman, and had many interesting experiences. An involuntary bath was the only misfortune she experienced, and she did not suffer from that. No one man or woman who has once taken an interest in fly-fishing ever becomes indifferent to it. A fresh source of pleasure in life has been gained and one that will continue to afford enjoyment until the end of the longest life.

The inhabitants of New York and vicinity are greatly favored in their opportunities for sport. Good salt-water fishing is near at hand and owing to the excellent facilities for travel a man can leave the city by the Newspaper train at four o'clock on any spring morning, spend a long day on good water a hundred miles away, and return in time for a late supper the same night. Of course, it is better and more agreeable to spend a night in the country, but it is not really necessary.

Business is so absorbing that many ardent fishermen can only steal a day now and then, in the early part of the season while fishing is at its best. The clubs on Long Island are largely patronized, but are beyond the means of the majority. Also a desire is felt to visit wild unpreserved waters, to get among the mountains and the evergreens. The angling fever is a very real disease, and can only be cured by the application of cold water and fresh, untainted air. I know a man eighty years of age who used to visit the Restigouche every year as soon as the ice was out. He often descended from his car at Matapedia to find himself in a snow bank, but his ardor was never chilled. On one trip he traveled many hundred miles, spent one day in a wet boat, caught one twenty-five pound salmon and a bad attack of influenza and was shipped home in spite of himself. He was quite as eager the next spring.

I am one of those who believe that all the vagaries of trout that seem so incomprehensible are capable of a rational explanation. For one thing, the eyesight of round-eyed creatures is not as good as that of almond-eyed human beings in some respects, although better in others. They are deficient in the sense of form, keen to detect motion and shades of color. A deer will not notice you if you are absolutely still, but the slightest motion sends him off at once. Trout are the same, only more so, if anything. A shadow alarms them greatly, and the position of the sun has much to do with our success, or the lack of it. If the rays of light are reflected from the water in a certain way, you can stand within easy casting distance of a school of shy trout in even the shallowest water; they cannot see you, nor can you see them. Prove this the next time you have an opportunity.

Trout take a fly when it is all chewed up sometimes. It does not look like anything to us, but to them it may be the exact color of a fly that is or has been hatching out, and they take it as larvæ or nymph just emerging from its case. I have, when not able to make a really good imitation of a fly upon which the trout were feeding, contented myself with a body of the right color and a few turns of almost any feathers of the right shade. This will kill better than a well-formed fly of the wrong color, though greater accuracy is desirable.

A FALL WITH GRACE

John W. Randolph

A former New York Times *outdoor columnist describes a fall that makes that of the Roman Empire seem small potatoes.*

A ndover, New Hampshire—Nothing makes an outdoor type feel so strong and so hardy as the knowledge that he has endured stoically a rude knock and thereby earned the applause of his companions. A visible bruise or cut, casually dismissed as a mere trifle, is a badge of honor.

A man can earn his badges on the Blackwater River if he exercises due carelessness. In some places, there are fine slippery rocks in fast water and good steep banks covered with brush and vines that offer unexcelled opportunities for minor injuries.

One of these is just below a certain bridge, in a fast riffle running between a falls and a deep pool. The bank leading to this riffle is about forty feet high and covered with loose dirt. The rocks below are irregular and slippery enough for all practical purposes.

The motives of John Brennan of the New Hampshire Planning and Industrial Commission in sending fishermen down this bank are not known. He is not a brutal type, and the publicity the state might win by the maiming of a single angler probably wouldn't be worth the trouble, unless fishing were particularly dull. Brennan says he sends them down because there are good brookies in that riffle, and there are, and maybe that is his reason.

Anyway, I was able to negotiate that bank with the agility, sure foot, and stout heart of a mountain goat. At the moment I wasn't even looking for honorable bruises, since there was nobody around to impress except Brennan. And he has been known to ignore a man with a broken leg in order to watch another catch an eight-inch trout.

The rocks at the bottom were equally easy to negotiate for an experienced rock-jumper. But somebody had moved one of them, and, when I stepped down onto it, there was nothing there except a patch of black water. If anybody could have recovered his balance at that instant, I probably could have; but nobody could.

The resulting flat dive onto the remaining rocks was executed with skill and grace. Some men might have been hurt, but not an old rock-faller. I even managed skillfully to lodge my six-and-a-half-foot Orvis bamboo rod in a willow bush on the way down, and to secure it there firmly by twining the leader among the branches.

That strategy freed my hands and enabled me to hit those rocks so softly that I was able to get up in less than ten minutes. It took me less than another ten minutes to free the rod.

Brennan watched this performance with admiration. He said that to fall in a place like that, I must have practiced rock-falling a lot. He said he had been down that bank thirty-eight times and had never been able to fall at all. He said he was fairly sure that he had seen people who were noisier after a fall like that, though he couldn't recall at the moment who they were. Brennan doesn't mind saying he likes a thing when he does.

Well, I caught eight good brookies, a couple of them weighing about a pound, in that riffle with a leader carrying two wet flies, rigged by Harry Darbee of Roscoe, New York. They were all natives and all full of fight.

That took me about an hour. Probably it was standing in one position all that time that made me begin to shake a little after the hour. But it was no great job getting up the bank again, and Brennan really didn't have to help.

He didn't have to say anything about how a man ought to know his own limits, either. There are certain badges of honor that could be shown to him, if I didn't scorn to do it.

DRY-FLY DISASTER ON THE DEE

George M. L. La Branche

and

A. H. E. Wood

A leading expert on dry-fly fishing for Atlantic salmon in Canada finds Scottish fish miss the point of his floaters.

In the summer of 1924, La Branche, one of the pioneers of salmon dry-fly fishing, was invited to fish several British rivers to demonstrate the killing qualities of floating flies. Due to local weather and water conditions, his best chance appeared to occur on the famous Cairnton water of the Aberdeenshire Dee. Here he was hosted and guided by the legendary A. H. E. Wood who had developed greased-line fishing—a fairly similar method of fishing a slim wet fly, virtually drag-free, just below the water-surface.

Although dry-fly salmon fishing has continued to gain followers on this side of the Atlantic, European anglers still find the dry fly rarely effective on their salmon river —though no one knows precisely why. Here, sixty-five years later, is the agonizing postmortem of that first, historic failure. (Ed.)

La Branche to Wood:

As you may not remember the things which I considered operated for and against success, I am putting them down again:

Conditions of Water

In my opinion—perfect. With no knowledge of climatic conditions or the effect of barometric pressure upon the fish in your river, my first look at the Dee at Cairnton made me not only hopeful, but almost confident.

The clarity of the water, its height, the character of the streams and the positive knowledge that there were fish in the pools and runs, so ideal was everything, that I could easily have imagined that I was at home on one of our own rivers. Notwithstanding this similarity I did not lose sight of the fact that I was on unfamiliar water, or that the methods which had proved so effective in New Brunswick might produce nothing in Scotland. So, while I had solid faith in the dry fly and its ability to rise fish in almost any river, this confidence was not unmixed with a feeling of apprehension that here, on your river, the whole theory might go smash!

In a measure it did, but not entirely, as I think you will agree. You saw enough I believe to satisfy you that fish can be killed on the dry fly. Of course, your own method, not so far removed from mine, would not be the wet fly used for comparison. I am speaking of the average salmon angler using the orthodox, downstream style. I am not ridiculing this method, I mention it only because I believe that during the season it will account for as many fish as any other, if not more—barring your method—but I do think that the dry fly will kill when our grandfathers' method will not—and I am inclined to believe that you will agree with me again.

Older Fish

By this I do not mean fish that through age in the river have become sophisticated. When the comparison is made between the runs of fish in your waters and those in ours, beginning in February in your case and not until the middle of April to June 1st in ours, you will understand that in July, when I was with you on the Dee, the season approximated September on our rivers, at the earliest—and our fishing is ended then by two weeks—by law. Fish that have been in the river for some time are more difficult to move than those fresh run, and if this is so, the longer they are in the river, the smaller chance one has with them.

Whether or not the dry fly will kill on your rivers, early, is something I would dearly love to know. I am sure you will give it a real test. In May or June, with the water in normal or even sub-normal condition, I am convinced that the method will prove effective. Some of the fish which rose to the dry fly in the Ballater Water, while not exactly fresh run, were certainly not "potted" fish and should have been killed (mea culpa).

100

_____

The Wind

Baffling enough in any method of fishing the high winds on the river during my stay at Cairnton absolutely destroyed any chance of placing the fly accurately—and I know you will agree when I say that placing the fly properly is most essential. It was difficult, too, with my light tackle, to place the fly on the water at all during some of the stiff gusts. At home we would have abandoned fishing entirely with the dry fly under those conditions, but I felt no desire to kill a fish except with those dry palmers! I might not have been able to rise a fish with the wet fly, even if I had used it, but that angle didn't interest me. Stupid, is it not? If I had killed one half or even one third of the fish which came to the fly I might now, if I thought of it at all, sit back complacently and congratulate myself and that is all there would be to it. But what does happen is that I don't sit in my easy chair, I cannot—I get up and walk around the room wondering what on earth it was I did or didn't do to miss them!

Audience

I am looking for an excuse for not having fastened to at least one of the fish. It is disconcerting to be watched as I was watched while attempting to take one of the many salmon that were lying in those two beautiful pools. *Your* close attendance meant nothing to me; it was not confusing. With you at my elbow I knew you were studying the method closely and would be able to discover any error which I was unable to detect myself. So please eliminate yourself from the picture. But with the Scottish gentleman, the ghillies and the onlookers on the other bank, my mind was certainly not completely on my work. All this may or may not have had any effect upon the actual killing of fish, but of one thing I am certain. After rising the fish that I did without fastening to any, I would, had I been alone, have taken chances, struck and struck hard, in an attempt to hang at least a solitary salmon. If I had I would probably have smashed as I did at the Cottage Pool when no one was looking, and as I did on the Wye at Hampton Bishop when after the only fish I rose.

Whether or not I killed one of your fish is really of no importance to me. The ability to hook a fish that rises certainly has its value, and I don't mean that I could be content to go on always merely rising fish and never laying one on the bank. What I am really trying to say is that had you and I been alone on the river I feel certain that at least a brace of fish would have been killed. I might have made mistakes which you would have recognized, and your criticisms would have helped, but I felt I was apparently on exhibition when I was met at the gate, as you will remember, with the request that I might be accompanied—to say nothing of the crowd watching from the cliff! I must admit I was nervous, and while this contributed somewhat perhaps to my failure ʰo fasten, I cannot plead it entirely as an excuse.

Lack of Practice

You will remember I told you that I had not been fishing for four years. Until I got to the Dee I had not even seen my favourite rod for four years. This inaction may have had something to do with my failure to hang a fish but I don't think so. Fly fishing is like swimming. If you do it, you always do it. My timing, perhaps, was a bit off, but I cannot understand, in the case of those fish that carried the fly completely under, why they were not hung when I straightened the line. They should have been solidly hooked.

On our rivers we don't get all the fish that rise, either. It is my opinion that when they are not hooked, however, it is not the angler's fault in all cases. My observations on the Dee led me to believe that your fish (and I saw this plainly) came at the fly with wide open jaws, but even after taking it did not close down on it. This occurred half a dozen times, and I am still unable to account for it, unless your theory of jaw dislocation is sound. As a matter of fact, this experience would lead me to believe that you had made a real discovery. I hope you have, because it will leave me a loophole to crawl through.

102

—— *Hackles Too Big*

I cannot yet subscribe to your belief that the hackles prevent the hook from taking hold. I will not, either, because it means abandoning my theory that the fly should "ride high." This is asking too much because I lean so heavily on it. When Hutton's keeper on the Wye voiced the same opinion I was a bit shaken, but feeling that he had never seen a dry fly fished before I dismissed the matter a little carelessly. What am I to do, however, when Marston* writes me in a recent letter: "I am puzzled at your not hooking our salmon—have wondered if your light rod does not pull the hook in when you strike, or whether the bushy hackles act as a guard to prevent the hook taking hold, yet you hook Canadian salmon all right." What am I to do? Set myself up as superior to you all and say you are wrong?

Do you remember the fish we tried for in the tail of the Cottage Pool at Cairnton? How he was moved so many times when the fly appeared over him though he evinced no desire to take? What do you think it meant when he

*The late Mr. R. B. Marston.

moved two or three times when I went above him and drifted the fly to him?

My recollection is that after we had tried a dozen times or more dapping after a fashion, he settled back into his original position, dove to the bottom and refused to move. Do you think he saw me, or did he recognize the whole thing as a fraud? There was just a moment when he looked as though he would take. This fish was teaching us a lesson, but I can't quite put my finger on it. What was your impression?

You suggest that I broke in two fish; that is not so. I did hook a grilse and had him on for an instant only, but the fish I broke in was a real salmon. In my eagerness (it was my last day) to grass just one fish I lost my head and smashed as he rose, because I struck hard and on a straight line. This fish was on the far bank and I cast *downstream* to him, and as the whole outfit straightened out he came to the fly and—I hope he has rid himself of it by now.

The other rivers I visited were absolutely impossible; the Annan was nearly stagnant... the Eden was nearly as bad, and the keepers told me they had picked up thirty-eight dead fish in a fortnight... the Wye was in bad shape also.

Wood's reply to La Branche:

I am still puzzling my head as to why you did not hook those fish. Watching everything very carefully as far as the line is concerned, all those fish that came at you, if they had come at my small fly would, I think, have been hooked, at any rate a large proportion of them, without my attempting to strike; and that is what beats me as my line on the water was more or less in exactly the same sort of position as your line was. Why should your fish have rejected the fly? The more I think about your hackle flies and your not hooking those fish it makes me think that it has a lot to do with the hackle, as Hutton's keeper says. One of the reasons that makes me think he is correct is that I tried some of the "Crosfield" light double hooks. These are very special light hooks and in using them when fishing in my downstream method I got fish on them but they never held long enough for me to tighten the line by the water; so I came to the conclusion that if I wanted to use double hooks I had to strike immediately I saw the fish go down with it, as they simply got rid of the fly directly they felt the bulk of it, i.e., the double hooks. Might not this be the same with your big hackles?

Now I am going to be rude at once and say that having seen those fish get the fly into their mouths and take it below the water I do think it was your fault that some of them were not killed. I say this, but at the same time I would say it of myself if it had happened to me, because I do think if any fish takes the fly it is *invariably* the fisherman's fault if he is not hooked. I have stated this fact before and it has caused me to puzzle out a method of hooking them where you want to hook them, so that although I cannot answer your question at the moment I am inclined to think that more attention must be paid to how the line is lying on the water, and that, in tightening, your strike should be made according to how the line is lying. On the top of this I am more inclined than ever to think that the stiff hackles of the fly prevent the hook getting home.

1 0 4

La Branche's reply to Wood:

While you saw that I was unable to do just what I wished to do, because of the wind, with the line and fly—you undoubtedly observed that it was quite as important to place the line in the proper current as it was to place the fly—and for two reasons:

First—to have the fly unhampered by drag; and

Second—to enable the angler to pick up the loose line so that the whole thing would be almost taut when the fish took the fly. I did the best I could under the conditions, and as a matter of fact, I did as well as ever I do on our rivers —but as we say over here, "there was a jinx on me" and nothing went right. On our rivers I have missed twice the number of fish I rose on the Dee and dismissed any idea that I was doing anything wrong; but we get so many rises and hook so many that a miss is always put down to the fish.

My experience on your river has given me a new train of thought because, coming as late as I did and rising as many fish as I did, I felt that if one third of them had been killed the method would have proved itself. In any event I think it is a fair conclusion that fish can be risen to the dry fly that might not be induced to look at a wet fly.

I remember one fish distinctly. It was the fish I rose in the lower pool at Birkhall when I was looking downstream and did not see the fly taken. When I did turn, the fish had taken the fly completely under, and my line was almost taut when I tried to set the hook, and yet it came away without my even feeling the fish. What was the lesson in this instance? On our rivers that particular fish would have been soundly hooked.

Is your theory of jaw dislocation even sounder than you think it is, or do you still persist in your belief that the hackles of the fly prevent the hook taking hold? I wish I could bring myself to think so, but I cannot except when I compare the taking of a fly by a salmon with the manner in which a trout takes one.

The trout not only lives in fresh water but feeds there, consequently when he takes a fly he clamps down hard on it as a rule and hooking then is a simple matter. The salmon does not suck the fly in as the trout does, nor does he close his mouth tight when the fly is taken. His jaws, or teeth, as dentists put it, do not articulate as does the trout's, so one must allow for this difference—as you do— and learn to hook the fish where one chooses, usually in the place where the hook will hold best. In your method of fishing you have been able to observe the actions of the fish as it takes the fly quite as clearly as we who use the dry fly, only you have learned that when a fish rises in one position he is more difficult to hook than if he rose in any other position.

I have not carried my fishing to such a degree of specialization as you, but I mean to do so in future; so it will be even more necessary to see that the line is in such water as will permit me to control my fly better.

We get so many rises on our rivers that we haven't felt that it was important to learn why we missed so many fish. We have discussed it, of course, but have blamed the fish for being the stupid things they are.

My experience on the Dee has changed my line of thought. I see now that, in July, under the conditions as they were when I was at your place, that to be able to say that the dry fly is really a method of taking salmon, one must kill a few fish. How is it to be done? By changing the pattern of fly? No! I cannot yet bring myself to that thought. I cannot yet abandon the thing I consider so important, the "high-riding fly." If we cut down the hackles to enable the hook to have a better chance of engaging, can we get what I consider so important? Isn't it, perhaps, our business to study from the rise of the fish just how the hooking should be done, and not merely depend upon a taut line and the belief that the fish has taken the fly well into its mouth?

You may be interested to know that on my river, the Kedgwick, in New Brunswick, this season, two of our best wet-fly men in the club lost two-thirds of their fish after having them on for a long time—long enough to know they were securely hooked. One chap told me also, that he lifted a twenty-five pound fish in the usual manner—finger in gills—and while he held it up to be photographed he felt his finger slipping slowly up to the point of the lower jaw, the flesh and bones parting until the fish fell at his feet—the lower jaw completely split. Doesn't this all sound like disintegration? And isn't it possible that if such a condition exists a fish may not be able to close down on a fly as it should —or as a trout would do—and account to some extent for our misses?

If this is so, then your belief that the hackles of my flies are really stiff enough to prevent the hook from engaging may be quite sound, but how are we to abandon these flies if, up to now, my theory is that big hackles are necessary to make the fish come up to them? Why not abandon dry fly fishing entirely and adopt your own method—so closely akin to it? And yet so different is it that you dress your flies thinly.

Wood again to La Branche:

I am greatly looking forward to seeing you in the Spring. I am having some flies made to see if there is any way of getting over those hackle flies of yours being so very solid, that is, compared with mine, as I am still puzzled as to why you did not hook any of those twenty fish that took your fly below the water; that is, why they did not hook themselves on your fly as they do on mine. You did strike on many an occasion when as a rule I do not strike at all until I see the fish going off with my line, in fact, in watching you I absolutely failed to understand why the fish did not hook themselves without your help.

I am still sending Dr. Rushton the jaws of the few fish we catch, and the later in the year the more dislocated everything is. I sent him a jaw yesterday of a 23 lb. fresh run fish, Autumn fish. This fish was not coloured and had not been long in the fresh water. I think I am right in saying it had only three teeth in its mouth. I can't help thinking that this dislocation or lack of teeth had nothing to do with your not hooking the fish. It might have had something to do with it but not much. However, the Spring will help us to decide better than letters.

Several years later, La Branche wrote this to Jock Scott, who was writing a book on Wood's greased-line method:

"My correspondence with Wood was confined, I think, entirely to those letters written in 1925. We never came to any conclusion as to why the fish were not hooked and I was never afforded another opportunity to rise so many fish.

"It is true that I fished the Dee with Wood for three or four years after my first experience, but always in July, with the exception of one season. Most of the time spent with him was occupied by me in studying his methods and perfecting my own casting and handling of the fly as instructed by him.

"I did finally kill a fish on dry fly, in 1928 (I think). This was on the Lower Ferrochs Pool on Cairnton Water. Mr. Wood's diary has a record of this... and the ghillie has the fly which took the fish.

"All this is unimportant except in so far as my Birkhall experience confirmed my belief that salmon can be risen to the dry fly on the Dee. It should be an easy matter to learn how to hook them. I daresay by now it has been done."

THE BOURNE

Harry Plunket-Greene

The delights—and the demise—of a perfect, small trout stream.

I can remember my first day on the Bourne well. I had no knowledge of its possibilities or peculiarities. It was virgin soil so far as I was concerned. I did not start till three o'clock, and began at the broad water just above the house. There were plenty of rising fish and I covered them all right, but I never rose a thing. I tumbled very early to the fact that they were "cruisers"; but even a cruiser runs his nose up against it sometimes, and I was much annoyed with them at the time for not playing the game. Later on I discovered that they were known as the "time-wasters," and deserved every word of it. What I chiefly remember of that day is that there were fish, real fish, everywhere, that they were "fine and far off" with a vengeance, that they were distinctly friendly—fish, like concert rooms, are either friendly, indifferent or sinister—and that any fish who lived in such a lovely stream in such a lovely valley would have been a blackguard if he had been anything else. In the end, however, I got four fish of 1½, 1¼, 1¼ and 1 lb., and fell into the water pretty nearly up to my neck.

Between the 12th of June and the end of August I fished

thirty-three days and got 124 fish, weighing 156½ lbs. They were mostly orthodox in their ways, but the biggest one was rather amusing. He was a 2¾-pounder, and he lived in the splash below the Beehive bridge on the Whitchurch road, where the horses and cows and engines stop for a drink and to cool their feet. He probably knew every inhabitant of the village by name, and he had a profound contempt for me in view of the number of futile shots I had had at him. He was a beautiful fat shiny fish, and I never could make out how he managed to keep in such perfect condition, for his waking hours seemed to be entirely spent in chasing marauders off his beat. Either he was a night-feeder or had some private store of his own; I never saw him burrow for a shrimp or rise at a fly until the time when he made his one fatal mistake.

On this particular occasion he had gone down-stream in a fury at an engine, which had not only stopped on the bridge—a matter of indifference to him—but had sucked up water under his very nose, and then illegally chucked cinders on top of his head, and I had faded away with him down-stream with a conviction in my mind that I was somehow or other going to get him this time.

He had a regular routine whenever he was disturbed. I knew it by heart. He would drop down about twenty yards to a certain spot by the weeds under the far bank and, when the obstruction was removed, would gently swim up as though butter wouldn't melt in his mouth and dash suddenly into his old beat, scattering the interlopers like rabbits. True to habit he paused for a time down-stream, and then began to move up. He was in an awful temper. He had lost all his serenity and made no pretence of having just arrived from the country. He kept lashing his tail and making short darts at imaginary foes, as though he were bayoneting sacks or punching the ball, working his way gradually up to the splash. I knew that my only chance was to take him on the move, so just before he got there I put a ginger-quill in front of his nose and a little to his right. He turned on it and snapped at it in a fury. I am convinced that nothing was farther from his thoughts than food at that moment, and that he simply meant to "land one" on anything that came along. He certainly frightened the life out of me. He had been sacrosanct for so long and he was such a bully that I was almost afraid to take him out of the net when the time came. It took about ten minutes to land him, and when I got back to the splash there was another fish almost as big as himself already in his place.

This stretch below the Beehive bridge, and the meadow below, were then, and often since, the best beats on the river. They held royal fish in those days, and when the lean years came they alone came through with credit if not with glory. They are sheltered by trees on the east bank, and the water is full of weed, and the weed of shrimp, and the gravel shines like gold. It was in the upper part below the splash that a friend of mine, the late Mr. Richard Grosvenor, tried his prentice hand with a dry-fly for the first time. The stretch is only about eighty yards long, and the bank on the near side is rather high, so that you have to keep very low and throw a long line. He managed this part of it all right, and the hospitable Bourne trout responded with such splendid loyalty that before he knew where he was he was into three two-pounders in succession. He hooked and lost each one in the space of about five seconds, and all in the same way. He was so excited when he saw them go for the fly that he leapt to his feet, staggered down the bank and fell flat on his back. He did this three times running, and each time the fly and the point went to glory, and as he was using my rod I was thankful when that particular beat was exhausted.

. I see that on the same day that I got the big one mentioned above I got three others of 2¼, 1½ and 1 lb. in these meadows, and another next morning of 2¼ lbs. When I think of the respect in which two-pounders are held in the deep heavy waters of the upper Kennet, and other great trout-rivers, I feel all the more admiration for the little Bourne.

This beat was remarkable in another way. The water was shallow and crystal clear, and the gravel patches acted almost as reflectors, so that you could see everything that the fish did and almost tell what they were thinking about.

If you kept far enough off you could experiment with any one of them and watch the whole process. It was both instructive and amusing to see how one fish would be indifferent to the fly which floated straight down over his head, but would at once display interest, or even enthusiasm, about a dun which came down a foot to his right; another would freeze from unconcern to suspicion the moment he saw it, and turn, apparently, to marble; another would let it sail a foot past him without a sign, then suddenly turn and follow it down-stream. It was often possible by a simple process of elimination to discover the one weak point in the defence of any individual enemy and store it away in one's mind to be used on a later occasion.

This stretch disposed for ever of the fallacy that the tailing fish will not rise to a fly. I have caught dozens of them in these two fields alone. It depends upon two things, first whether you can see the whole fish, his entire personality, not merely his tail wagging about in the air as he burrows, and secondly the pace and energy of his excavations. If he is really shrimp-hungry, and keen on his job, and dashes his nose down into the weed, exploring every inch in slow time as he goes, you may give him up. But if he is sauntering up the water, and lazily nosing into the weed at casual intervals, you are as likely as not to get him; indeed, more likely than if he is rising regularly at fly, for his active mind is so reposefully switched on to shrimp that he subconsciously sucks in the passing fly without thinking, and you are under his guard before he has time to pull himself together. He is so lazily absorbed in shrimping that you can take far greater liberties in the matter of approach than if he were rising. I have followed a tailing fish fifty yards up the Test, and got him in the end, and I have known from the beginning that I was going to get him if I kept long enough at it. On the other hand, how many times have I followed his like, casting over him and always just going to get him, with the result that he has either come to the top of his beat and turned round and swum past me, incidentally getting the shock of his life at the ugly apparition on the bank, or he has dropped gently back, and I have dropped back with him and on to my back over a stump or a stone! I have never found the expedient of whacking a great big fly with a splash over a tailer's nose of the slightest use. He either takes no notice of it or bolts for cover. He certainly never takes it. It is the fisherman's sixth sense which tells you which tailer you can tackle and which is a "time-waster."

• • •

In the winter of 1904–5 we re-stocked the water. We put 2,000 yearlings and 500 two-year-olds into the Bourne and Test—chiefly into the former—and 200 Loch Levens into the broad water below the park. What happened to the latter I do not know. They either resolved themselves secretly into the ordinary brown trout, as is their wont, or departed from the Bourne in disgust. We never saw them again.

It is easy to tell what happened with the others. It is written for those who run to read. In the light of bitter experience I could preach a world-polemic against overstocking. Common sense is all that is needed, and yet when it comes to replacing fish that are caught the average fisherman becomes a megalomaniac and a glutton, blind of one eye and staring through the wrong end of the telescope with the other. Let us take a few simple facts and put them side by side, and we shall see the tragedy of the Bourne and how it came about.

The Bourne, as said before, was a small narrow stream, so shallow as to be wadeable in short waders throughout its course, except for a quarter of a mile of the broad water and 100 yards by Savage's cottage.

The number of fish taken out in the season by all the rods combined could not, at the highest estimate, have exceeded 1,000. There was practically not a pike in the water; I never saw one of any size. There were a number of spawning-beds, models of what spawning-beds should be, scattered through the river, and these were covered with trout in the winter. The hen-fish lays on an average about 2,000 eggs. Grant that only 1½ per cent., or 15 in 1,000, or even only 1 per cent. if you will (Mr. Donald Carr of Blagdon puts it as high as 3 per cent.), of these survived and grew up, there would be, in view of the numbers on the spawning-beds, hundreds more fish brought into the water than ever the rods took out. And yet we put in 2,000 year-lings from outside at the time of year when the big fish were all away and they had the river and whatever food was in it all to themselves, and 700 semi-adult to adult fish as well!

We asked for trouble and we got it. Nemesis pursued us from that moment. The season of 1905 was awful. It was one long series of gales and bitter cold and "not a fly on the water." I quote from the diary: "There was no surface food for the fish, and, in addition, we were rather overstocked" —when I read this I do not know whether to laugh or to cry—"so the big fish never came into condition, and got to look like miserable eels. The young ones got all the little food there was." In the last sentence can be summed up the whole indictment.

As everybody knows, the chalk-stream trout, when he grows to a size of authority, takes up his quarters in a comfortable place with his tail against a stone, or a pile, or a patch of weeds, where the current will bring him down the food without any bother on his part. This beat he will hold against all comers and here he will stay at his ease, sucking in whatever the gods send him, without ever moving away, except to chase off interlopers or make an occasional tailing excursion into the weeds after shrimp, and returning in each case to his old stand to take up position again. If the food comes along in plenty, he gets strong and fat; if it does not, he starves, for he will not go to look for it.

That was the pitiful history of the Bourne from 1905 on. The figures tell the tale:

1905: 170 fish weighing 218¾ lb., the best of them being taken at Bransbury Common several miles down the Test.
1906: 180 fish weighing 189 lb.

One could see the game being played under one's eyes— the old fish in position slowly wagging his tail and waiting for the millennium, and the little two-year-olds darting about in front of him and snapping up everything eatable before it reached him. One saw him early in the season chasing them away furiously and dropping back to his stand; and then, as time went on and he grew weaker, his rushes would become fewer and shorter, till at the last he just lay there enervated, inert, blue and blind, and one lifted him out in mercy in the landing-net and put an end to him.

I remember one in particular. He was slowly swimming about in circles on the top of the water, black and stone-blind. I netted him out, and when I took him in my hand he gave a horrible cry like some warm-blooded animal. No doubt it was something to do with pressure in the air-passages, but it made my blood run cold, for it felt like a vivid impression of the curse which had descended upon the water.

Signs of *saprolegnia* appeared at the end of this year and the beginning of 1906, and we shot a good many bad fish and managed by luck to eliminate it before it had got too far; but the real cause of it all was contained in the report from Fishmongers' Hall, to which we had sent a typical "diseased" fish: "This fish died of starvation."

What a pitiful picture that brings to the mind! When I think of those gallant gentlemen with whom we fought so often, and who beat us far oftener than we beat them, bright, bonny and bursting with health and spirits, and remember that we let them starve, with all the misery it must have meant to them, it comes between me and my sleep. The vision of those old warriors, lying on the top of the water, blind-eyed and emaciated, haunts me to this day.

The explanation was patent and so was the solution. Lord Portsmouth was, as usual, ready to do whatever we agreed should be done, but we could never get a unanimous decision from the rods. To make assurance doubly sure, I asked Hugh Sheringham down to report on the river, giving him no information as to our respective views. His report was that the river was badly overstocked, and that a good half of the fish ought to be taken out and disposed of. He could have come to no other decision, and if his advice had been followed the Bourne might still be the best trout-stream of its size in the kingdom.

But it was not to be. The mischief went on, the fish died of hunger, and the proud little Bourne fell from her high estate and went to the workhouse.

Here is an average quotation from 1906—naturally the damage would be more apparent the year following:

"Aug. 3. Got three miserable fish, 1 lb., ¾ lb., ¾ lb."

We had to look the other way and call ¾ lb. fish "pounders."

"Aug. 6. Same thing. River deteriorating day by day. Fishing a farce. One fish, ¾ lb."

I do not claim any credit for superior knowledge. I was guilty of the original sin like all the rest, but at least I repented. I would earnestly, nay passionately, urge the owners of the smaller, and even the larger, trout-streams, to think twice before re-stocking. When you eliminate the pike you leave nature free to make up the deficit caused by the work of the rods. If the spawning-beds are good, you can leave re-stocking to her. Colonel Grove-Hills told me that in all the years he had the Ramsbury Kennet he never put in a fish, and yet that water to-day is full of them. I have never seen a black fish there and hardly ever a lean one, once the season was in swing. It is, of course, deep, heavy water, and there would probably be food enough to go round even if fresh fish were put in, but nature preserved the balance, and always will if you leave her alone.

It is a strange thing, particularly interesting to me, that the physical economics of singing are precisely the same as these. There is a popular belief that the trained singer fills himself up with breath as full as he can, holds on to it like grim death, and lets it out in infinitesimal quantities in the making of vocal sounds. As a matter of fact, he does not want any breath at all beyond what he happens to have normally in his lungs at the moment for five out of every ten phrases that he has to sing, and every extra barrelful he imbibes helps to strangle him and all his means of expression, tone, rhythm, thrill and diction. Nature is essentially an economist. She hates to be either hustled or crowded. Whether you sing a song or fish a river your greatest enemy is overstocking.

Let the man who is about to re-stock ask himself a few questions:

Has the river good spawning beds?

Has he extirpated the pike and other coarse fish?

If he can answer these in the affirmative, let him then ask himself:

How many fish does he take out of the water?

Do the spawning-beds hatch out enough to fill the gaps his rods have made?

If his bag was smaller this year than last in the matter both of weight and numbers, was there nothing to account for it? Was there a poor rise of fly throughout the season, and were many more fish tailing than before? Was there less shrimp in the weed? Was the water low? Were there any signs of tar or other pollution?

If, at the end of it all, he decides that fewer fish are coming into the water naturally than he takes out artificially, and that the average of weight is going back, let him look at his spawning-beds and his weeds and bring his family to birth in healthier conditions and feed them better as they grow up. There would not be such infant mortality or so many starving tramps under the hedges. Above all let him not turn in others to divide the little that there is.

The tragedy of the Bourne is a striking example of what it costs to go one better than nature. If we could have doubled the volume of water and planted it afresh with weed, and turned in a few million shrimp, we might have made another inexhaustible Kennet. But the Bourne was not made that way. It was a wise schoolboy who said, "Man cannot live on stones alone." No more can a Bourne trout.

That was thirty years ago. Think of it! Thirty years to emerge from the swoon of starvation to which we sent her. And she can never be the same again; for up above the viaduct the trees and the flowers and the snipe and the wild bees are gone and the great silver trout with them, and the place thereof knoweth them no more.

1 1 7

THE FATHER OF
THE FLY ROD

Sparse Grey Hackle

*Profile of the man who invented and per-
fected the classic, hexagonal, split-cane
rod—by the late dean of American fly-
fishing writers.*

"In sunshine or storm, feasting or starving, he was
always good-hearted and willing to do more than
his part. No man ever had a better camp mate."
Wouldn't any sportsman be proud to receive
such a tribute? It was written, by an old friend,
about the inventor of the six-strip bamboo fly rod and
you ought to know him better, for he was not only a real
genius but a most interesting individual and a rare character.

Gentlemen, meet Hiram Lewis Leonard.

Although he is known today only as the inventor, de-
signer and first manufacturer of the modern fly rod, he
was also a genius in several other fields: a dead shot and
an accomplished hunter, a splendid woodsman, a talented
musician, a student of the natural sciences, and a leader
and inspirer of men. And he had his full share of that
sharp individuality which gave the men of the last century
self-reliance, confidence, and initiative, before mass education and regimentation existed.

Leonard had the soul of a poet, according to a lifelong acquaintance, although the active and purposeful nature of his life makes it clear that he was no dreamer. He was passionately fond of music, playing several instruments with talent, and this was apparently a family trait, for both his daughter and his granddaughter were accomplished pianists.

In fact, Leonard's musical nature is responsible for the most appealing and human glimpses of him that remain on the record. Manly Hardy, an old-time associate of Leonard's during his years as a professional hunter, once said of him that "in the woods he always carried his flute, and played it well. Many is the night when I heard him wake the wilderness with *Nellie Gray, The Irish Washerwoman, My Old Kentucky Home,* and other tunes now seldom heard."

Too, Leonard held the entertaining belief, often expressed, that no man was capable of making a good fishing rod unless he loved music and could play at least one instrument. In the Golden Age of rodmaking, when he was making rods in Central Valley, New York, everybody in the shop was musically inclined and they had quite an orchestra, which used to practice regularly at the Leonard home with Leonard himself leading on the violin and his daughter, Cora, playing the piano.

It must have been the Golden Age of industrial relations, too, with the skilled workmen associating with their employer on terms of equality (one of them, Hiram Hawes, married Cora Leonard) and finding their diversion together in amateur theatricals, casting tournaments, and any amount of rifle shooting with the old-fashioned, heavy-barreled, Scheutzen rifles. One of them, Ed Payne, was so famed for his song and dance about Old Black Joe that he was nicknamed Joe.

Leonard's health was somewhat frail in his early manhood, and doubtless influenced some of his habits. He abhorred liquor, and "had no use" for anyone addicted to it. He did not like tobacco, and disapproved of its use. Certainly it was the consideration of health that made him a lifelong vegetarian, for he always claimed that his long life and the good health of his later years were due to abstaining from the use of meat. He seldom or never ate it, and would not even permit the use of fat in the preparation of his food if it could be avoided. His old hunting associates said that when he was camping he even cooked his beans without putting in any pork.

Possibly it was the farm isolation of his boyhood, or his even more isolated existence as a market hunter and trapper, that made Hiram Leonard fond of social contacts—a fondness which there is ample evidence that he possessed, for in addition to the orchestra practice-sessions and the amateur entertainments of Central Valley, he was a member of a number of those fraternal organizations which were an outstanding feature of American life a generation or two back. He was a Mason for fifty years, a charter member of Central Valley Lodge of the Independent Order of Odd Fellows, a Knight of Pythias, and a Red Man. It must be presumed that his evenings were actively occupied!

He was a believer in spiritualism, a cult which in bygone years had a large number of followers in the United States. In fact, Miss Nellie Brigham, "the eminent spiritualist lecturer of New York," assisted the Reverend Charles R. Ross, a local minister, in conducting Leonard's funeral services in 1907.

But above everything, he had genius in his fingertips. Whatever he did, he did extremely well. "Very few men who ever entered the Maine woods were as good still-hunters, canoemen and woodsmen as Hiram Leonard," an old associate said of him, and added that men were scarce who could carry a heavy load so long a distance as he could; it is recorded that in 1856 he carried a quarter of moose meat weighing 135 pounds from Little Spencer Pond to Lobster Lake, a distance of seven miles—and he a vegetarian! He was a taxidermist "and did excellent work"; a gunsmith who could make every part of a rifle "and few men could do as fine work." And the first fishing rod he ever made so impressed a Boston sporting goods firm that they commissioned him to make rods for them and thus started him on the road to fame.

The Leonards are an old American family, three brothers having come from England during the early days of the Bay Colony. Lewis Leonard, Hiram's father, was born in Roxbury, Massachusetts, but when he grew up he went to Maine, then a new country, to raise sheep. Subsequently he turned to the manufacture of oars and eventually came to specialize in the production of racing sweeps, at which he was so proficient that his fame spread, first through this country and then to England. Considering the remoteness of America from the British Isles in those days, and the then-prevalent English contempt for anything American, this was a very substantial achievement and it indicates that Lewis Leonard possessed a high degree of craftsmanship. It also indicates that Hiram Leonard got from his father some knowledge of the properties of wood and the design of a "catenary lever."

Hiram Lewis Leonard was born January 23, 1831, at Sebec, Piscataquis County, Maine, but when he was three or four years old his family moved to Ellenville, New York, and some years later to Honesdale, Pennsylvania. I have been unable to discover any reference to fishing as applied to his boyhood years, although it scarcely seems possible that a man who was an accomplished woodsman in early manhood, according to reliable reports, could have been raised in the heart of the Catskills, among the classic trout streams of America—the Esopus, the Neversink, the Basherkill, the Rondout, the Schoharie—without having learned to love the thrill of taking the native speckled trout of those waters. He was described as an expert fisherman by one of his old friends, yet he said himself that he made his first fishing rod, for his own use, in 1871 in Bangor, Maine. I think we may assume that he fished the waters which we now love.

But before he was twenty-two years old (one chronicler, indeed, states it was at the age of sixteen) he was in charge of the "machinery department"—probably mechanical superintendent or master mechanic—of the Pennsylvania Coal Company. If this refers to the present company of that name it probably was an important concern even in those days, and consequently there is an implication that he was skilled in mechanical matters even as a youngster.

Very little information is now available concerning this period of Hiram Leonard's life, but my inquiries disclosed a single fact that supplies the key to unlock what otherwise would continue to be a mystery.

My interest in Leonard and the early history of the fly rod was originally formed through my friendship with Everett Garrison of Yonkers, New York, a deep student of rod design and a top-flight custom rod-maker. In the course of his studies, and also through his work in repairing, restoring and copying many early Leonard rods, he has minutely investigated them, even to steaming some of them apart to note their internal characteristics.

Not once, but many times, Garry remarked, "I cannot understand how Leonard could hit on the true design of a rod without being an engineer. I suppose he used the method of trial and error, but even so, he must have had a tremendous amount of luck. It doesn't seem possible.

"His early rods are out of date now, but remember that they were designed for a different kind of fishing—short casts on small brooks, fishing the wet fly in constant motion against the current. There was no need to shoot line and indeed, the old ring-and-keeper guides made it impossible. Furthermore, it was a fad in those days to use a very thin line, which was thought to be invisible to the fish. For that kind of fishing, with that line, Leonard's design was absolutely right and couldn't be improved upon today.

"I wonder if there wasn't an engineer in the picture somewhere that we don't know about."

As Garry is himself a civil engineer, and a good one, these remarks stuck in my mind. Imagine my exultation, then, when I found among some papers in the possession of the Leonard family a brief statement that "he studied civil engineering." This is corroborated by a statement of a friend in Bangor that "by profession he was a civil engineer." Here was clear evidence that the Leonard rod designs were indeed not hit-or-miss, trial-and-error affairs, but were calculated by a mind schooled in the natural sciences.

When Hiram Leonard was twenty-two years old, that is to say, in 1850 or 1851, he removed to Bangor, Maine, and worked as a taxidermist and gunsmith. In the meager data on his life there is no actual statement that poverty dogged the family, but there is a sort of implication to that effect —a likely one when we recall that the United States was then a poor country, subject to frequent and drastic panics and depressions. Too, there is reason to believe that he was delicate in health.

So behind the brief statement of his removal I seem to see an impecunious young man, maybe out of employment because his shops had shut down, restless to visit new scenes and perhaps wistful for the climate and surroundings of Maine, which his father may have described with longing and regret. What more natural than that he should resolve to convert a hobby into a business, capitalize on his manual skill, and at the same time make a living in healthful surroundings?

No specimens of Leonard's taxidermy are in existence that I know of, but the old-timers declared that his mounted animals were so lifelike as to deceive the beholder. As to gunsmithing, I personally believe that he was an even better gunsmith than a rod-maker, for I have handled and closely inspected a weapon which he made, and do not believe that its workmanship could be excelled by Neider, Adolph, Howe, or any of our other topnotch gunmakers. It was a work of genius.

He worked as a gunsmith with Charles V. Ramsdell in Bangor for several years, but apparently business was slow, for he then decided to become a professional hunter. At that time Maine was largely an uninhabited wilderness, there were no game laws, deer were thicker than fleas on a dog, and hunting venison for the Boston market was a perfectly legitimate occupation.

The manner of his entry into this calling is interesting. At the time of Leonard's death in 1907, an old-timer in Bangor recalled entering the woods in the '50s with a party of eight men and a wagonload of supplies, to spend the winter hunting for the market. As they were preparing for their first night on the trail a tall, pale, quiet-spoken

man with a heavy pack on his back came up to their fire
and said he would like to become a member of the party.
This was Hiram Leonard, and the way in which he induced
these strangers to take him into their party is evidence
that even then he could handle men.

"We stayed there all winter and shot 131 deer, sent them
to Adams & Chapman, Boston, receiving a good price for
them," the narrator declared.

Part of the contents of Leonard's heavy pack, according
to this associate, were a kit of tools and pieces of steel.
Along the first of the winter, when the snow froze and became too noisy for hunting, he took a smooth-bored He-
menway gun barrel, rifled it and made a "double-shot"
rifle right there in camp. This type was undoubtedly that
in which two loads were put into one gun-barrel, with separate caps and nipples arranged to fire them. The bullet of
the bottom load served as the breech for the top load. In
some contemporary sources he is credited with the invention of the "two shot from one barrel" principle but I cannot find elsewhere any corroboration of it although he was
certainly capable of doing such a thing.

The subject of Leonard's two-shot-from-one-barrel guns
invites a digression. Apparently this was a favorite style
with him, for Manly Hardy relates that when he hunted
with Leonard in 1857, the latter carried "a three-barreled
revolving two-shotter" of which he had himself made every
part.

A two-barreled over-and-under rifle of the two-shot type
which he made is still in the possession of the Leonard
family. When a catch is released the barrels may be ro-
tated by hand on a pivot so that each can be fired in turn.
Each barrel has two nipples for percussion caps, one at the
breech and the other a short distance up the barrel. The
lock is arranged so that it automatically fires the upper
and then the lower load, in turn.

Leonard made a shotgun of the same type as a matched,
companion piece to the rifle. It fell into other hands at
some undetermined time later, a man in the South wrote
to a Bangor newspaper, enclosing a photograph of the shot-

gun, stated it was marked "H. L. Leonard, Bangor, Me." and inquired if any reader could throw light on it.

He stated that the shotgun had been lent to a man to go turkey shooting; he failed to return, and was not found until the snow melted off the next spring. He had been shot, and from the circumstances it was deduced that he had fired at a turkey and, while he continued to stalk, the second load in the barrel had been discharged through its wadding having taken fire from the first discharge and smouldered until it reached the powder. This is quite probable; arms collectors declare that guns of the two-shot type, which were quite popular for a few years, went out of use because of this defect.

Leonard was a deadly shot and renowned for his hunting ability even among men who were all good shots and hunters; he was a splendid woodsman, and reputed the best of them all at hitting the trail. Many tales were told of his prowess. In these years he encountered Thoreau; in "The Maine Woods" the writer describes, without naming, a "slender and delicate-looking" young man who assisted in the rescue of some people who had broken through the ice in a horse-drawn vehicle.

In the summer of 1858 Hiram Leonard went on an exploring trip up the Tobique River in New Brunswick and returned immediately to arrange a hunting trip into that territory with Manly Hardy. Leaving Bangor early in September, they went by canoe to the headwaters of the Tobique and the Nepisguit "and spent some months exploring what is now called 'the newly discovered hunting grounds of New Brunswick,'" Hardy related in 1907. "It was on this trip that he did the first fishing that he ever did in the Province." And one wonders if that included any of the now-famous salmon waters. He made at least one salmon rod (a tremendous *two-piece* eighteen footer, in splices) very early in his rod-making career; it is still in the hands of his grandson.

The following year, on September 25, 1859, Hiram Leonard married Miss Elizabeth Smith Head of Bangor. In 1860, he contracted measles, a serious illness in an adult, and the disease, with ensuing complications, left him in delicate health. His physician prescribed an outdoor life for him.

Accordingly, Leonard arranged a fur-hunting and -trading expedition into New Brunswick and "the wilds of Canada" on an ambitious scale. He and at least one other member of the party, Samuel Whitcomb, were accompanied by their wives and the party went in with oxen and numerous supplies. They settled on a branch of the Kedgwick River and remained there "for several years."

The exact date of this expedition is in doubt, one member of the party placing it "in the later years of the Civil War," while Leonard's daughter puts it in the earlier years of the conflict. The period of "several years" may have been considerably longer because when he returned to Bangor he commenced taxidermal work in a room "above Pol's store" and soon afterward made the fishing rod that started him on the way to glory.

126

Matching up the various stories of Leonard's contemporaries regarding this rod, the facts seem to be that he became interested in a description written by W. H. H. Murray of the fishing rods made by Conroy of New York, declared that he could make one as good, and immediately set to work. According to Leonard himself, this was in 1871. The rod, of ash and lancewood, was intended for his own use, but a friend of the sporting goods firm of Bradford & Anthony, in Boston, advised him to send it to them for inspection. They were immediately interested, and when their salesman came to Bangor he looked up Leonard.

They had been having trouble in getting well-made split bamboo rods of the four-strip type and wanted to know if he could make them. After inspecting samples which the salesman showed him, he replied in no uncertain terms that he could, and forthwith he was in the rod business. He began that same day, with his only tools a small vise, a hatchet for splitting the bamboo, and a rasp and "a crooked knife" to work out the strips. (If this was the Ojibway crooked knife, it was a sort of one-hand, miniature drawknife or spokeshave, in the use of which a great deal of skill may be employed.)

His business grew and he began to employ help. He ceased to sell his rods to Bradford & Anthony, and for a time marketed them through Abbey & Imbrie of New York; characteristically, he broke off with the latter firm because they wanted him to mark his rods "Abbey & Imbrie." Then the rod-maker demonstrated that the description of him as "a genius but not a business man" was correct by entering, in 1877, into a partnership with a Boston man named Kidder, without stopping to realize that the name of H. L. Leonard Rod Co. which he had broken with Abbey & Imbrie to retain, thereby became as much the property of his partner as of himself. The partners continually disagreed and a year later, in 1878, Kidder sold out his partnership interest to William Mills & Son of New York.

The growth of Leonard's rod business under Mills' handling made his location in far-off Bangor a matter of great inconvenience and they urged that he move his plant closer to New York. Leonard asked them to suggest a location and Thomas Mills replied that he had a sister living in Central Valley, New York, and it was a likely community for his purpose. Leonard came down on a trip of inspection, agreed, and forthwith, in 1881, moved his plant and a number of his employees to that location.

Mills supplied the business ability and trade contacts which Leonard lacked and in the ensuing thirty years up to his death they spread the name and fame of him and his rods throughout the civilized world. They acquired the remaining interest in the business after Hiram Leonard's death. A nephew, Ruben C. Leonard, has an interest in the corporation which succeeded the original partnership.

Central Valley and its mile-off neighbor, Highland Mills, constitute a sort of shrine of rod-making. The Leonard plant is still in Central Valley; Jim Payne, the son of that Ed Payne who was one of Hiram Leonard's skilled rod-makers, has his shop in Highland Mills. All of the old rod-makers except Fred Thomas are buried in the Cemetery of the Highlands, in Highland Mills—Leonard; Payne; Will Edwards, the stormy petrel who was "always shifting about," making rods at different times for Spaulding,

Abercrombie & Fitch, Winchester, and Bristol, and starting photograph galleries between-times; Hiram Hawes,
who came from Honesdale, Pennsylvania, to work for
Leonard and married his daughter Cora; his brother,
Loman Hawes; and Frank Oram (he joined up with Ed
Payne after Hiram Leonard's death), who died with Leonard's gluing secret locked in his breast, according to a legend which has absolutely no basis in fact.

Hiram Leonard died at his home in Oak Clove, Central
Valley, on the morning of January 30, 1907, at the age of
seventy-six.

Probably no man deserves better the thankful memory
of sportsmen than the Yankee genius who invented, per-
fected and provided for them the rod that revolutionized
the art of fly fishing and made possible the kind of fly casting that is the basis of our sport. It must always be a matter of regret that he did not survive long enough to apply
his magnificent talents to the problems of two developments of later years which would have delighted his soul
—the use of Tonkin cane instead of the Calcutta bamboo
that he knew, and the rise of dry fly angling.

To leave the reader with the full flavor of Hiram Leonard's individuality, I have saved until the last a curious,
undated and unsigned fragment of autobiography which
his wife apparently wrote at his dictation, for the document is in her handwriting. Through the courtesy of Mrs.
Hiram W. Hawes, I am privileged to reproduce it, as follows:

"I made my first rod in Bangor, Me. Material used was
ash and lancewood. I made it for my own use, not intend-
ing to make a business of rod manufacturing. I, however,
sent it to Bradford & Anthony of Boston who kept a sporting goods house, being advised to do so by a friend of
theirs.

"Their salesman said, 'The man who made that rod understood the business and ought to be able to make split
bamboo rods.'

"I had never seen one, he showed me two; I examined
them; he asked me if I could make them. Answered, 'Yes,
and better than those.' I commenced making them from

that date—opened my shop in two rooms on Main Street in Bangor—worked alone at first, was there about a year, then moved into Strickland's block on the bridge, hired one man at first. As business increased, 6 or 7.

"Stayed there three years then moved to Dow's block on Hammond Street. Employed 11 men, 1 woman. In 1877 went in company with Mr. Kidder of Boston, remained with him until 1878. Then he sold out to William Mills & Son, New York.

"In 1881, removed from Bangor to Central Valley, N.Y., built factory which was moved in 1899 to present site. Am with Mills, yet.

"The rods I first saw were in four strips but in splitting up the bamboo I found where it was burnt there were weak places, so made the rods in six strips, the first ever made, and from the very commencement the demand has been so great for the Leonard rod that I have not been able to fully supply it.

"My rods took the first prize at Vienna, London, and at the world's fair, Philadelphia, and in all contests for fly, or bait casting, they lead the world."

SEA-RUN

CUTTHROATS

Roderick L. Haig-Brown

Praise for the unsung, "second-best" trout of the Pacific slope by western Canada's late fishing laureate.

May is a great and generous month for the trout fisherman. In the English chalk streams the fish are coming to their best and the hatching May flies drift in squadrons and flotillas and armadas, their proudly upright wings a mark that stirs both fish and fisherman. In the Adirondacks and the Catskills trout fishermen are out with the Hendrickson. Here in British Columbia the interior lakes are warm enough, but not too warm, for good fly-fishing, and the great native-stock Kamloops trout come up out of Shuswap Lake to their fierce feeding on sockeye and spring salmon yearlings at Little River and off the mouth of Adams. On the coast the summer steelhead are running. In May each year I used to return to General Money his big thirteen-foot salmon rod; through the winter months it was mine because, the General said, he was too old to give it proper work to do, but by mid-May he would be thinking of early summer fish in the

Stamp and would take the big rod over there to fish its easy, graceful way down the Junction Pool or the General's Pool. In May I turn to a smaller rod and go to the Island Pools to find our own run of summer fish, little fish seldom over five pounds, seldom under two, but sea-run steelhead just the same and brave fish that hit the fly hard and jump freely in the broken water. The twenty-fourth of May, a good Canadian holiday, is a day I have often celebrated with the little steelheads of the Island Pools.

The Pacific coast is great trout country. If we consider the chars as separate from trout—and I am quite certain that we should—there are in the world only three species of trout, the brown, the rainbow and the cutthroat. Of these, two are native to the Pacific coast and the slope of water west of the Rocky Mountains. This, by itself, seems to argue that the Pacific watershed has in full measure whatever it is that trout need and like; all the testing and sorting processes of evolution have left it with two trouts and given only one to all the rest of the world. The variations of environment in the watershed have developed at least two subspecies of each of these native species: the rainbow or steelhead of the coast proper becomes the Kamloops trout at medium elevations and the mountain Kamloops at high elevations; the Yellowstone cutthroat and the mountain cutthroat, as their names suggest, bear similar relationship to the coast cutthroat, the type of the species.

I suppose it is most improper to talk of degrees of nativeness. A fish or a bird or a mammal is native to a country or not native, and that is all there is to it. But for many reasons, most of them emotional and quite illogical, I feel that the cutthroat is the most native of Pacific coast game fish, just as I feel that the ruffed grouse is the most native of the continent's game birds and the cougar and the raccoon are the most native of the mammals. The cutthroat, the coast cutthroat of tidal waters particularly, is such a down-to-earth, workaday, unspectacular fish; he fits his environment so perfectly and makes such good, full use of it, following the tides and the salmon runs and the insect hatches to the limit of their yield; and he has not been, as the rainbow has, more or less successfully transplanted to all parts of the world. He lives in his own place in his own way and has his own special virtues. He is a little like the burned stumps and slash and new growth of the old logging works in that one must know and deeply love the country to appreciate him properly.

In writing of the "Game Fish of British Columbia," Professor J. R. Dymond gives an opinion of cutthroat trout that is undoubtedly shared by many anglers:

> Were it not that it (the cutthroat) occurs in the same area as two of the hardest fighting game fish known, its qualities would be more highly regarded. At times it does leap from the water when hooked, and often puts up quite a prolonged struggle before being landed. It generally rises quite readily to the fly, although as a rule it takes the fly sunk and drawn as a minnow, more readily than the dry fly.

1 3 2

The implication of this is that the cutthroat is not to be compared with either the Kamloops or the steelhead as a game fish. My own opinion is that, at his best, he is in every way comparable; and under some circumstances a discerning angler may even find him superior.

The qualifying phrase "at his best" is important, because the cutthroat is too often caught when he is not at his best. When the humpback fry are running in March and April, anglers catch two- and three-pound cutthroats that are thin and feeble after spawning. Many cutthroats are caught in low-producing lakes where the average fish are too small to give a good account of themselves and the larger fish are always in poor condition; and many are caught, quite unnecessarily, with spinner and worm or other such clumsy gear and have no chance to show what they can do. The cutthroat is at his best in a river that is open to the sea; he should then be a short, thick fish of two pounds or more, not too long in fresh water, with a clean white belly and a heavily spotted, green- or olive-brown back. Such a fish will come nobly to wet fly or dry—better to the dry fly than will Kamloops trout and far better, certainly, than steelhead—and when you set the hook he will run as boldly as any fish of his size, and probably he will jump too. Beyond this he has a way of his own that is fully as dangerous to tackle as the more spectacular antics of the Kamloops, a way of boring down and out into the heaviest stream against the lift of a fly rod and sometimes twisting his body and shaking his head in solid, sulky strength. I have had more moments of straining anxiety with big cutthroat trout half played out than I have with any fish, except, perhaps, big brown trout among the weed beds and other obstructions of the chalk streams.

The cutthroat's habit of going to sea is what makes him a really fine game fish. There are good cutthroats and good cutthroat fishing in the cold mountain streams that drain into the big lakes and even in ordinary landlocked rivers that owe nothing to lake or stream; but the true sea-run cutthroat is a very special fish and makes very special fishing. He is not truly migratory, like the steelhead and the salmon: that is, he does not run out to sea from his river in early youth and range freely through deep water until grown to full maturity. He is at once less businesslike about his migration and more practical. Somewhere toward the end of his first or second year he finds that the food available to him in fresh water is not enough, and he simply moves downstream to find more. In tidal water or in the sea just beyond the mouth of his river he finds what he is seeking, so he stays there awhile and feeds; sometimes he moves on out as far as five or ten miles from the mouth of his river, feeding as he goes; he may even (though I am not sure of this) school with other cutthroats to feed for a while off the mouth of some stream quite distant from his own—certainly schools of big cutthroats lie at certain times off the mouths of little creeks that seem far too small to support them even as a spawning run.

But in spite of all this wandering there seems to be no sharp break between the salt-water and fresh-water life of the migratory cutthroat. He may return to the fresh-water pools of his river at any time: in spring when the salmon fry hatch, in fall when the ripe salmon run, in summer when the sedge nymphs crawl thickly over the round rocks of the stream bed. And he is seldom beyond reach of the fly-fisherman's search; by studying the tides and his movement in them you may catch him at his feeding in the estuary; by knowing a favorite bay or sandbar and his chosen time there you may even find him right out in salt water. In Puget Sound keen cutthroat fishermen search water as far as six or seven miles from any stream, trolling a small spinner until they hook the first fish, then changing over to the fly.

My own first meeting with sea-run cutthroats was in the Nimpkish River. I was working in a logging camp seven or eight miles away and started out for the river immediately after work on my second Saturday in camp. I took a blanket and enough food for a meal or two and promised myself a well-spent Sunday. On Saturday evening I fished one pool in the short hour or so before dark and caught three fish of about a pound. The Sunday was a bright, warm day and I started early. The Nimpkish is a broad, fine river, fast and fierce in most places, but with a few long, slow pools. On the first of these pools I wasted far too much time, but there was a strong deep run below it that spread into something less than a pool, no more, really, than a slackening in the rapid. Right in the deepest and fastest water a fine fish took, and I landed a three-pound cutthroat. At the head of the next pool was another deep, broken run, and there the second fish, a little larger than the first, came boldly to my fly. From then on I fished the fast, heavy water whenever I could find it, and by the end of the day I had four cutthroats and two rainbows, all over three pounds and one of them over four.

Since then I have caught sea-run cutthroats in the salt water, off the mouths of tiny creeks, over the tide flats of big rivers, in fresh-water pools and in the brackish water of shrunken river channels on the ebb tide. About ten years ago I used to fish the mouth of the Campbell regularly with Cliff Whitaker, who was my next-door neighbor at that time. Cliff had learned to fish and hunt in Alaska and was a good man at both sports, aggressive and determined, a fine woodsman and a tireless walker. He also loved human competition in hunting and fishing, which I do not, but we found a way around that which left both of us happy and comfortable.

There are half a dozen or more good places to catch cutthroats in the tidal part of the Campbell; two of them are sloughs, which make dull fishing; three of the good places are best fished from a boat; and only one offers the real variations and complications of current that one hopes for in river fishing and can, at the same time, be fully covered by wading. On a fair run-out of tide the river breaks into a sharp rapid just below the upper slough, and this runs for two hundred yards or more—water where there is always a chance of picking up one or two fish on the wet fly. At the tail of the rapid a small creek comes in, and since the creek has a run of cohos, the cutthroats wait near its mouth when the fry are moving down. But the best of the fishing was in a fairly big pool below the rapid. The main current of the pool swung away from the bank from which we fished and left a wide eddy where feed collected; this was a good place. The run of current itself was fairly good and became very good where it spread out among the short butts of rotten piles at the tail of the pool. All this water was uncertain; on a good tide during April or May the fish were sure to come into it, but just where they would be and how they would be feeding depended on the stage of the tide, the strength of the river and the type of feed that was most available. The mood of the fish also seemed to depend on just what kind of hunting they had had during the full tide before the ebb—a fish with a really fine bellyful of sand launce or sow bugs or sand hoppers could be a very fussy feeder when he came into the pool.

Cliff and I made a habit of going down to the pool whenever there was a good tide, and it wasn't long before we were getting very fine results on the last two hours of the ebb. We caught most of our fish on flies of the streamer type, tied, not in the American way on a long single hook, but on two or three small hooks in tandem, what the English and Scottish sea-trout fishers call "demons" or "terrors." Several Hardy patterns were very deadly: one with long dark badger hackles laid back to back, two tinsel-covered hooks and a red tag on the second hook; another with long blue hackles, strips of light mallard and three hooks each tinsel-covered and with a red tag; a third, called the "dandy" and made up of two hooks, mallard strips and a red hackle at the throat, was deadliest of all. But in the course of this fishing two things become evident: first, that streamer-type flies were altogether too effective under certain conditions, particularly when fish were taking freely on the last of the ebb; and second, that we were not catching fish at all well on the start of the flood, though big ones commonly moved up into the pool and began a lazy sort of feeding at that time.

Cliff and I discussed the deadliness of the streamers and agreed that we had better limit ourselves by giving up their use. At about the same time we discovered we could pick off some of the lazy feeders of the flood tide very nicely with a dry fly. From then on, all Cliff's competitive instinct was directed toward catching the fish by more and more delicate methods. We almost gave up fishing the ebb and always gave our main attention to the glassy slide of water near the piles at the tail of the pool; as soon as the tide began to slow the current there, we went down and waited for some sign of fish moving in.

They came early one day, and Cliff saw a quiet rise just behind the lowest pile. He dropped a brown and white bivisible into the rings and hooked his fish almost as the fly touched the water; it was a three-pounder. His fly was hardly out free and dried off again when another fish rose within reach; Cliff covered him, played him and netted another three-pounder. Ten minutes later he dipped his net under a third of the same size. "That bi-visible's too deadly," he said. "Guess we'll have to quit using it."

And we did. The bi-visible we had been using was brown and white, tied on a size 9 or 10 hook. We turned to other flies on size 15 and 16 hooks and did less well with them, though still well enough. And we finally went one stage farther still, to upstream nymph fishing with flies as small as size 17. The nymphs were more attractive to the fish than were the small dry flies, but the fishing was actually more exciting and more difficult, because light and water conditions made it hard to tell when a fish had taken the nymph; we were usually wading deep and looking toward the sun across smooth water whose reflecting surface concealed the faint flash of a moving fish that the nymph-fisherman generally depends on.

That seems to show that you can go to almost any refinement of fly-fishing and still find sea-run cutthroats willing to meet you halfway. But in spite of the sport they give in tidal waters, I still prefer to catch them when they have left the estuaries for the fresh-water pools. Tidal waters can be very beautiful. I remember an evening below the falls of Theimar Creek, when the sunset light was blood red on the shiny wet sand of the tide flats and big cutthroats were rising in the narrow channel all down the length of a seaweed-covered log. I remember an August sunrise in the mouth of the Campbell, off the point of the Spit, when big cutthroats in perfect condition came to our flies so fast and hard that we each had a limit within an hour or two; outside the tyee fishermen were passing up and down in their white rowboats, and a little westerly wind came up to scuff the water of Discovery Passage as the full daylight made it blue; behind us the mountains of Vancouver Island were black and white with rock and snow, and across from us the Coast Range was jagged and tall and endless from farthest south to farthest north. Those were good times. But in the comings and goings of the cutthroats in fresh water there is something more than good fishing, something more than any simple beauty of surroundings. Each movement is an outward sign of a change in the year's cycle; more than a sign, it is an actual part of both change and cycle. And knowledge of the movements in any particular river is the seal of one's intimacy with the country at least as much as it is a test of one's knowledge as a fisherman.

In March and April and on into May the cutthroats are there because the salmon fry are coming up from the gravel and moving down; the fishing is often quick and fierce, with a big wet fly quickly cast to a slashing rise and worked back fast. Fish show in unexpected places, in short eddies behind rocks in the rapids, off the mouths of little creeks, and in all the expected places as well. Sometimes the May flies hatch thickly and not a trout will stir to a wet fly, though fish after fish will come to a dry blue quill or a little iron blue. Then on some hot day in May, the big black ants put out their wings and make their brief mating flight; for a day, or perhaps two days, the river is full of drowned or drowning ants, and the fish feed on them and come to a dry fly that is not too tidily tied and not too well greased, something bedraggled and half-drowned like the ants themselves. After that there is a change, and there seem few cutthroats in the fresh-water pools of the Campbell. I used to say of June and July: it's hardly worth going up—there won't be any fish. But the days are so good and the river is so bright that one goes sometimes just for the pleasure of being out in the sun and the summer, with running water all about one and the trees green on the banks.

I have been surprised so many times now that I am careful what I say about June and July. It was a June afternoon that I went up to the head of the Sandy Pool, lay on the beach for a while in the sun and at last walked lazily down into the water to make a few casts before going home. Just as soon as my fly reached out into the fast water a trout took hold, a good trout, short and thick and over two pounds. I went on fishing and soon hooked a second fish, the most beautiful cutthroat, I think, that I have ever hooked; he was a two-pounder, like the first one, but shorter still and thicker, splendidly marked with a rich pattern of heavy spots all over the deep and shining green of his back and sides. That was all for that afternoon, but it was enough to leave the short June hour as clear and sharp in my memory as any fishing time.

Two years ago a July day looked good, and I went to the Island Pools, just to look them over. I told myself that the fish wouldn't come in for a couple of weeks yet. So I worked along the bar and floated a Mackenzie River bucktail down the runs, dancing it back to me from wave top to wave top on the upstream wind, lowering my rod to slack the line and let the fly ride the rough water down again. It seldom finished the ride. The big cutthroats, three-pounders, some

of them nearly four pounds, came at it like fiercer creatures than any fish, leapt right out of the water with it,
fought me for possession of it and yielded only to utter exhaustion and the lift of the net.

So I have no wisdom that will let me write of June and
July, even in my own river that I know well. And the wisdom I once had for August and September is shaken a little
and likely to grow shakier yet as I grow older and learn to
watch more closely. Sometimes in the second week of August the humpback salmon run into the river. With them, I
used to say, come the big cutthroats that are maturing to
spawn in the following February—magnificent fish that
have attained their full weight and strength and a cunning
or dourness that makes them hard to catch on bright August days in the Canyon Pool. I argued that they came into
the river because of their maturity, following the maturity
of the humpbacks rather than in any hope of feeding on
salmon eggs that would not be dropped to the gravel for
another two months. It was a nice theory, but in the last
two or three years I've noticed the cutthroats before the
humpbacks. I asked General Money about that, and he had
noticed the same thing. So I no longer know why they come
in then—I only know that I try to get away to the Canyon
Pool as soon as I can after the first of August.

That August fishing in the Canyon Pool is the finest cutthroat fishing I have had anywhere. The fish are very
big—I have killed several that weighed within an ounce of
four pounds and have lost some that I know were over five
pounds—and they can be superlatively difficult. They are
not feeding, for only very rarely is there so much as a
May-fly nymph in a stomach; they lie in water six or eight
feet deep, unrippled by the slightest stir of wind and bur-
nished by the full glare of summer sun. When they rise,
they come right up from the bottom, and every cast that
covers them is a really long cast. When they feel the hook,
they turn and run with a pull that makes every one seem a
ten-pounder, and at the end of that first long run, well
down at the tail of the pool, they jump with a coho's wildness. That part is easy. Coaxing them back up the pool
again, trying to keep them from disturbing the rest of the

water, meeting their plunging, boring, heavy resistance and yielding no more than must be yielded to save 2X gut is the hard part, the part that makes fingers clumsy and trembling and the heart quick in the chest when it's time to reach for the net.

After August you may perhaps find cutthroats again in October, when the cohos run up on the first heavy fall rains. They seem less important then, because their season is almost over and you're fishing a big fly and heavy gut for the cohos anyway—tackle too clumsy for a trout—so you turn them back to live and spawn. And again in steelhead time, in December and January and February, they are there, heavy with spawn now, dark, with red gill covers and golden bellies. I hold them hard and bring them in fast, then reach down for the shank of the hook and twist the barb quickly away from them so that they can go back without harm to their important affairs. But recently a few big cutthroats have been caught and killed as steelheads in the Campbell. I saw one two seasons ago that weighed six and a half pounds. This season there was one that weighed well over seven pounds. I hope that next August, or one August soon, in the Canyon Pool...

FLY FISHING FOR BASS

Dr. James A. Henshall

Long before the streamer and bass-bug were invented, big wet flies were the standard killers. Over a hundred years ago, "Mr. Bass" described the state of this art.

I t is useless to cast for Black Bass from high elevations near the water, as a bold bank, a projecting rock, a damn, etc., under ordinary circumstances; for the angler must remember that the most commanding situation for seeing the fish also furnishes the best facilities for being seen in return, and *vice versa*. In fishing from a boat, it must be kept in deep water, while long casts are made in-shore, toward the feeding grounds. We should never fish with the sun at our back, or in such a position as to throw the shadow of our rod or person upon the water.

From what has been said in the chapter on the "conditions governing the biting of fish," it will be apparent that it is absolutely necessary that there be a breeze sufficient to ruffle the surface of the water. It is perfect folly for the angler to cast his flies upon a smooth surface, if the water is clear enough for fishing. A gale is better than no wind at all, and it does not matter from what direction the wind blows, if the condition and temperature of water are right. A good breeze is the angler's best ally, for by rippling the water it breaks the line of sight, to a great extent, between him and the fish.

The angler should endeavor to cast his flies as lightly as possible, causing them to settle as quietly as thistledown, and without a splash. After casting, the flies should be skipped or trailed along the surface in slightly curving lines, or by zigzag and tremulous movements, occasionally allowing them to become submerged for several inches near likely-looking spots. If the current is swift, allow the flies to float naturally with it, at times, when they can be skittered back again, or withdrawn for a new cast. Two or three times are enough to cast over any one spot, when a rise is not induced.

When Bass are biting eagerly and quickly, whipping the stream is to be practiced, that is, the casts are to be often and rapidly repeated, first to one side, then the other, allowing the flies to settle but a moment. In casting and manipulating the flies, the line must be ever taut; for often a Bass will thus hook himself, which he never does with a slack line.

STRIKING AND PLAYING

The angler should strike by sight, or by touch; that is, he should strike the moment he sees the rise; for the Bass has either got the fly in his mouth, has missed it, or has already ejected it, when the rise is seen; it very seldom happens that the rise is seen before the fly is reached by the fish. The angler must also strike at the moment he feels the slightest touch or tug from the fish, for often the Bass takes the fly without any break at the surface, especially if the flies are beneath the surface.

Striking is simply a twist of the wrist, or half-turn of the rod, either upward or downward (upward with stiffish rods, and downward with very willowy ones), which is sufficient to set the hook if the rod and line maintain a proper state of tension; but when the careless angler has a slack line, and, consequently, a lifeless rod, he must necessarily strike by a long upward or side sweep of the rod, called "yanking"; and should he succeed in hooking the fish, the chances are that it will shake the hook out again before the slack can be reeled up.

The top of the rod must always be held upward, so that the rod constantly maintains a curve with the line; and never, under any circumstances must the rod point in the direction of the flies after they reach the water, for this allows the direct strain of the fish to come upon the line or leader. When a Bass is hooked, he must be killed on the rod; the rod must stand the brunt of the contest; the more pliable and springy the rod, the less likelihood of its breaking, for a stiff rod is more easily fractured than a flexible one. Give the Bass more line only when he takes it; make him fight for every inch, and take it back when you can; hold him by the spring of the rod, and do not hesitate to turn the butt toward him to keep him away from weeds, rocks, snags, or other dangerous places; this will bring him up with a round turn, and is called "giving the butt."

143

Don't be in a hurry to land him; the longer he resists, the better for your sport; take your time and only land him when he is completely exhausted; for if he is well hooked, and the proper tension of rod and line maintained, he can not get away; on the other hand, if he is tenderly hooked, the more gingerly he is handled the better. Therefore, never be in a hurry, and never attempt to force matters; always keep a bent rod and taut line; if the Bass breaks water, the best plan is to lower the tip, so as to slack the line, and immediately raise the rod and tighten the line when he strikes the water again, for if he falls on the tightened line he is most sure to escape; this is one of his most wily tricks.

REMARKS, HINTS, AND ADVICE

It has been doubted by some that the Black Bass will rise to the fly, or at best that they are uncertain in their modes and times of doing so, as compared with the Brook

Trout. These doubts are mostly raised by those who angle for the Black Bass in precisely the same way as for the Brook Trout, upon the supposition that the two fish are identical in habits and instincts. But while their habits of feeding are very similar—both feeding on the bottom, in midwater, or on the surface, on crustacea, larvæ, minnows, insects, etc.—they differ greatly in other habitual features and idiosyncrasies.

The Black Bass will rise to the fly as readily, under any and all conditions, as the Brook Trout, when fished for understandingly, and under proper precautions. There are times, seemingly favorable, when neither Bass nor Trout will rise to the fly.

One reason why the Bass is thought to be uncertain in rising to the fly is this: While he is fully as wary as the Trout he is not so timid. A Trout darts incontinently away at the first glimpse of the angler, and is seen no more; but the Bass will retire but a short distance, and as often will stand his ground, and on balanced fins will watch the angler vainly casting his "brown hackle" or "coachman" over him, perhaps laughing in his sleeve (shoulder girdle) at his discomfiture. The truth of the matter is, the Bass is not uncertain, but he is too knowing to be deceived by his flies, so long as the angler is in sight.

Fish are more suspicious regarding objects on the surface of the water than of those beneath. I have often demonstrated this, causing them to skurry away, by holding a long stick immediately over them, above the surface; while I could introduce the same stick underneath the water and even prod a fish with it, without alarming it much. This is why more caution is necessary in fly-fishing than in bait-fishing; the bait in one instance being on the surface, and in the other, beneath. If a Black Bass, in rushing to the surface for the fly, sees the angler, he at once stops in his course, and thenceforth the daintiest flies, never so deftly thrown, will be cast in vain while the angler remains in view.

In a recent issue of the London *Field* appeared an article, written by the able editor of that valuable paper, Francis Francis, Esq., on the frightening of Brook Trout by the flashing and reflections of a varnished fly-rod, when wildly waved by the angler in casting, and which, at first sight, would seem to be plausible enough; but upon mature consideration, and with all due deference to so eminent an authority as Mr. Francis, I am convinced that there is not much in it, and that instead of proving the matter he seems to be rather begging the question.

The main rules to be observed in fly-fishing I conceive to be these: on narrow streams to keep entirely out of sight, and on open waters to make long casts; in either case, the fish, not seeing the angler, will not be alarmed at the flashing of the rod; the finer the water the greater the caution that must be used on the one hand, and the longer must be the cast on the other.

Mr. Francis does not offer any remedy for the varnished rod, but merely suggests that it might answer to paint it sky-blue, or a dull, smoky tint, without polish; but this, I know, will not do. I have seen rods that had the varnish scraped off and were painted a delicate pea-green, to harmonize with the foliage of Trout streams, and I have seen the bark left on alder, elm, and tamarack poles when used in bait-fishing, but they were not more successful than the varnished rod.

Split bamboo and other jointed rods must of necessity be varnished to preserve their elasticity and beauty. Think of a delicate split bamboo tip coated with sky-blue paint! The very thought is heresy, and an offense against the eternal fitness of things that would make even the spots on a Brook Trout blush more deeply crimson. American split bamboo rods are the finest made rods in the world, and the numerous foreign orders received by the manufacturers fully attest this fact, and show, moreover, that they are duly appreciated abroad, as well as at home, highly varnished and flashing though they be.

There is one feature of this subject that is peculiarly gratifying to me, and I heartily thank Mr. Francis for the article in question. It concedes the fact that fish, having eyes, can see, and are not the near-sighted dupes that most writers would have us believe; this concession could not be put in a stronger light than by the assertion that they are frightened at the flashing of a varnished rod, and that a rod, therefore, should be rendered as nearly invisible as possible by painting it a sky-blue or cloud color. But if this were done, what a quantity of brash wood and poor workmanship, and what a multitude of sins of omission and commission would this sky-blue mantle, like charity, cover!

When fish are frightened at a fishing-rod at all, it is when its shadow is suddenly cast upon the water—which all prudent anglers are very careful to avoid doing, especially on small streams—and, viewed in this light, a sky-blue rod has not even a fancied advantage over the most highly-polished one.

The most important rule, then, to be observed, first, last and all the time in fly-fishing, is: *Keep out of sight of the fish;* this is the first and great injunction; "and the second is like unto it": *Keep as quiet and motionless as possible.* "On these two" laws depends all your success in fly-fishing. Let your necessary movements be deliberate and methodical, avoiding all quick, sudden, or energetic motions. Fish see and hear much better than we give them credit for. To keep out of the fish's sight we must be screened by such natural objects as bushes, trees, rocks, etc., or by keeping well back from the brink and making long casts. In wading the stream it is also necessary to make long casts. The latter is the best plan of fishing a stream, as the angler, being so near the water, is not so apt to be seen.

It is best, always, to fish down stream, even with the wind against one, for fish always lie with head up stream, and will be more apt to see your flies. The current will, moreover, take your flies down stream, and so keep your line taut. It is also easier to wade down, than up stream. Many other reasons might be given, but these will be sufficient. Cast just below ripples and rapids, over eddies and pools, along the edges of weed patches, under projecting banks and shelving rocks, near submerged trees or driftwood, off gravelly shoals, isolated rocks and long points or spurs of land; it is useless to fish long, deep, still reaches of water.

The most favorable time for fly-fishing for Black Bass is

146

during the last hours of the day, from sundown until dark, and also on bright moonlight evenings. On streams, an hour or two following sunrise, in warm weather, is quite favorable. On dark, cloudy, and cold days the middle hours are best. Bright sunny days, especially in hot weather, are not favorable to fly-fishing, except in quite cool, shady, and breezy situations. In short, the best conditions are a mellow or dusky light, a good breeze, and translucent water; while the most unfavorable are a bright sun, a still atmosphere, and a smooth and glassy surface, with the water either very fine or very turbid.

And now, in concluding this portion of my subject, let me say a parting word to the beginner: Cast a straight line; keep it taut; strike upon sight, or touch; kill your fish on the rod; take your time. It is better to cast a short line well, than a long one bunglingly. Should you cast your fly into a branch of a tree overhead, or into a bush behind you, or miss your fish in striking, or lose him when hooked, or crack off your tail-fly, or slip into a hole up to your armpits —keep your temper; above all things don't swear, for he that swears will catch no fish. Remember, yours is the gentle art, and a fly-fisher should be a gentleman.

THE CONSTANT
NYMPH

G. E. M. Skues

*Eye-opening observations from the man
who brought us modern nymph fishing.*

I t has long been a conviction with me, based upon observations over many seasons, that the part of a river which has the wind across it will present better opportunities for finding rising fish than a part where the wind is blowing straight upstream or straight down. The obvious and straight-forward inference is that a cross wind, whether direct or up or down, will sweep the duns, hatching all over the surface of the river, into those strings which go sailing along in the glass edge —the cushion of calm—under the lee bank.

If that were all that could be deduced it would be something, but not much; but it is far from all.

The trout is a gentleman who never wastes energy on unproductive exercise. He takes up a position where his food is brought to him and can be secured with the minimum of trouble and exertion to himself. It follows that the more rapid parts of the stream will, in general, bring him his food in the form of nymphs more steadily and copiously than the slower portions. On the other hand the trout, to spare itself undue exertion, must lie out of the strength of the current, if really a strong current, only exposing itself to it momentarily in order to secure a tit-bit in the form of nymph or dun. So one sees that it is to be found during the time of the take for the most part under that bank against which the push of the current sets. This observation has to be qualified by the fact that where the stock of trout is large the younger and smaller fish are not permitted by their elders to occupy posts of vantage under the banks, and are therefore driven to make their living in mid-stream. That is a reason why during the day-time the trout rising in mid-river are generally small ones. The same conditions apply in the evening when a hatch of duns is proceeding, with this qualification that, when there is no wind, the trout will not have the duns driven for them under the banks and must spread themselves over the river. I have seen a strong evening rise when every trout was taking nymphs and scarce a hatching fly was to be seen.

When, however, there is no hatch or no swarming of nymphs to the surface, but there is a heavy fall of spinners, these, falling on the water all over its surface will not be carried by the wind under the banks, and then one finds feeding trout in the river cruising with neb to the surface and feeding greedily on spinners. Yet even in this case the stronger current will bring if not the larger yet the quicker supply of food and the best fish will, therefore, be found where the current sets strongest.

The same conditions will recur on a still day when there is no hatch of fly, or only a small one, and a heavy fall of spinners. I recall a still morning in April when the trout were rising all over the river, and my companion and I were quite defeated until we diagnosed spinner.

But during the day-time there is another matter to be considered! Are the trout nymphing or are they taking hatched ephemeridæ? My conclusion is again reached by consideration of the trout's prejudice in favour of the con-servation of energy. Which form of food will pay it best? Obviously that which is in greatest quantity for the time being at the point where it can secure it with least effort. The nymph on the point of hatching is not the active wrig-gling creature one extracts from sand or weed or mud, but a more or less inert and comatose being, tossed hither and

thither by the current and apt to drift out of the strength of
the current into the bays and eddies under the banks
where the trout lie in wait. If it were out in the stream the
trout would have to exert itself more, and the supply will
be nearly, if not quite, as great in the neighbourhood of its
shelter. It is only in the very height of its summer condition and in the presence of a strong rush of nymphs that
one finds the larger trout willing to face the current where
it is strong. It will not do it for the subimago, but invariably for the nymph.

But, to proceed with our inquiry, what brings the trout
on to the floating fly? Doubtless if it be hungry and the
food supply for the moment be small or inadequate for its
appetite it will take nymphs or hatched fly indifferently.
But given a copious supply of nymphs it is obviously its
policy to feed on these and confine itself to them (with
the casual exception of a floating sedge or bluebottle
coming within range) until the surface food becomes
more attractive through being greater in quantity than
the subaquaeous nymph. Then, and then only, *me quidem
judice,* does it turn to feeding steadily on the floating fly.
And that occasion is brought about invariably by wind
which sweeps the hatched insects from the entire surface
and concentrates them in strings under one bank or another.

I had two instructive instances lately in support of my
conclusions. In the first instance there was no rise of fly on
a day in early May until 3:30 p.m. (S.T.) when there was a
strong hatch of dark Olives. The stretch which I was fishing ran due north to south. The wind, which was strong
enough to produce high waves in mid-stream but not
strong enough to tear one's line off the water, came from
slightly east of south and seemed to drive every hatched
fly on to the grass edge underneath the west bank on
which I knelt. In a few moments a string of fish were rising
under my bank definitely taking surface fly and surface fly
only, and in the half-hour or so during which the rise
lasted I hooked three brace, killing a leash. In that half-
hour fish were rising occasionally in the high waves in
mid-river, but though I offered them time and again the fly

which their banker relatives accepted so greedily I got no offer from any of them; and I was driven to conclude that these mid-stream fish were smallish trout taking nymphs hatching or ready to hatch, the hatched fly being blown off before they had a chance of securing them.

In the other instance there was again a strong wind, this time from the north-north-west. I selected a length where the wind cut straight across, and I began fishing with the wind straight across river, using a nymph pattern. I found a few risers, and being fortunate in my selection of nymph, copied from some taken from a trout on the previous day, I at once began to get fish. The risers, however, seemed very few and I looked down-stream to the next bend where the wind, instead of driving directly across, set across and down at a slight slant. Here I found the rising fish not only numerous but busy. Yet even here they were nymphing almost exclusively and I found in the five trout which I took in only one winged dun; the remainder of their contents being entirely nymph. The rising to nymph went on till noon, when I had secured my modest basket and put back some of the smaller trout. Then they came on to the floating subimago, and the virtue of my nymph seemed to have gone out of it, and I got no more fish—the cast across being too long to drift the fly successfully without drag over the fish which ranged from a yard to two or three yards up or down. It is clear to me that until noon the hatch of fly had been insufficient to produce such a steady stream of floaters as to counteract the strong attraction of the constant Nymph.

Another question occurred to me, not for the first time, and that is this; is there not evidence to suggest that the trout, whether by instinct or experience, has a pretty good notion where, within limits, to take up its feeding quarters having regard to the set and strength of the wind?

One thing, however, is clear beyond all controversy, and that is that the nymphs which come to the notice of the trout are far more numerous than the hatched fly that do so. To begin with, the trout consume innumerable nymphs before they reach the surface; and of those which reach the surface many get into the upper air before covering a trout, and these are often snapped up by swift, swallow, martin or other small birds of the river side, while many of those which attain the spinner stage incur some tragic fate, and do not survive to get back to the river to die upon it. It stands to reason, therefore, that unless there be a definite rise to the hatched subimago or the spinner, the angler who offers his trout a proper pattern of nymph stands a better chance of sport than does one who offers it a floating fly. It is, however, in my judgement, quite as important to offer the right pattern of nymph as the correct pattern of floater, or even more so, for the trout gets a clearer view of its subaqueous food than it does of its surface prey.

FATAL GESTURE

John Taintor Foote

The equally hilarious sequel to the world-famous "A Wedding Gift."

Some ten years or so ago, it was my painful duty to report certain episodes in connection with the marriage and rather brief honeymoon of George Baldwin Potter, passionate angler, and his bride, the fair Isabelle.

From time to time since then, sympathetic readers of the narrative have inquired as to the subsequent relationship of that unfortunate couple.

Such solicitous inquiries have taken, as a rule, the following form: "Did George and Isabelle get together again?" To this question, as the years have passed, I have been able to answer, with increasing satisfaction, in the affirmative.

I have become almost lyrical, I now recall, over the continued felicity of the Potter union. One may judge, therefore, with what misgivings I learned of recent disturbing developments in the domesticity of George and his still-lovely better half.

The indisputable source of my information was George himself. I came upon him skulking—no other word describes it—in the shadows of the deserted club library. Since it was now close to the witching hour of midnight, I looked at him with some astonishment.

"Hello," I said. "What are you doing here?"

He did not return my greeting. Eying me with a sort of

furtiveness, I thought, he muttered something unintelligible and attempted to edge from the room in a slinking, unobtrusive manner that suggested burglary or worse.

Now, I had left some excellent pheasant shooting on Long Island and come in to town for the night to attend the début, musically speaking, of a female friend of a female friend. Still simmering with the just wrath which the notes of the incipient songbird had brought to a boil earlier that evening, I seized George roughly by the arm.

"Why are you sliding around here in the dark like a crab?" I demanded. "What's the matter with you, anyway?"

George collapsed into a leather lounge chair with a groan. "Why do I always run into you," he inquired, "at times like these?" He groaned again, but sat erect to favor me with a brooding stare. "You're asking me," he said bitterly. "Now I'm asking you. What are you doing here; why should you be snooping around at all hours when a man just wants to be alone?"

"I'm sorry to have forced my way into your private club," I said. "I'm deeply mortified. I blush at admitting it, but I'm spending the night. If you can believe such a thing, I've taken a room here. I hope you'll forgive my—"

Sarcasm seemed wasted on George.

"So have I," he interrupted, and added with mournful dignity, "This is now my home."

"Your what?"

"I said, 'my home.'"

"Since when?"

"Since day before yesterday. I have left Isabelle."

"Not really, George!"

He nodded.

"For good?"

"Absolutely!"

"Why?"

George rose from the chair and faced me. "Her mother," he said simply. He lit a cigarette with shaking fingers and repeated, "Her mother."

My irritation of a moment before had fled. "Life," I thought, "never changes. The old, old story! It goes back to the head of the family, crouching, club in hand, at the mouth of the cave."

Aloud I said, "But, George, why let an interfering old woman, no matter how obnoxious, destroy your—"

"You're all wrong there," said George. "You're barking up the wrong tree. As a matter of fact, she had ptomaine poisoning."

I simply stared.

George grew uneasy under my eye. "Damn it all," he said, "I suppose I'd better tell you everything! Let's go up to one of our rooms. I have a bottle of Scotch."

"Make it your room," I said.

An elevator bore us aloft. George unlocked a door and snapped on a light. We entered.

There are, no doubt, drearier abiding places on Manhattan Island than its various club bedrooms, but I have not, as yet, been forced to occupy one of them. I was able to take in the furnishings of George's sleeping quarters at a glance. Its general color scheme was a corpselike gray, warmed only by a variegated cataract of neckties wedged between the dresser mirror and its support. On the dresser were two ebony brushes, a comb and one peculiarly significant item. It was Isabelle's picture in a tooled-leather frame. She was smiling.

Gazing at the picture and uplifted by the implication of this face beaming upon George dressing, George undressing, George slumbering through the night, I now assumed a manner indicative of gayety and cheer.

"You old mud turtle," I said, nudging him in the side, "you certainly have a lovely wife."

George dashed me to earth.

"Had," said he, and turned the picture face down upon the dresser. "You take the chair," he commanded; "I'll sit on the bed. But wait a minute—" He went to the telephone. "Do you want soda or ginger ale?"

"Never mind ordering anything for me," I told him. "Plain water will do."

"Suits me too," said George. He reached under the bed, pulled a traveling bag into view and withdrew a bottle from its interior. "Ought to be a couple of glasses here...."

Oh, yes, they're in the bathroom." Presently he was sitting on the bed staring down into his glass.

I sipped in expectant silence. "Well?" said I, at last.

"It's a brownish-yellow thing with shelves," said George suddenly. "Below are two doors with wooden catches. That's all there is to it. I give you my word, that's all there is to it. Don't think I'm exaggerating. I could make one myself out of two—well, maybe three—dry-goods boxes. What do you think of that?"

"Nothing as yet, George," I told him patiently.

"Well, you will before I get through, and don't you forget it. It's called an Early American cupboard. It was to go in the breakfast room. Two of 'em. She had bought one already. The other was to go at the other end of the room. She had done the room over for 'em—new paper, new paint. Yellow walls with Colonial-white woodwork, she said. Think that over. But that's nothing. You may not believe me, but it's the truth as God is my judge. She was going to have a perfectly good hardwood floor ripped out and wide boards with knots laid in place of it. I had it from her own lips. Wide boards with knots, was what she said.

"I remember asking her, 'Why knots?' To show you I had perfect control over myself, I laughed when I said it. I laughed and said, 'Pretty good, eh, darling—why nots?' Can I take it? I'll say I can.

"She didn't laugh. She didn't explain about the knots. She put her head on one side, then she put it on the other. She said, 'George, can you imagine what the delft plates are going to look like on those warm yellow shelves against the mustard-colored walls?'"

George paused and slowly shook his head. "Well, I suppose life is like that," he said, and paused again to stare unseeingly at the floor.

"But, George," I said, "somehow I'm not getting this straight in my mind. Somehow I don't seem to get anything from what you are saying. Downstairs you told me it was Isabelle's mother. Where does she come in?"

"She'll come in all right. She'll come in plenty....Where was I?"

"Frankly, George, I don't know."

"Well, what was I talking about?"

"I think," I said cautiously, "that cupboards had something to do with it."

"Something to do with it! I'll tell the cock-eyed world! They had everything to do with it."

"Well, then," I said, "suppose we start with cupboards. Begin right there."

"But, my God," said George, "I've been all over that once."

"My fault, no doubt, but it isn't altogether clear to me even now. Suppose you get this cupboard business straightened out for me. She had two cupboards—was that it?"

"It was not," said George firmly. "She never had two. She had one. I said so distinctly. I'll say it again. She had exactly one cupboard. One—count 'em—cupboard. C-u-p-b-o-r-d—cupboard. Have you taken that in?"

"You left out the 'a' in cupboard," I said.

"I don't care what I left out, so long as I get it through your thick head that she had one of 'em."

"Don't get excited, George," I said.

George set his glass down on the small table beside the bed and threw his arms despairingly in the air. "I give up," he said. "I give up completely. I've lost my wife. You force yourself into the one home I have left, and when I try to tell you, as a friend—as a friend, mind you—coolly, calmly, clearly, exactly what happened, you sit there drinking my Scotch and tell me I'm excited. I simply give up."

"Don't give up, George," I urged. "I've had a trying day, what with one thing and another. I suppose my mind isn't all it should be. Make allowances for me and go ahead, like a good fellow. First, if you don't mind, just skim over this cupboard business again. Where did she get them—it, I mean."

George eyed me dubiously but went on.

"She got the one cupboard—one, mind you—from old Mrs. Touchard, up in Connecticut. The depression had the old lady on the ropes. She was selling her furniture a piece at a time. She'd part with an old, rickety chair that you couldn't sit in three minutes without dislocating your spine, as though it were her life's blood, and live on the money until it was gone. Then she'd let go of a sort of curlicue bed. Isabelle called 'em—let's see—thread beds?... No, that isn't it.... Rag beds?... No, that's the messy sort of rugs they go crazy over."

"Spool," I suggested.

George looked at me admiringly. "I guess the old bean isn't so dead, after all," he said. "Now, how did you guess that?"

"One of them," I confessed, "severed diplomatic relations between two branches of my family."

"That's it!" said George. "You're beginning to get the idea. Well, listen. Did you ever happen to see a picture I saw once? It was an old buffalo standing in the snow. All around him were wolves, just sitting there waiting for him to topple over. Well, the women Isabelle trains with were like that about old Mrs. Touchard. They just waited. They knew every stick of furniture she had. They'd argue about who was to get what. When the old lady had to sell something, there was a riot.

"I think Isabelle was the leader of the pack. She simply lived at the old lady's. She took her port wine—six bottles, pre-Volstead, I had left—until it was gone. She took her jelly and soup and cold chicken. Once I said, 'Listen, darling; your system's all haywire. Just take her cocktails as an appetizer, and let it go at that.' She said I was heartless and disgusting. That's what you get when you try to help a woman."

George broke off, reached for his glass and drank deeply.

"Well, maybe I was wrong, because Isabelle got the prize package. It was this cupboard I told you about six or seven times. Mrs. Touchard had two of them, exactly alike, and Isabelle got one. The rest of the women would hardly speak to her after she told 'em. She sent it somewhere to have it waxed—I think she said—and started in doing over the breakfast room. She said, 'I'm planning the room for both of them, George; one at each end." I said, 'How do you know you'll get the other?' She said, 'That's what those silly women are being so absurd about.' Then she told me she'd called a meeting and persuaded the crowd to enter into a ladies' agreement that if any of them got one cupboard, it would be a sort of option on the other. She said, 'You see, they're companion pieces, George; they simply have to go together. They all saw how reasonable and fair my suggestion was at the time.' I said, 'Well, then why are they so snooty about it now?' Isabelle said, 'It's all that Grace Witherbee's doings—the cat.' She wouldn't say anything more for awhile, but at last she told me—well, not told me, exactly; I sort of got it out of her—that Tom Witherbee's wife had found out that Mrs. Touchard had already promised Isabelle one cupboard when Isabelle called the meeting. Can you possibly beat that?"

"What did you say?" I asked.

"Not much," said George. "I didn't get a chance. When I suggested—just suggested, mind you—that the transaction might be—well, a bit shady—she went all to pieces. She said, among other things, that it was simply business. That's what she said—simply business. She said I made her sick. She said I did things at the office like that right along and thought it was clever, but that when my wife showed a little foresight—that's what she called it, 'a little foresight'—I talked like the Sermon on the Mount. Then she went up to her room and locked the door, and when I tried to get in, I heard her weeping. . . . How about another snifter?"

"Not yet," I said. "Go ahead!"

"Well, the unexpected happened. Old Mrs. Touchard died. I asked Isabelle if she thought losing the cupboard killed her, and Isabelle didn't even smile. Funny thing about women—you may have noticed it—absolutely no sense of humor. The old lady died without any warning. They simply found her in the morning. Isabelle had to bring back some pound cake, I think it was, she'd taken up to her. Isabelle said, 'It's such a shame. She adored cake. What on earth am I going to do now?' I said, 'About what?' She didn't answer. She asked a question instead. She said, 'What do they do about estates?' Now, I ask you to try and answer that one. I started in to straighten it out. I said, 'To begin with, who are they?' Isabelle said, 'They are whoever does whatever they do.' I said, 'Darling, that doesn't even begin to make sense.' Isabelle said—I'll give you her exact words—she said, 'George, I wonder if there is anyone else like you anywhere? I wish there was—I'd love so to meet his wife.'" George paused reflectively. "After what's happened," he said at last, "I keep going over things she's said lately, in my mind. I've wondered about the remark I've just repeated to you. What do you make of it?"

"If you don't mind," I said, "I think I'll have that drink you offered me a minute ago, now."

"Why, sure," said George, reaching for the bottle.... "Where was I?" he wanted to know, when our glasses were filled.

"She'd asked you about estates."

"Right-o! I found out what she was driving at a week or so later. The executor sent what was left of Mrs. Touchard's furniture to an auction company here in New York, to be sold under the hammer. Isabelle found out the day it was to be sold, and that was that. She put a ring around the date on her desk calendar, and she'd go into the breakfast room, right while the painters or paper-hangers were at work, and stand by the hour. The day before the sale she got a sales catalogue from the auction people. She was sitting in the living room that evening, poring over the catalogue, when the telegram came. A maid brought it to her on a tray." George lapsed into silence. He stared down into his glass for a moment, then looked up haggardly at me. "I can see that telegram on the silver tray now," he said. "I can see her take it and tear it open. Little did I think that—" He broke off, was silent for a moment, then raised his glass. "Here's to life," he said, adding, with the glass at his lips, "and a hell of a mess it is."

I joined him in a toast that left him with a beaded brow and an expression that marked him as one of the doomed.

"Nothing," I offered weakly, "is ever as bad as it seems."

George snorted in derision.

"Oh, is that so?" he said. "Well, listen! The wire was from her father. I've still got it somewhere. It said: 'Your mother ill. Wants you. Come at once.' That's what it said. That's what it said exactly. What do you think of that?"

"I don't know what to think yet," I told him. "Suppose you—"

"Hah!" George burst out. "You don't, eh? Well, you will, I promise you that. Get this: It meant she had to go to New Rochelle that night. It meant she'd have to be there all the next day. All the next day, mind you. Now what do you think?"

"Why, George," I confessed, "I've been to New Rochelle once—I stayed a whole week-end, as a matter of fact. I don't see why she couldn't stand it for—"

"You're right," George broke in. "There is something the matter with your head. Well, try and take this in: The other cupboard was to be sold at auction the next day. Now think this over. Of all the days in the year—in nine years, when you get right down to it—that was the day her mother picked out to have ptomaine poisoning."

I remained speechless.

George rushed on: "While a maid was packing a bag for Isabelle, she told me what I had to do. The cupboard was No. 827 in the catalogue. It would be sold, she said, somewhere around four o'clock next day. But she said not to take a chance. She said something might happen to advance the hour. She said, 'George, the sale starts at two. You be there at one o'clock and simply stay right there until they put it up.' I said, 'Darling, surely you don't expect me to sit there twiddling my thumbs from one o'clock until four?' Isabelle said, 'I didn't know that even you would talk about thumb twiddling. I didn't know any one had ever mentioned it since Thackeray or Dickens. I never asked you to do a single important thing before, and now, when I do, with my own mother dying, for all you know, you bring up thumb twiddling.' Well, of course, that settled it. I told her I'd be there at one o'clock, and she told me to find the cupboard as soon as I got there and then keep my eye right on it until it was put up for sale. How would you like to sit and watch a cupboard for three hours? Now, as man to man, how would you?"

George paused momentarily, but was off again before I was equal to a reply.

"I told her I'd do it. That's exactly what I told her. I want you to notice that in this whole business I never crossed her once. Her wish was my law. That makes what finally happened all the more— But never mind that now. I not only said I'd keep an eye on the cupboard, I also promised I'd top the bid of Grace Witherbee or any of the rest of them, if it took my entire bank balance. And listen; this isn't 1929. I expect even you scribbling fellows know that."

"Yes, George," I said, "we do."

"Well, it only goes to show my attitude. It ought to be clear to you by now that I was for the little woman, lock, stock and barrel, let the tail go with the hide, hook, line and sinker." A spasm swept George's face like a passing cloud at his last metaphor. "Just imagine," he said, "fishing with a sinker. Imagine plopping such a thing into a stream. And yet, up on the Ausable, one day—" George's expression changed. The anxious look left his face, the rigidity went out of his figure. He settled himself comfortably on the bed. "I'll simply have to tell you this. It's really good. I was fishing the ski-jump pool. I was using a No. 12 fan wing, Royal Coachman—early in the day for it—still that's what I was using, I remember. I'd hooked a small native and was taking him off when I saw what looked like a good fish rise about thirty—well, perhaps, thirty-five— yards above me, close to a rock on the right-hand side of the stream. The native had messed up the fan wing some. I was drying the fly before working up *slowly* to where I'd seen the rise, when a fellow came out of the bushes just above me, carrying—think this over—a steel rod with a hunk of lead about as big as a—"

"George," I interrupted, "if you get started on that sort of thing, we'll be here all night."

"Eh?" said George, as though returning suddenly from another world. "What did you say?"

I repeated my previous comment.

George sighed.

"All right, all right," he said. "I was only going to relate a—But as you say, perhaps this isn't the time for—Where was I?"

"You'd promised Isabelle to be at the auction rooms by one o'clock."

162
____

"Precisely; and, believe it or not, I was there at quarter past. The first thing I did was to locate the cupboard. Naturally, I expected to be knocked dead by it. I had it in my mind's eye as a sort of massive, shiny thing, with carving all over it. I poked around until I came to something with No. 827 pasted on it. I took one look at it and went straight to a young man who seemed to be in charge. I said, 'I'd like to call your attention to a mistake.' He was a pale, thin, unpleasant young man, with light hair and sort of pinkish eyes. He said, 'Really. What sort of a mistake?' I said, 'Oh, nothing very serious. If you'll follow me I'll show you.' I took him over to the thing I'd found and pointed to the number in my catalogue. Isabelle had marked a heavy ring around the number and then underscored 'Early American Cupboard' three times. I said, 'You see?'

"The pale young man looked at the number. His eyebrows went up in a most extraordinary way. You'd hardly believe it—they seemed to go right up into his hair. He said, 'Really, I'm afraid I don't.' I began to get annoyed. I said, 'What kind of a place is this, may I ask?' Then I explained patiently that 827 called for an Early American cupboard. The young man said, 'Quite so,' and stood looking at me with his eyebrows up. I said, 'But damn it all, you've got the number on this thing here.' He said, 'Quite so,' again. Then he ran his hand down the thing I'd found and said, 'Absolutely authentic; about 1780. One of the finest pieces we have ever handled.' He let down his eyebrows and went away. I suppose I stood and took in the Early American cupboard for ten minutes. I've told you what it was like. I tried to figure out why on earth any one would give it house room. I gave up and went and sat in one of the camp chairs that were standing in rows from the front to the back of the place. . . . Cigarette?"

"Thanks," I said, helping myself from his proffered case.

"Drink?"

"Not yet."

George lit a cigarette and inhaled deeply.

"Have you ever," he wanted to know, "been in one of these auction rooms?"

"Not that I remember."

1 6 3

"Well, it's depressing," George told me. "So much old furniture and knickknacks and whatnots all around, and the rows of camp chairs and the kind of pulpit thing up front. There were only a few people there—mostly old men with milkish whiskers and thin old women with lorgnettes— poking about and looking at the things that were going to be sold, and not making a sound. I'll say to you I never wanted a drink more in my life. I'd have given ten bucks for a good, stiff pick-me-up. I'd have given fifty if I'd had a flask with me.

"I got out my pipe and started to fill it, but the pale young man, who had been keeping an eye on me in an annoying manner, came and said, 'Sorry, no smoking.' So I just sat there sucking on the empty pipe.

"And now get ready for the most surprising thing you ever heard. I had begun to look through the catalogue just to keep from rushing out to a speak-easy, and all of a sudden I read: 'Consignment of rods and fishing tackle. Estate of the late Andrew B. Jenks.' That is exactly what I read, no more, no less. Can you believe it?"

"I don't see why not, George," I said. "What's so surprising about that?"

"Plenty," George told me. "In the first place, I would have expected to find fishing tackle at the morgue quicker than where I was. In the second place, I'd never heard of Andrew B. Jenks. I still don't understand that. Not in view of what followed. I remember actually smiling, after my first shock of surprise, at what the rods and tackle of Andrew B. Jenks would be like. Yes, sir, actually smiling." George looked at me and shook his head. "Pride goes before a fall," he said, and helped himself to more Scotch. "I think of that smile," he presently confessed, "with humility and shame; but I've got to admit it. I'm telling you now, I once smiled with contempt at the rods and tackle of Andrew B. Jenks." He drank deeply, placed his glass on the table and again shook his head. "I said I'd tell you everything."

I nodded.

"Well, believe me, I am. I hate to admit what I thought next. I thought: 'After all, I haven't anything else to do.

Why not go and look the stuff over?' That was exactly the condescending attitude I took. I'll say that's making a clean breast of it. Of course, you know Spinoza is dead?"

"Why, yes, George, I think I do. He died in sixteen seventy something, wasn't it? At—"

"I suppose you're trying to be funny," George broke in. "I'm not talking about that one—whoever he was. I'm talking about Spinoza the rod maker. He's been dead seven years. Of course, the business is in charge. As a matter of fact, they still put out the best rods on the market, but the rods made by the old man himself have something—well, it's hard to explain. They're just different. You simply know, when you get one in your hand, that you've got hold of the sweetest thing that ever shot a line. Not too whippy, not too stiff, sensitive tip with plenty of backbone in the middle, handle heavy fish for years and years and keep straight as a string. Oh, man, those old Spinozas! I've got nine of 'em—no, ten, now—I'll come to that. I'm simply getting you prepared a little for what happened.

"I went over to where I saw the pale young man and said, 'Where are these so-called fishing rods you're selling here today?' His eyebrows went up again. He said, 'The Jenks consignment is in the rug room at the right. We've been informed that it is a particularly fine collection.' I don't know why this fellow irritated me so. It was his eyebrows as much as anything else, I suppose. At any rate, I smiled coldly and said, 'No doubt.' Then I went into the room he had indicated. It was a big room with piles of rugs everywhere you looked. At one end I saw something that startled me. It was a row of leather rod cases standing against the wall—leather, mind you. They ran from one side of the room clear to the other. But that's nothing. That isn't a starter. I went over and began uncasing those rods. Before I'd looked at a dozen I was shaking like a leaf. Listen. You won't believe it, but listen. Every rod I looked at was a Spinoza—made by the old man himself. Every single rod. I remember I thought I was dreaming. There I was alone in that room with forty or fifty old Spinozas. I simply folded up. I had to go and sit down on a pile of rugs. I have never had such a sensation in my life—never.

1 6 5

"I must have sat on that pile of rugs for five minutes just trying to pull myself together. I had sense enough to look in the catalogue and go down the list of rods. Outside of one or two cheap bait rods, everything there was a Spinoza —everything. Light, medium and heavy trout rods. Light, medium and heavy salmon rods. They ran from fairy weight to heavy tournament. I said: 'Oh, my God!' and sat on the pile of rugs staring at the rod cases, for I don't know how long, not thinking especially, just sitting there, sucking on my empty pipe, in a sort of daze. You can imagine the shape I was in. We can only stand so much. A thing like that simply flattens a man.

"After a while I began to think. It began to dawn on me that I was face to face with the chance of a lifetime. It came to me that now I could do something that really counted for the little woman. Get that—for the little woman. That's how my mind was working. How does that strike you?"

"But what had fishing rods to do with Isabelle?" I asked.

"I'll explain it," said George. "It's simply this: No single human being is perfect. Am I right?"

"George," said I, "you are."

"Well, then, I'm going to tell you that I have a—call it a weakness."

"Not really, George?"

"Absolutely!"

"You astound me!"

"It's a fact, just the same. I admit it. I'm not trying to hide it from you. I come right out with it. The fact is, I keep buying fishing rods. Some men drink; some men gamble. I buy fishing rods, and there you are. It has been a constant source of friction between Isabelle and me. Whenever I buy one, I try to slip into the fishing room quietly, without her knowing it. I do it to spare her feelings, naturally. But she has a sort of sixth sense about a new rod. I defy any man to get one into the house without meeting her in the front hall.

"We've had it out dozens of times. At first she used to say, 'But, George, you have heaven knows how many rods now. Why do you buy another one?' That's a hard one to answer. The fact is, I don't know myself. Sometimes when I get home with a rod, I ask myself the same question. But it's too late then. For some years now she doesn't say anything when I come in with one. She just looks at the rod case and then looks at me, while I go past her to the tackle room. Then she goes upstairs and locks herself in her room and stays for hours. Once I said to her, 'Darling, suppose I was a booze fighter, or a woman chaser?' She said, 'Well, that would be more human than this sneaking in with rods. It's queer. It's like taking drugs. It makes me want to scream!' Hell, isn't it? Or, rather, it was. It's all over now." George sighed deeply, drained his glass and lapsed into silence.

"You started to tell me about planning to do something for Isabelle," I urged, at last.

"Yes," said George, coming out of his reverie, "I decided to end my rod buying once and for all. It was certain the old spooks I'd seen in the auction room wouldn't know a Spinoza from a cane pole. I told myself I could buy every rod there for a few dollars each. I thought it all out. Of course, there would be the expense of enlarging the tackle room; but that wasn't to be thought of when you consider what I was doing to spare Isabelle's feelings for years to come. I told myself I'd like to see some slick sporting-goods salesman sell me another rod. I thought I'd let him put it together and wave it in front of my face and then hand it to me. I thought how I'd take it and test it and say, 'Not bad,' and then hand it back to him and march out of the store and go home to Isabelle and my fifty or sixty old Spinozas."

George broke off and indulged once more in rueful head shaking. "Just a dream," he said. "Just an idle dream.

"Well," he went on, "by the time I got back into the auction room, the sale had started. There were a lot more people there by then, all sitting in the camp chairs. Just the same kind of timid-looking old washouts I'd seen before. I sat down in a chair, still in a sort of trance. But pretty soon I got interested in that auctioneer. I don't think I've ever seen any one who impressed me more, at the time. He knew so much, it was simply appalling. It gave you an inferiority complex just to listen to him. No sort of jim-crack could be put up that he couldn't give you the inside facts about. If a Smyrna rug came up, you'd think he'd spent most of his life in Smyrna. The same for Chinese rugs. He knew the province a rug came from like his own back yard. Same about any old rickety piece of furniture. It might be a hundred years old, but he knew the man who made it by his first name, and the day of the week he turned the thing out. There wasn't a corner of the world or a thing in it that could fool him. He'd take a piece of brass, or glass, or china, and glance at it, and that was enough—just a glance and you'd get the facts as to where it was made, and when, and what it was worth. And that wasn't all. He handled the whole thing like Mussolini. No monkey business; no backing and filling—just biff, bang, snap! I remember, I thought after a while that here was the man to lead us out of the depression. I'm telling you this as a warning. It'll teach you never to judge a man too hastily. You'll find out what this fellow turned out to be presently.

"I was awfully cheered by the prices. The way things were selling was a crime. The auctioneer said so. They were going, he said, for a fraction of their value. Judging by the difference in what he said a thing was worth and what it sold for, I figured I'd get my Spinozas for about fifty cents each, case and all. I remember thinking how strange life is. There I was, practically the owner of half a hundred old Spinozas at an outlay of a few dollars, and I had cursed Isabelle's mother, earlier that morning, for getting me into what I thought was a frightful jam. I made up my mind right there I'd invite the old lady to come and stay several days with us—just as soon as I'd got the tackle room enlarged. That'll show you whether or not my heart was in the right place. Why, I know a lot of men who have apoplexy if they hear their wives' mothers are going to spend the night. I'll bet you do too. Now, don't you?"

"Well, something like that," I said.

"There you are," said George. "That goes to show you. Of course, I've got to admit one thing. I've got to admit I didn't think of Isabelle's mother, or Isabelle, for that matter, much longer. But I'll ask you, when you hear what happened, whether you think any man could think of women or their vague, impossible notions at such a time? I'm going to ask you, as man to man, and I want a frank reply.... Where was I?"

"You were thinking of having Isabelle's mother for a visit."

"Correct. And right there I got a shock. I hadn't noticed any one come in and sit down, but all of a sudden I realized that there was some one next to me with a pipe in his mouth. I turned like a shot, and there was John Woodruff. The spent-wing Woodruff is named after him. It's a good fly at times. Why, one day over on the Broadhead, I simply couldn't raise a fish. I tried a Cahill first, I think it was—nothing doing. Next I tried a spent-wing Lady Beaverkill—nothing doing. Then I tried a Skews Hackle, No. 14, for twenty minutes or so—nothing doing. Next I tried a—"

"George!" I broke in warningly.

"All right, all right," said George. "Where was I?"

"A man named Woodruff had just—"

"I'll say he had. There he sat. No getting away from it. I could feel the sweat break out on my face. Beyond him was a row of old ladies with lorgnettes, and he sat there with his pipe in his mouth just as though he owned the place. I said, 'Listen. They don't let you smoke in here.' He said, 'Am I smoking?' I said, 'You've got a pipe in your mouth.' He said, 'I've got shoes on my feet but I'm not walking.... What are you doing in here?' I told him I had dropped in to see if I could pick up something for the little woman. He said, 'Me, too,' and began to read a catalogue. I tried to see what page he was looking at. But he kept the catalogue tilted away from me. I thought to myself, 'Maybe he doesn't know. Better divert him from that damn catalogue.' So I said aloud, 'Did you hear about the twenty-inch rainbow I took on the East Branch of the Delaware this season?'

"Well, he simply grunted. But I went on to tell him how I took the fish. Naturally, I gave him all the details. I told him which pool it was and where the fish was lying. I explained how I had happened to see the trout rise while looking at the stream from the road. I told him what fly I had tied on—a No. 10, brown-and-white, Bi-visible—and I

showed him just how I'd made my cast to avoid some hemlock branches. In doing so, of course, I raised my arm and
made the proper gesture for a loop cast. Do you know just
what a perfect loop cast should be?"

"Why, no, George, but—"

"Look!" said George. "Here's your fish." He laid a hastily
gathered Gideon Bible on the bed. "Now, then, here's
where your fly should light." He dented in the bedclothes
with his thumb. "Please bear in mind that it's the leader,
not the fly, that, as a rule arouses suspicion in a trout.
That being so, how are we going to place the fly here with
the fish here, and not let the leader—"

"George," I interrupted, "I'm going to ask you again to
postpone any fishing experiences, any instructions as to
the pursuit and capture of fish, to a more suitable hour and
place."

George laid the book slowly back on the table from
which he had taken it. He rubbed out the dent in the bedclothes. He eyed me silently for a moment and said at last,
with a slight shrug of his shoulders, "Well, it takes all
kinds of people to make a world."

"True," I agreed. "But after all, isn't that a blessing?
What if we were all anglers? Think of the consequences to
art, medicine, philosophy, business!"

"Business, hah!" said George bitterly. "Why bring that
up? Well, anyway, I'll get on with what I've been telling
you. As I said, I'd made the gesture for a loop cast. A moment later the pale young man interrupted me just as I
was telling Woodruff what the fish had done after I'd
hooked him. It seems I'd bid in something when I'd raised
my arm. I told the pale young man there had been a mistake. He told me I had one of the greatest bargains of the
sale. I said, 'I don't care how much of a bargain it is, I don't
want it.' His eyebrows simply disappeared. He said, 'My
dear sir, what do you think would happen to us if people
made it a rule to come in here and bid in articles and then
repudiate their bids?" Well, that did stump me for a minute, and his damned eyebrows got my goat, I suppose, because I told him I was not in the habit of repudiating
anything, and asked him what he claimed I'd bought. He

said, 'You have purchased an absolutely brand-new, golden-oak sideboard with heavy beveled mirror, for the ridiculous sum of twenty-six dollars.' I said, 'All right, here's your money,' and gave him my address. He thanked me and that settled that.

"I started in to finish telling Woodruff about the big rainbow, but he had disappeared. I was delighted, of course, but suddenly I wondered whether he had really left the place or taken another seat for some reason. I stood up to look around and see if I could locate him, and I got what will probably be the most fearful shock of my life. . . . I'm going to have a snifter before I tell you. Join me?"

"Not just yet, thanks."

George replenished his glass, sampled its contents and lit a cigarette.

"Any one might have expected what I discovered when I looked around that auction room," he told me through a cloud of smoke. "Any one that hadn't been turned into a plain dope by finding what I had stumbled across that day. You couldn't put up half a hundred kohinoors at auction and keep the business dark, now could you? Well, this was the same thing, only more so. The first thing I noticed was that the last three or four rows of camp chairs were filled with men with pipes in their mouths. Then I saw men with pipes simply massed at the back of the room. And then I got the shock I mentioned. Half the Anglers' Club of New York were there. And that wasn't a starter. There were men from dozens of other clubs—upstate, Jersey, Pennsylvania—I knew most of 'em. There was a lot of the crowd who put up at Keener's and fished the Big River from Roscoe down, and about as many more who stay at Phœnicia and fish the Esopus from the Reservoir up. They stood there not saying a word, not looking at one another—just staring straight ahead—waiting. My heart simply sank into my boots.

"In staring around, I noticed a woman—she was not a bad-looking woman—so my eyes came back to her automatically. I thought vaguely that I'd seen her somewhere before. Then she bowed to me. It was Grace Witherbee. To show you what can happen to a man's mind at a time like that, I remember wondering what she was doing there. That will give you a faint idea of the strain I was under.

"Just then a man sat down in the chair Woodruff had left. He got out a pipe and looked hard at me. Then he said, 'Hail, hail, the gang's all here! My name's Blodgett. Ever fish the Ausable?' I said, 'I have.' He said, 'Ever fish the Margaree in Nova Scotia?' I said, 'I have.' He said, 'Ever fish the Big Sturgeon in Michigan?' I said, 'I have.' He said, 'Ever fish the St. Margarite in Quebec?' I said, 'I have.' He said, 'Ever fish the Gunnison in Colorado?' I said, 'I have.' He said, 'Ever fish the Wahoohoo above Squidjum Lake?' I told him I had not. I told him I had never even heard of it.

"He said, 'Neither have I, brother. I was just putting the acid test on you.' Then he whacked me on the back and asked to see my catalogue. I gave it to him without a word. I had taken an instant dislike to the fellow. As he began to turn the pages he started in to tell me about losing a big salmon up on a Gaspé river. I stood it for some time and then interrupted him. I told him this was not a suitable occasion to listen to fishing exploits. I said my mind was too fully occupied with matters of the moment to profit by anything he might say. He slapped me on the back again, said, 'I get you,' and pointed to the Jenks' rods in the catalogue. Then he looked toward the back of the room and said, 'Boy, we're as safe here as on a trench raid.' I made absolutely no reply of any sort.... Your glass has been empty for ten minutes. How about it?"

I hesitated and was lost.

"Make it a short one," I said.

With our glasses filled, George went on:

"I have had some trying experiences in my time," he confessed simply. "But for pure mental torture, nothing has ever equaled the sale that day of my old Spinozas. The auctioneer made a speech when he came to them. It was then I began to realize he was not the man I had taken him for. The speech was little short of pathetic. He said the late Andrew B. Jenks had been a celebrated fisherman—not angler—fisherman. He said the sale of his paraphernalia —think that over—'paraphernalia'—offered other fishers

—get that—the chance of a lifetime. Mind you, he used the very phrase that had occurred to me, and I'm no word painter. It was—well, feeble, I felt, from him. Fifty old Spinozas, and I had heard that auctioneer grow really eloquent over cracked dishes and rickety furniture. He wound up by saying, 'I am now about to sell the collection of that celebrated fisherman, the late Andrew B. Jenks. Page 47 in your catalogues.'

"I was sitting there in a short silence that followed. My heart had begun to pound like fury, I remember, when the Blodgett fellow said, 'Ever read his *Brown Trout of the Pyrenees?*' I said, 'Whose, pray?' He said, 'Jenks'.' I told him I had not. Blodgett said, 'Not so hot.' Then he slapped the catalogue and said, 'But Andy had the tools.' My dislike of him was increased by his flippancy at such a time. I said, 'When you are entirely through with my catalogue, I'd appreciate just a glance at it.' He said, 'Sure, brother, I know 'em by heart, anyway. There's a twelve-footer that I'm going to wade through blood after.' I took the catalogue without a word.

"And now get this: The first thing put up was a two-piece, seven-foot, two-ounce, dry-fly rod. A man stood on the platform next to the auctioneer's pulpit and waved it in the air in circles—in circles, mind you—and this is what that auctioneer said. He said, 'Now, then, what am I offered for the little fishing pole? Who'll start it at a dollar?' He called a fairy-weight Spinoza a fishing pole. I'm asking you to think that over—and, remember, I'd admired him.

"Well, there was an awful silence for a minute. Then a voice boomed out of the stillness—it was really terrific, everything being so quiet that way, after we'd been listening to the squeaks over doodads and whatnots that had been going on. The voice said, 'Listen, you; twenty-five dollars.' Another voice like a Jersey bull's said, 'That's getting him told. Thirty-five.' Now, that fairy weight had cost fifty dollars new. What do you suppose they took it up to?"

"I haven't an idea, George."

"Well, make a guess."

"Oh, forty-five dollars."

"If it didn't sell for seventy-five dollars, may I never step into a trout stream again. And listen; that auctioneer was just a spectator. He never opened his head. He just sat there with his mouth open until he finally said in a weak voice, 'Are you all through? Sold to the tall gentleman in the gray hat on the right.'

"The Blodgett fellow looked at me. I looked at him. He said, 'Get the cripples and children back of the ropes.' I said, 'This is an outrage. It's plain lunacy.' He said, 'If it wasn't for the depression, they'd use poison gas.' I remember feeling more warmly disposed towards him. I suppose it was because we were—well, fellow sufferers, if you get what I mean."

"Yes, George," I said.

"There is no need of going into the rest of it. It was all just as senseless, just as exasperating, as that first performance. One remarkable thing was that as it went on, I felt more and more drawn to Blodgett. After each rod sold for some stupefying figure, he'd never show that he was being cut to the quick. He'd give a sort of dry laugh he had and say something extraordinary. He must have been in the war, because his talk was like that. He'd say, 'Third platoon forward, and don't step on the wounded.' He'd say, 'Into the shell holes, men; it's shrapnel.' Once he said something I didn't understand. I don't think it had anything to do with the war. It was when two men started bidding on a rod after every one else had stopped. It was a sixteen-foot, wet-fly, salmon rod, and they took it above a hundred dollars. Blodgett said, 'It's better than a natural; it's a grudge scrap.' Now, what would you make of that?"

"I think it has to do with prize fighting," I said.

"I believe you're right," George agreed. "I remember, now, he added something about throwing science to the winds and slugging toe to toe. He was an unusual person. I admit that even though he did turn out to be a stubborn jackass."

"How, George?"

"I'll come to that presently. I want to tell you one thing that happened that threw a little more light on the auctioneer. That first rod had knocked him out of his stride, but he came back and took charge of the next sale. It wasn't long till he was handling everything like Mussolini again. He kept calling the rods 'poles,' but he'd start each one at twenty-five or thirty dollars and say that seventy-five dollars was just a fraction of what a rod was worth. Once Blodgett said, 'I'll bet he ate up the third grade. He's hell on fractions.'

"Well, anyway, at last the man on the platform began to wave a steel bait rod about. It cost three or four dollars new. I can't imagine why a man like Jenks should have had such a thing. The auctioneer simply rose up in his pulpit. He said, 'Now, gentlemen, I have the privilege of offering you a steel fishing pole—think of it, gentlemen; a fishing pole of the finest compressed steel. Such a pole should last several lifetimes. What am I offered for the steel fishing pole? To be used and passed on to your grand-children. Who'll start it at fifty dollars?' I give you my word, that's what he said. You could have heard a pin drop any place in the room. The crowd was simply stunned. The auctioneer said, 'Well, then, forty dollars?' No one said anything, of course. The auctioneer said, 'Thirty-five,' and waited. He said, 'Come, come, gentlemen. Make an offer.' There was another silence, and then a voice said, 'Fifty cents to get it out of the way, and you keep it for your own grandchildren.'"

George broke off and chuckled. "Not bad, if you ask me," he said. "You should have seen that auctioneer. It took all the Mussolini out of him. He said, 'I'm licked. I quit. Make your own prices, gentlemen.'" George chuckled again, then suddenly sobered. "That was the only light moment of the rod sale. All the rest was just a sort of horrible nightmare, as far as I was concerned. You can understand that, after what I'd planned to do for Isabelle."

"Yes, George," I said, "but what about Blodgett disappointing you in the end?"

"Disappointing me!" George exclaimed. "Well, I hope so! I told you he proved to be a stubborn jackass. I'll tell you what happened and you can decide whether I've overstated it or not. You remember I'd looked at a dozen or so rods before the sale. Well, one of 'em had impressed me particularly. I had even noted its number in the catalogue. It was a twelve-foot, dry-fly, salmon rod that was just simply a poem. It was a two-handed rod—make no mistake about that—two-handed. Of course, there is a school of thought that's trying to foist single-handed, dry-fly, salmon rods on the anglers of this country, and what do you suppose they advocate? They favor a longer butt that fits into a hollow in the actual butt of the rod after you hook your fish. Of all the cock-eyed notions, that beats them all. In the first place, a single-handed rod at the required weight will simply break your wrist in two before you've fished it half a day. In the second place—"

"I know, George," I said, "but what about Blodgett?"

"But you don't know," George informed me heatedly. "You don't know the half of it. You don't know a tenth of it. I haven't even started to tell you. Why, I could keep giving you reasons from now until morning, why single-handed salmon rods, dry or wet, are simply—"

"That's just it, George," I managed to break in. "I couldn't possibly sit here until morning. Get back to your friend Blodgett, like a good fellow."

"Don't call him my friend," said George. "Not after— Listen. I'd been sitting there in a sort of torture chamber, watching my old Spinozas go, one after another. I'd make an extravagant bid on one now and then, but mere extravagance wouldn't get you a ferrule off one of those rods. If you wanted a rod you had to go hog wild.

"Well, they'd worked so far down the list of rods that I knew something had to be done or I'd walk out without one single old Spinoza to show for all my plans and the hours I'd spent there.

"I decided, finally, that I'd take home the twelve-foot salmon rod that I'd liked particularly, or bust a G string. When it came up, I let it go to forty dollars, and was about to bid when Blodgett, out of a clear sky, said, 'Fifty.' I thought, 'He doesn't know I want this rod,' so I gave him a friendly smile and said, 'Sixty.' He looked at me quickly. He didn't smile back. He said, 'Seventy.'

"I felt my earlier dislike of him begin to return. I gave him a look in which there was no smile, I assure you, and asked him, coldly, a point-blank question. I said, 'Why are you bidding?' He said, 'This is the baby I've been waiting for, major.' I said, 'I'll have to tell you I particularly want this rod.' Then I bid, 'Seventy-five.' Blodgett said, 'Eighty.' I said, 'Are you going to keep on with this?' Blodgett said, 'Report to G. H. Q. that we're holding our position in the face of heavy fire.' I bid eighty-five. Blodgett bid ninety. I bid ninety-five. Blodgett bid a hundred. For a moment I hesitated, I confess it. The rod cost seventy dollars new. Then I thought about Blodgett using, or rather misusing, that old Spinoza—casting short, sloppy casts with it, no doubt. Letting the fly and leader smack down on the water, in all probability. I turned and looked him in the eye and bid one hundred and twenty-five dollars in a loud, clear voice. Blodgett got up from his seat. He called out, 'Stretcher bearers, stretcher bearers!' and went out of the place with every one looking at him. Curious performance, wasn't it? His stubbornness cost me about fifty dollars."

George refreshed himself from his glass and went on.

"When all the rods and a lot of reels, lines, leader boxes, et cetera, had been sold, the gang paid at the cashier's window for what they'd bought and then made a bee line for the rug room to test their rods. I put mine together, tested it for a moment or so, and then started to show it to men I knew. Not a man was interested in my rod. They all, without a single exception, tried to get me to look at theirs. Extraordinary how self-centered most men are. Have you noticed it?"

"Well, yes, I come across it now and then," I confessed.

"I regret what followed," George went on. "I admit it frankly. It had a decided bearing on what finally happened to Isabelle and me. I feel certain that despite the strain I'd been under, I should have remembered the purpose of my visit to the auction rooms shortly after the rod sale was over. As a matter of fact, I did remember eventually. It came to me with startling clearness. I'll get to that presently. The fact remains that my mind was confused, not to say numbed, by all that had happened. You can readily understand that. It was now further distracted in a quite unexpected manner.

"It seemed that Woodruff, whom I had encountered ear-

lier that afternoon, had not left the auction room. He had
remained for the sale and had bought a seven-and-a-half-
foot, two-piece, three-ounce, dry-fly rod. He somehow con-
ceived the idea of rigging the rod with a Vomber reel and a
Gebhart tapered line, Size F, he had secured from the sale
of tackle, and after tying on a leader and fly, standing at
the edge of one rug and casting for a medallion in the
center of another rug.

"Well, the idea took like wildfire. Presently it became a
series of casting matches for a stake. Each man put a dollar in the pool. He was then allowed one cast. The best
casts were marked on the rug with a piece of chalk. The
nearest cast to the exact center of the medallion won the
pool. You'd be surprised how absorbing those competitions
became. Each pool contained about thirty dollars. Woodruff, I noticed, won most of them. I was not lucky enough
to win a pool for some time. I had contributed twenty-two
dollars, I remember, before I succeeded in winning. This

left me eight dollars to the good. At that precise moment it
came to me that I had to go back to the auction room to
purchase the cupboard for Isabelle.

"I excused myself, returned to the auction room and was
really startled to find that the cupboard had already been
put up and sold. The thought occurred to me that if I could
find the purchaser I might yet get the cupboard by offering
an advance over the price paid.

"I went to the cashier's window and asked for the name
of the purchaser. The cashier referred to her slips and told
me No. 827 had been sold to Mrs. Thomas H. Witherbee.
She started to give me the address, but I told her it wasn't
necessary, and asked to use the telephone. I called up the
Witherbees', but Grace was out. I went home and called up
again, and she had just returned. When she came to the
phone, I explained what I wanted and asked her if she
would take a very substantial advance over what she had
paid, for the cupboard. This is what she said. She said, 'All
the money you've got, George Potter, wouldn't buy that
cupboard, and please tell Isabelle I said so.' Strange about
women. Apaches aren't a marker to 'em.

"Well, I was pretty sick, after Grace tomahawked me

that way, but just before dinner a truck drove up with the sideboard I'd bought. I'd forgotten the thing completely. I told them to put it in the breakfast room and went in to look at it when it was unwrapped. I was worried, I admit that. Naturally, I didn't want to disappoint Isabelle, even though I'd done everything humanly possible to get the cupboard for her. I was worried, as I say, until I got a look at what I'd bought. Then I cheered up mighty quick. The pale young man hadn't overstated it a particle. I want to tell you that sideboard looked as though it had just come from the factory. There wasn't a dent or a scratch on it. It had a polish you could see your face in. And the brass handles on the drawers looked as though they'd never been so much as touched. The beveled mirror was there, just as the pale young man had said, and it was a corker. Furthermore—and now get this—the sideboard was yellow—you'll remember how she had gone on about the yellow shelves. It was just a happy accident, I thought. I was just luckier than I really deserved to be.

"When you consider what I'd been through that day, I felt pretty good after dinner. Fact is, I was kind of anxious to have Isabelle get back and see what I'd bought her for twenty-six dollars, instead of her dilapidated cupboard. I got out my newest old Spinoza and put it together. I took it into the front hall where I'd have plenty of room to swing it.

"I was standing there testing the rod, when the front door opened. It was Isabelle. I hadn't expected her, of course. I thought for a minute that her sixth sense about rods had brought her all the way from New Rochelle to arrive just when I had it in the front hall. Well, naturally, I began to explain at once. I told her it was an old Spinoza. I said, 'Think of it—an old Spinoza, darling. They were selling them at that place you sent me to. Can you believe it?'

"She never even looked at the rod. She said, 'Oh, George, I've been perfectly awful. Mother had ptomaine poisoning.' I said, 'Well, darling, you didn't give it to her, did you?' Isabelle said, 'She's better, but I shouldn't have left her; I simply couldn't wait. Where is it?' I said, 'Where is what?' She said, 'Where is my cupboard—my Early American cupboard? Don't tell me it hasn't come yet. I couldn't bear it.' I said, 'Now, I'll explain about that, too, darling. There was a little slip.' I'll give you my word, she went as white as a sheet. She said, 'You didn't get it?' I said, 'I'm afraid I didn't, darling. Grace Witherbee beat me to the cupboard. But don't you worry. Don't you worry for a minute. I got something else.' She stood there just opening and closing her mouth in the queerest way. Then she said, 'George, not Grace Witherbee?' I said, 'Never mind her, darling, you wanted something yellow, didn't you? Well, that's exactly what I got, and not a scratch on it. It's in the breakfast room.'

"She went to the breakfast room without a word. I took the rod down and followed her. When I got to the breakfast-room door, she was standing in front of the sideboard staring at it. I give you my word, she didn't look human. Her eyes seemed to be starting from her head. She was saying, 'Oh, God! Oh, God!' over and over again. And now listen carefully. Here is exactly what I said, no more and no less. I won't add or subtract one syllable. I said, 'Don't you like it, darling?' that's what I said. Is there anything in the slightest degree offensive in that question, I ask you?"

180

I was gripped by emotions too deep for utterance. I could only gaze at George and maintain a frozen silence.

"You needn't answer," said he. "Obviously not. And yet, those simple words unloosed on me such a tirade, such abuse, as I had never dreamed could pass a woman's lips." George ceased abruptly and dropped his head in his hands.

I waited for several moments.

"After all," I offered at last, "mere words aren't to be weighed against ten years of—er—devotion."

George raised his head and looked at me with bloodshot, haggard eyes.

"Mere words!" he said. "Do you know what she called me?"

"No, George, I don't, but—"

"I'll say you don't, and you never will—she was once my wife. But I'll say this much: I don't yet know where she ever learned such words. I can't yet understand how a girl of breeding—a girl who had led a sheltered life—ever heard such appalling epithets, let alone use them."

"But after all, George," I said, "this is a modern age. Women are no longer helpless, overly nice creatures. You must consider that when—"

George held up his hand to stop me.

"Useless," he said, with quiet dignity. "Absolutely useless. I appreciate your motives, but—" He broke off, regarded me cautiously for a moment, looked around the room as though to assure himself that no possible eavesdropper shared our privacy, then, "Listen," he said hoarsely, "you don't know everything yet."

"Is there more?"

"More? You haven't heard anything. I thought I wouldn't tell you. As I've already said, she was once my wife. Naturally I don't like to blacken her character beyond a certain point. But, after all, facts are facts. We've got to admit that."

"Yes, George, but don't tell me anything you don't care to."

"H-m-m," said George doubtfully. He got up, paced the room nervously for a moment, took a drink and returned to the bed. "I think I'll tell you," he said at last. "I owe it to myself."

"All right," I said. "Go ahead!"

George unconsciously lowered his voice and went on.

"I was standing there simply stupefied by the things she was saying—simply stupefied. She kept it up until she ran out of breath. Then she began to stare at the sideboard again. She seemed to be looking at the mirror. She said, 'It isn't possible! It just isn't possible!' Suddenly, without the slightest warning, she snatched the middle joint of the rod from my hand and crashed it with all her strength into the sideboard mirror. Can you conceive of such a wanton, such a monstrous, act? Now can you?"

George rose and again took to pacing the floor. "Unbelievable!" he muttered, mopping his brow. "And yet I saw it with my own eyes. The middle joint of an old Spinoza!"

"Did it break the mirror?" I asked innocently, after giving him time to control his feelings.

George halted in his stride and whirled upon me.

"The mirror!" he roared. "Do you suppose I looked at the damn mirror? She broke the rod joint in two about three inches below the upper ferrule. Of course that ended our married life." He sank down on the bed and again buried his head in his hands.

"George," I said after a silence, "time works wonders. Just now you feel—"

"Don't talk about time," said George. "Do you think any man could ever forgive such willful, wicked, inhuman destruction? Never mind what she called me. Let that go. Just take the breaking of that middle joint—nothing else. Why, it will be years before I can bring myself to see her again, let alone—"

The telephone bell exploded suddenly within the narrow confines of those four drab walls. George leaped from the bed to the instrument as though galvanized.

"Hello," I heard. "Yes, Isabelle, this is George....Oh, darling, not really!...Oh, darling, so am I!...Will I? In twenty minutes. Maybe fifteen."

George hung up abruptly, turned and dove under the bed for his bag.

"Lonesome!" he shouted at me. "Lonesome! What do you know about that?"

In not over one minute from the end of that telephone conversation between husband and wife I found myself alone. I had become the sole occupant of the late sleeping quarters of George Baldwin Potter. The neckties, I noticed, were gone. The empty dresser missed those warming bits of color. I recalled seeing the ends of several of them trailing from a closed traveling bag as it was borne, like a hurricane, toward the elevator.

THE MANNERISMS
OF BIG TROUT

Huish Edye

Where, and how, to find the largest, fly-eating trout in a stream.

The mannerisms of the bigger trout of a stream —whether the half-pounder of the Dart or the three-pounder of the Kennet—are peculiar to each stream, and must be learnt separately for each. The angler cannot evolve them from his experience of other streams. To help him in his search for good fish, such experience can teach him where to look. Local knowledge is required to tell him what to look for.

The term "good" as applied to trout is relative to the

RIVER	CHARACTER	GOOD FISH	MASTER FISH
Dart . .	Peat	½ lb.	¾ lb. and over
Irfon . .	Peat and limestone	¾ lb.	1 lb. and over
Culm . .	Limestone	¾ lb.	1 lb. and over
Otter . .	Limestone	¾ lb.	1 lb. and over*
Coln (Glos.) .	Chalk	1 lb.	Over 1½ lb.
Wylye . .	Chalk	1½ lb.	Over 2 lb.
Kennet . .	Chalk	2 lb.	Over 2½ lb.

*This is a very accurate classification. Trout of about 15 oz. are plentiful. Pounders are decidedly rare.

stock of any given water. A good fish is something considerably bigger than the merely adult trout—an exceptionally heavy trout. Above him I like to classify a higher
grade of "master" fish—*very* exceptionally heavy trout
that are beginning to qualify for the glass case. Above is a
suggested classification for a few typical streams.

General experience teaches us the living conditions to
which a trout aspires. These are:

1 A holt in deep water with cover of bank, an undercut rock, or
   a dense patch of weed.
2 A feeding station, preferably shallow water, with a line of retreat as easy as possible to (1). The shallowness probably
   gives a sense of security on the blind or under side.
3 A set of the current at (2) that brings concentrated food (especially surface food) within his reach.
4 And if he is elderly, spacious shallows accessible for the hunting of minnows or other small fish.

Quarters which provide all these amenities are scarce,
and are taken more or less in order of seniority. That is to
say, they are taken by the most aggressive trout; which
generally, but not always, means by the biggest trout. Less
desirable quarters fall to lesser trout by precedence of val-
our. Amenities attract, I think, in the order in which I
have set them out, and no trout of any pretensions will
dispense with (1). The smallest and immature trout have
to put up with such accommodation as they can get, and
generally have no permanent residence at all.

For success in trout fishing the finding of good or (if you
are ambitious) of master fish is at least half the battle. On
a stream like the Wylye, where merely warrantable trout
—of a pound or so—are very numerous, and grayling add
complications, it is much more. In the search for a worthy
quarry in unfamiliar water, I take as a general guide principles based on the trout's way of life as just summarised.
If I find a stretch of undifferentiated shallow water, I feel
that I am losing nothing and saving time by disregarding
it. A big trout must have a bolt-hole, deep relatively to his

surroundings, and protected from observation. But before you disregard it, make sure that the shallowness is *really* uniform. I can think at once of three stretches, each in a different river, which are habitually neglected by nearly all anglers as being—and casually examined they appear to be—too shallow to hold even a warrantable fish. One of these, on the Wylye, is a new acquaintance. The keeper told me it was useless, and as I walked along it I saw no reason to question his judgment. For about a hundred yards the river broadens out; the water appears to be nowhere more than twelve inches deep, is slack and lifeless, and swarms with small grayling. Nervous shoals of minnows scurried from the margin as I passed. I was on the left bank. The right bank is bushed and treed, and quite unapproachable. About half-way up this reach a pebble in one of my waders became unbearable, and I sat down to eject it. It was not till then that I noticed a steady current flowing smoothly close under the far bank. I walked out to investigate this. I was within a yard of the other side before the water topped my ankle by more than a few inches; then the river-bed begins to slope downwards into the bank, beneath which it is relatively deep. The bank itself is undercut and a mass of gnarled roots. I took a brace of good trout from the stretch that morning. And it is so generously endowed with trout amenities—a choice of perfect holts, shallow feeding stations alongside in a current which draws to itself a concentration of surface food, and spacious hunting water beyond—that if anyone will lay three to one against my catching a master trout in it before the end of the season, I am prepared to make it a bet.

The second stretch I think of is on the Otter. It extends along the foreshore of a small meadow on the right bank, below a weir which diverts at least half the river into a big mill-leat. It is very weedy and shallow. *But* a close examination will show that it is not uniformly shallow. On the right bank is a shelving shingle; the left has at some time been reinforced by timber. Close under the timber is a quiet, very unostentatious current that forces for itself a relatively deep channel through the weeds. This stretch is almost wholly neglected. Most unjustly: the last time I fished the water (about three miles on both banks) out of nine trout killed, seven, averaging over $\frac{3}{4}$ lb., were landed in that meadow.

The third stretch is on the Dart. This differs from the two I have described in that the river-bed is not tilted towards one bank; nor is it particularly weedy. The stream moves quietly over clean gravel, such as trout love to have beneath them when they feed. What gives the flat its character is the dispersal over it of pairs or larger groups of boulders, between which little runs form and beneath which hidden cavelets have been washed out by the friction of the accelerated current. Wading up the slacker water I have killed here as many good and master fish as in all the rest of the Dart put together.

At a place where the Plym runs close under the road one used, looking down through the trees, to see a file of good trout dimpling the surface right against the bank. A few years ago winter floods altered the character of the pool. The bed is no longer canted towards the roadside bank. It is now almost flat—perhaps very slightly concave. The good trout have disappeared. Instead, numbers of immature fish splash clumsily in midstream.

While it profits always to neglect water that is uniformly shallow, it profits only as a general rule to neglect water that is uniformly deep. Most of us are lured by the heavy swirls to be found below weirs and hatches. There is no doubt that the deep hole under the sluice often houses an exceptionally big trout. But he does not feed, in my experience, in the swirl itself. He should be looked for in the shallows further down the stream, where the force of the current has petered out. Such is a likely place to choose for that usually disappointing gamble, the evening rise. It is true that Leviathan, if he drops down, will probably be after a meal of minnows rather than of spinners. Even so, a fat alder may tempt him.

But one should certainly not neglect the long, gently flowing pool above the weir; and this is an important exception to the rule of discrimination against uniformly deep water. What precisely attracts master trout to mill pools I cannot see. That there is such an attraction does not admit of doubt.

Be slow to leave a bank that has been protected against erosion—generally by stone-walling in peat, by rough timber in limestone, and by what I believe is called "camp-sheathing" in chalk streams. The protection indicates that there is a strong set of the current towards the bank, and a consequent concentration of surface food that clings to the face of the protecting material. Here big trout will waive their objection to feeding in deep water. Camp-sheathing seems to be particularly attractive to them, and I like to wait for the rise where I can command a length of it; and nowhere is it easier, when the rise begins, to identify the fly on the water.

These are the general principles that should govern, I suggest, the search for good and master trout. But, as I began by saying, subject to these principles the big fish of every stream have mannerisms of their own. A station much favoured by the *élite* is where a patch of scum is held up by a snag or a dipping bush and deflects the bankside current outwards. Here, in all limestone or peat streams, and among chalk streams in the Coln, it is well to watch for a rise. But in the Kennet and Wylye such a station seldom seems to be taken by a distinguished tenant. In the Wylye the most likely place for a master trout is probably off the tail of a group of weed patches. The Wylye has problems of its own. It swarms with grayling, which generally avoid weed; and elderly trout do not like to be jostled by this plebeian company. In the Kennet I have not noticed that the really big trout have any marked preference. They may be found almost anywhere—even in apparent defiance of the general principles set out above.

The glassy water at the tail of a pool, just before it slides over into a lower pool, is in many rivers, but by no means in all, a likely place for a good rather than a master trout; especially when there is a fall of spinners. Such places are not a feature of chalk streams, but are most pronounced. I can think of no two streams where the bigger fish break the surface in exactly the same way. In the Dart they make, without showing any part of their persons, a very

appreciable hole in the water, which gives the impression
that a heavy body is behind it, and to the experienced is
unmistakeable. In the Otter the rule is wholly different.
The smaller the break in the surface, the bigger the trout;
till the dimple made by a master fish is so delicate that
even a keen and careful watcher may miss it. Here I have
covered a rise for an hour or more, uncertain whether it
was the work of a monster or of a minnow, but quite certain that it was the work of one or the other. In the Wylye
the bigger trout—but not grayling—though making a
very small hole in the surface, expose the tip of the snout.
This is not obvious from above, but is clearly visible if you
look upstream with your head close to the water. In this
attitude you will sometimes, in slack water, see a snout,
but no rise-form at all.

Such mannerisms can be recognised easily only after
experience of the stream you are fishing. Meanwhile on
an unfamiliar stream there are other helpful though less

reliable aids to appraisement. It is an amusing and remu-
nerative practice to give points for certain favourable
characteristics (assuming that you are generally satisfied
with the rise-form): say 40 points for likeliness of station;
30 for constancy of position (a big trout is jealous of his
station; he may move about a little, but only in a fixed
orbit); and 30 for methodical and persistent feeding (the
man or fish who does not enjoy his meals and like to get on
with them is not worth worrying about). If the rise scores
over 80 points, launch your attack; if less, look for another.
Following this practice during my first season on a chalk
stream (helped latterly by some little knowledge of local
mannerisms), I have so far knocked on the head 79 trout as
being comfortably over the pound, and returned 15 as
being undersized and 9 as being otherwise undesirable. If I
could quote the number of grayling knocked on the head
without respect for age or sex, the figures would be much
less flattering. But grayling are a very exceptionally disturbing element in this water, and I think my method of
marking has justified itself as a provisional measure.

Above all, do not, O brother, waste your time over a
"oncer." You will not catch him. And if you do, you will put

him back again. Listen to the oldest member, who will tell you to do as I have told you. And do not be dissuaded from following his advice when, happening to see him at work, you find that he himself does nothing of the sort.

EVERGLADES

Red Smith

What do Florida fly-fishers cast to when they've had their fill of snook and tarpon? Alligators, of course.

There's a man down here casts for six-foot alligators with a seven-and-a-half-foot fly rod, and lands them on six-pound-test line. Being a sportsman, Rocky Weinstein scrupulously returns his catch to the water, unharmed except for a cracked lip that hurts only when the gator laughs. A game warden might take a dim view of an angler with six feet of reptilian ugliness stuffed in his creel. However, the law says nothing about scratching one in the face with the barb of a little streamer fly. Nowhere in the Florida Fish and Game regulations is anything said about fly-fishing for gators, probably for the same reason that New Jersey has no open season on elephants.

This is exactly the sort of country where one might expect to encounter a fly fisherman like Rocky Weinstein, who can thread a needle at 120 to 140 feet. Everglades is a hamlet on the banks of the Barron River, a few miles removed from the Tamiami Trail. It is tidewater country, where the blue Gulf of Mexico spills across the green wilderness, meandering in twisting channels among matted mangrove islands.

The resident population includes fish and alligators, snakes and every conceivable variety of waterfowl and varmint, along with seagoing wild hogs that live on seafood. The hogs' table manners are deplorable and if you're within a quarter mile of one crunching oyster shells on a sandbar you think something is scraping a blackboard with a rusty nail.

In addition to the normal population, Everglades currently has an abnormal one made up of movie actors. Budd Schulberg is filming a story of his called *Across the Everglades,* which his friend Roger Donoghue describes as an adult Eastern, with good guys and bad guys and egrets instead of horses.

Two of the bad guys are Sammy Renick, the former jockey-turned-television-personality, and Tony Galento, the matinee idol who once knocked Joe Louis down and later toured the country sparring with a bear. They're outlaws in the picture, and these naïve movie people, mostly strangers to the jocks' room, are astonished at the realism Sammy gets into his role.

Tony has an inch or more of wild black stubble on a visage which, even in the bloom of his youth, suggested a detour on Highway 30. Right now he looks like an abandoned hobo jungle. One glance at this former golden boy of the heavy-weight ranks, and Arthur Brisbane's gorilla would run screaming into the underbrush.

Author-producer Schulberg, an incorrigible sports fan and fight buff, obviously enjoys this company. He and the fly rod expert, Weinstein, have become close friends.

"I was in my cottage one night," he said, "when Rocky came banging on the door, shouting that he had something for me. I opened the door and he was holding an alligator five feet long.

"'Here,' he says, 'just grab the tail with one hand and keep the other behind the head, like that. There you are, that's fine.'

"'What'll I do with it?' I hollered, standing there with my arms full of alligator. 'Toss it in that clothes closet,' Rocky said. I pitched it in and slammed the door and you should have heard that thing slapping and banging around inside.

"Next day when the maids came in to clean up I warned 'em not to open that closet, and then I worried that maybe I'd stirred their curiosity, like Bluebeard's wife. I had to go to work, so my brother Stuart propped a chair against the closet door and stayed there reading script. We built a pen for the gator, but he got out and went home."

One night Budd was fishing with Weinstein when they spotted an alligator, its eyes gleaming red in the darkness. Rocky made a half-dozen casts, putting the fly right on the critter's nose again and again. Annoyed, the brute snapped.

As the rod and gun writers say, the reel sang. Somebody interrupted the story at that point, and it never was explained how Rocky gets the hook out of that unfriendly face when he releases his prize. Perhaps a demonstration can be arranged.

Across the canal which runs along the highway the forest was a matted wall of mangrove and gum trees and occasional palmettos, but every little way the car passed a break in the green thicket, where a creek or ditch carried water down out of the glades. Rocky Weinstein said minnows bred by the thousands up these ditches, and the big snook in the canal loved to congregate at the openings to lunch on their little cousins.

Snook and tarpon are Rocky's tribal enemies. Widely known as a master of the fly rod, he won an award called the Greater Miami Sportsman's Release Trophy, not by releasing sportsmen but by catching and returning to the water hundreds of these two game-fish species. Spotting a fisherman at one of the openings, Rocky turned onto the highway shoulder and parked.

"Anything up, Pat?"

The fisherman was Pat Henning, of the cast of the movie *Across the Everglades*. Shooting had just ended for the day and this dedicated fish-killer was still in the tattered costume he wears as "Sawdust," a former lion-tamer on the bum. He hadn't even paused to remove his makeup.

Occupants of cars whizzing past may have been startled by the sight of a barefoot Walton in grimy rags with the long, livid scar of a lion's claw creasing his forehead.

Working fish made occasional bubbles on the surface of the canal but they weren't snook, Pat said. His bucktail streamer had attracted no interest as yet.

Rocky rigged a pair of glass rods, a nine-footer and another cut down to seven and a half. He was about to give a fly-fishing lesson to a pupil whose flailing casts have spooked off fish and hung flies in treetops from Lapland to the Antipodes.

Rocky's square name is Maurice and he is out of Richmond, Virginia, a stocky, smiling man somewhat less than medium height, with muscles. He was a first-rate croupier at dice tables in Las Vegas, but suckers never impressed him as game fish and so he came down here and set up as guide, tackle consultant, flytier and companion of anglers like Ted Williams.

He can't throw a tuft of feathers quite as far as Williams can drive a baseball, but his casts get better range than some of the rockets that have been launched lately in this state.

"Watch my left hand," he said, and began an illustrated lecture. He talks rapidly, gaily, with the enthusiasm and warmth of the dedicated teacher. And he casts. His fly is a guided missile that soars sweetly out to distances of 120 to 140 feet on casts meant to reach fish, not win tournaments. He can float a fly high so it wafts down like a loose feather; he can skip it over the water; he can shoot it in against the far bank under a tangle of brush that barely clears the surface.

Nobody this side of NATO disagrees so violently as fly fishermen. There are two or three tenets in Rocky's religion which would stir dissent in some quarters, but he can argue for his convictions.

Rodmakers, he believes, can put better backbone into glass than any other material but they make the tips too soft, so he cuts off the tip and compensates by shortening the butt.

Taking the fly off the water with an overhead lift, he argues, greatly diminishes the efficiency of the backcast. "We're little guys," he told his pupil. "Look how this picks up all that heavy line and straightens it out high behind me." He used a sidearm backcast. "And this," he said, "is the double haul."

New to his pupil, the double haul is no invention of Rocky's. It's a technique to impart speed to the line, which is essential in "shooting" line on a long cast. As Rocky's right hand starts the backcast, his left simultaneously strips line up through the guides, doubling the speed of the fly leaving the water. As his backcast straightens, he lets the left hand ride back toward the bottom guide, still holding the slack line, then he strips line in again sharply as he starts the forward cast. The speeding fly rockets out, slack hissing through the guides.

The tide ran swiftly down the canal, carrying green blotches of water hyacinth spinning toward the Gulf. Small fish broke the surface, bulging and splashing, but the snook weren't working. Now and then a mullet came hopscotching down the current like a happy child bound home from school. The sun had gone down. A chill was putting teeth into the evening, and there hadn't been a strike.

It didn't matter. Rocky's pupil threshed away happily with his stick, stripping line awkwardly, mistiming the backcast, snapping off Rocky's bucktails, now and then doing everything right by accident and shooting line half again as far as he's ever cast a fly before.

There would be hours of practice on the frozen lawn up home. For a fellow fishing the comparatively small streams of the Catskills, casts such as Rocky makes aren't necessary at all. Must be wonderful to know how, though.

NO WIND IN THE
WILLOWS

Russell Chatham

*The catching of a record striper while
eighteen-wheelers thunder by overhead.*

Outside a blizzard is raging. The familiar edges
that normally define my yard, its fences,
woodpile and barns, have long vanished beneath the snow. My house, the last on an unpaved road among aspen and pine forests
along the northwestern perimeter of Montana's vast Absaroka wilderness, is well on its way toward becoming a
smallish speck on the surface of a preposterous marshmallow.

Unable to go out, perhaps I will simply sit, reminisce
and revisit. A word recurs, an idea, insisting upon the situation: *remoteness*. I moved to the Big Sky Country to get it.
As an angler reflecting upon the fabric of American sport
afield, I recognized the essential thread to be a romance
with far places. In short, I'd identified the Mainstream and
wanted in.

Early on, my fishing days were spent in a northern California cabin snugged against the hillside beneath stands of
redwood. On a bookshelf beside its fireplace was a pile of
old magazines, sporting journals mostly, and some outdated tackle catalogues. It seemed fishing was more plain
and intimate then. For example, the invocation, "Take a

boy fishing!" required but a few Bass-O-Renos and perhaps a small outboard motor, called a "kicker," for immediate implementation.

This pastiche of allusions then, was rife with visions of adventure in which the canoe loomed large as a vehicle of escape. A guide, invariably of French descent, dressed appropriately in a red- and black-checked wool shirt, took us to lakes and rivers teeming with unusually large brook trout or northern pike somewhere in the vastness of the Canadian outback.

Portage! How much more a vision of unsoiled landscape this word promises than . . . ecology.

But before I founder completely in fatuous recall, it occurs that until very recently, among the hundred-odd thousand words placed by the Oxford Unabridged at my disposal, the adjective least correct as a predicate to my own angling past is *remote*.

San Francisco Bay: It is four-thirty in the morning on June 21, 1966. I am later than planned because of the time it took to clear myself with the policeman who pulled me over in San Anselmo for "suspicious behavior." Was it the generally fishy odor about the car which, in the end, convinced the law of my salient innocence? I don't know. In any case, we had parted amicably.

Now I am parking the car near a maintenance station on the Marin County end of the Richmond-San Rafael Bridge. I expect to be joined soon by an acquaintance but since he hasn't arrived I decide to walk out to the bridge itself for a quick preview.

On the way, rats scurry for cover behind a shabby row of shrubs. These would not be your big Norways, the kind you might see in the tropics sitting boldly in a palm while you sip your rum and tonic on the veranda below. No, the pusillanimous little rodents that people my morning are inclined to cower behind slimy rocks near the freeway, struggling on an equal footing with Marfak for control of the last strands of seaweed, or waiting in crevices for the next high tide.

I brush past the PEDESTRIANS PROHIBITED sign, jump the low guard rail and trot to the second light post. There is no visible traffic but from the north I hear a diesel truck shift down just before the crest that will bring him into view and then onto the bridge approach. He will be doing seventy when he reaches me so I hook one leg over the railing, grip the light standard and try to become inconspicuous. I would rather not be sucked under the rear wheels of a truck and trailer full of rutabagas. He goes by with a blast and the bridge vibrates ominously as I watch his lights diminish toward Richmond.

I run out to the next light and look down. As I'd hoped, half a dozen dark forms are finning in the shadow beneath the bridge. I am especially excited by the largest, which is a striped bass upward of thirty pounds. To my right, a pod of smelt moves near on a tangent certain to prompt an attack. The little fish are attracted by the brilliant light overhead. In their lack of purpose they seem ephemeral, like a translucent curtain quivering near a window, while the heavy predators lurking in the dark are deliberate and potent. In a moment the black shapes explode outward, sending the smelt showering away in a radius of flashing bodies.

Satisfied, I turn back toward the approach in time to see the California Highway Patrol car coming at me, its nose down under heavy braking.

"What are you doing out here, buddy?"

"Going fishing soon as it's legal time."

"Is that your car parked back at the maintenance building?"

"Yes."

"Well it's illegally parked. Better move it. Now get going and don't walk out here any more."

On my way to the car I see the patrolman who'd questioned me get out and look over the railing. Then the amber light is flashing and the driver is out too. Together they lean over the side, pointing.

I recognize Frank's blue sedan come down the off ramp and turn south. When I reach him he is untying his boat and I begin to do the same. In a few seconds we will have them in the water.

In order to launch we must trespass. The land belongs to

the state of California and although I've never been ver-
bally warned off, any number of KEEP OUT signs are posted.

For about eight years I kept a boat chained and locked
behind a large sign reading CABLE CROSSING. Once a year
they would repaint this sign getting white paint on the
chain.

Some yards away in a square blockhouse belonging to
San Quentin Penitentiary, trustees worked during the day.
Each season they planted a handsome little vegetable gar-
den which I was careful never to disturb.

I often talked to one convict in particular. After fishing
it would take some minutes to put the boat behind the sign
and then carry everything else up to the car. He would call
a greeting and I'd perhaps comment on the progress in the
garden. Then he'd ask, always rather plaintively, about the
fishing. He said he liked to go fishing before he got "inside."

One December we had a severe storm, accompanied by
especially high tides. Afterward, I went over to check the
boat and all that was left was the chain. I was poking
around the beach when I heard my friend's voice.

"Looking for your boat?"

"Guess it's gone," I replied sadly.

"No, I saw it break loose and caught it. Then I dragged it
up there." He said, "Only thing I couldn't find was the
seat."

Beyond the garden, I could see the trim little *El Toro*
upside down on a pair of two by fours.

In recent years there have been no inmates at the blockhouse and the garden lies fallow beneath wild anise. In a
sense this has meant more license to trespass but I stopped
keeping a boat behind the sign when I knew there would
be no trustees to look after it.

It is a windless, overcast morning. Sunrise, such as it
will be, is in an hour but the eastern horizon over San
Pablo Bay is still dark. Bursts of flame glow against a
cloudy ceiling above Point Molate, tangible evidence that

behind the latter's headlands lies the Standard Oil Company of California's research center, in a bitter sense, petroleum's ode to the cubists with its sprawl of cylinders, cones and rectangles.

At Point San Quentin, the flaring fires have become a familiar greeting like the dew on a chokecherry bush that starts off the trout fisherman's day in the Rockies.

"Did you look?" Frank asks.

"They're there."

We row around the tilted bow of a derelict tugboat, then past rotted pilings left from the ferryboat days. Over on the approach a yellow bridge patrol truck moves slowly, flashing its warning lights. Switching on a spotlight, the driver scans the water, catching sight of Frank and me. Then the light is off and the truck starts toward the toll plaza.

Unseen overhead, a black-crowned night hawk rasps its singularly forlorn call.

The smell of an institutional breakfast wafts unappetizingly across the water from San Quentin, an odor not unlike that of a cow barn in winter. No croissants and chilled grapefruit sections this morning, to be sure.

There is a fast tide and we must row smartly to pass beneath the bridge, where it is always dank and dripping. Sounds are magnified and echoed, especially that of wavelets slapping against pilings. Reflected light plays on the girders overhead, and just before we emerge I see several bass hovering at the edge, but Frank rows into the dark while I decide to try a few casts at the first light. The piling directly beneath the lamp attracts my attention so I drop the large bucktail fly where the current will swing it into the shadows.

Instantly there is a take and I set the hook twice. This is always the moment when you wonder if the bass will go under the bridge and break off on a sharp barnacle. But I've learned that initial light pressure generally encourages them to dive toward the boat.

Now my bass pulls around into the dark, and I try to gauge its size. It is, if nothing else, a stubborn fish that resolutely resists all the strain I can manage on a fifteen-pound tippet. Eventually, however, I land it and mentally record a weight slightly above twenty pounds.

Frank is anchored under the third light, where I see angular splashes as fish erupt under a school of bait.

It was Walt Mullen who showed me the bridge and how to fish it shortly after it was built. When we first met I was sixteen and he was more than eighty. Coincidentally, Walt had taken my father fishing and hunting back in the twenties when the latter was going to Stanford.

Mullen was an old sign painter, wiry and spry, surely no more than a hundred pounds soaking wet. I wanted to learn the sign business so I'd hang around his shop. But my patience proved short and my business acumen entirely nonexistent so we always ended up talking about fishing. He loved it more than anyone I'd ever met. In the front pocket of his coveralls he always had a tide book, dog-eared and paint-smeared.

"See here," he said one day, pointing out the numerals. "There's a good tide in three days. If the water's clear and it's not too windy, I'll take you out to the bridge."

At that point my own experience was primarily academic insofar as fly-casting for striped bass was concerned. Walt didn't fly-fish but he knew instinctively I would catch fish on the streamers I showed him.

I'd read about certain pioneer anglers on the East Coast who caught striped bass by fly-fishing. I knew also that Joe Brooks, the noted Virginian, was much interested in stripers and that he caught one of twenty-nine pounds six ounces in 1948 out of Coos Bay, Oregon. This fish was acknowledged as the fly-rod record.

For several years Walt and I fished together regularly. Then I married and became too busy and he closed his shop, moving the business to another county.

Occasionally I'd see him at the bridge. His eyes were failing and he didn't trust himself in a boat any more so he'd cast from the rocks, often a futile gesture since fish rarely fed close to shore.

One windy, choppy evening Bill Schaadt and I were in our boat at the third light.

"Look." Bill pointed.

On the bridge, hunched against the railing, oblivious to speeding traffic and thoroughly unable to distinguish Bill or me, was Walt clutching an enormous spinning rod. Cocking it back, he used it to drive his lure in a trajectory which carried it over a school of bass I'm sure he never saw. His face was locked in an expression of determination that did not make him look any less like an angling Ichabod Crane.

"Boy," Bill said, "Now there's a guy who likes to fish!"

Then as we'd hoped and anticipated, Walt hooked a striper whereupon he stalked grimly back to the rocks and landed it.

Several years passed during which time I did not see Walt Mullen. Then one cold spring morning I was out at the bridge alone. To avoid the noisome mob of trollers, with whom the bridge had become a favorite haunt, I'd begun going at odd hours and poorish tides. When it grew light I saw a figure on the rocks, casting. Walt! Excitedly I drew up my anchor and rowed in, circling widely so I wouldn't spoil anything. Close in, I turned but could no longer see anyone.

Going ashore, I called out with no response. I looked under the bridge and finally crossed the freeway to search the other side. There was no one. I felt a deep sense of loss, an uneasy melancholy. I went home.

Later I found out Walt had died earlier that spring.

I row around behind Frank. The bass are there and I see the heavy swirls as they feed.

Traffic on the bridge is picking up. Early commuters. They are too low in their cars to see us but the truck drivers give a wave or short blast of the horn. It is getting light, a gray dawn that I imagine could be heavily depressing to a man looking forward to eight hours on the production line.

"The coldest winter I ever spent," wrote someone, "was a summer in San Francisco." I wonder momentarily if this, in part, explains the high suicide rate and high alcohol intake for which the City on the Bay is known.

We are virtually within sight of well over a million people, yet alone. We are perhaps, out of step, ill placed and ill timed, in a sphere where cogs must mesh and all parts syncopate to keep the system running smoothly. Even within the framework of angling as a popular endeavor, our methods are archaic: fly rods and rowboats. But we are touching something unrestricted, wild and arcane, beyond the reach of those who carefully maintain one-dimensional lives. There is, I tell myself, someone in the city nearby whose one contact today with unreconstructed nature will be to step into a diminutive pile of poodle excrement.

When I looked into the mirror during the late fifties I saw a striped-bass fisherman who often imagined, wrongly, that he was doing something remarkable and unique.

At the time an old gent by the name of Ellis Springer was pier keeper for the Marin Rod and Gun Club, which was situated only a few feet from the bridge. He let me use the club's launching ramp, dock and fish-cleaning table even though I was not a member.

Ellis was never seen without a light-blue captain's hat and stubby cigar. He talked often of the days he'd spent in the Spanish-American War but his manner of speech was so unique that you could understand nothing of what he said. I didn't think he knew what fly-fishing was and wanting to let him in on my little discovery, I gave a demonstration one day off the dock. He looked properly astonished and when I showed him my flies, he became incoherently excited, exclaiming, "Yeeehhh! Hoopty poopty! Hoopty poopty!"

These exclamations became a permanent part of all subsequent conversations.

"Hi, Springer."

"Eeeeehhh! Hoopty poopty!"

I used to carry fish around in the back of my car the way other kids my age carried a six pack of Country Club. I'd show Ellis and he'd become truly frantic.

"Yeeeehhh! Hoopty poopty! Hoopty poopty!"

Gradually I became aware of the fact he called everything that was not strictly a sardine fillet a hoopty poopty.

Frank hooks a bass. I put my anchor down out of his way but still close enough to reach the school. I see two powerful boils and cast the bulky fly on a slow loop toward the swirl closest to a piling. I overshoot so the fly tinks against the bridge hanging momentarily between the rail and roadway, then as it flutters downward I see the number 9 stenciled above on an abutment.

The take is authoritative and my response lifts the clearly visible fly line from the water, curving it abruptly to the left as a sheet of droplets limns the fish's first long run. It is not a frenetic contest as the striper stays deep, far from the boat. But I am not inclined to carry out these contests gently and soon have the fish nearby. Once, glowering, he shoots away beneath a crescent of spray only to be turned in a verticle wallow. After all, nothing in their lives really prepares a fish to deal with the relentless affixation of being hooked.

203

Oddly, I am reminded of how Walt Mullen described playing a fish. "Then it fooled around and fooled around," he would say. And that is exactly it.

In the boat the fish is big.

"It's more than twenty-five," I say to Frank.

Earlier we had discussed a twenty-five pound striper caught accidentally by a fly-fisherman in the Russian River. It seemed more appropriate that a fish taken by design should receive top honors for the season. Naturally, we both expressed the hope that one of us would catch such a fish.

Back at the beach we lay three large bass in front of the sign that reads CABLE CROSSING.

"That one's bigger than the one I caught last season," says Frank.

Getting his Polaroid camera, he takes a picture of me holding the fish, which comes out a minute later looking distant and journalistic. Then after promising to call him as soon as I get the thing weighed, I head for San Rafael and he goes off to work in San Francisco.

Later, I call.

"It's big isn't it?" Frank asks right away. "I've been looking at this snapshot all morning."

"Yes. Thirty-six pounds six ounces."

The record Joe Brooks had held for eighteen years was
broken. When I got to know Joe he would always introduce
me as "a great salt-water fisherman," which was embar-
rassing because while he was alive he was so clearly one of
the greatest. Now others have caught bigger bass, elimi-
nating my personal stake in the matter. It is a relief to be
reminded that competition in angling is entirely beside the
point and that I'm simply an angler of average persuasion
and ability who happened to cast a fly near a large, hungry
fish one morning.

Besides, there are too many other things to think about,
like a certain broad shovel on the porch. I finished all the
Jack Daniel's last night and this morning we are hope-
lessly snowed in.

THE BEST RAINBOW TROUT FISHING

Ernest Hemingway

Vivid reporting on fishing for giant rainbows by the twenty-one-year-old Hemingway.

Rainbow trout fishing is as different from brook fishing as prizefighting is from boxing. The rainbow is called *Salmo iridescens* by those mysterious people who name the fish we catch and has recently been introduced into Canadian waters. At present the best rainbow trout fishing in the world is in the rapids of the Canadian Soo.

There the rainbow have been taken as large as fourteen pounds from canoes that are guided through the rapids and halted at the pools by Ojibway and Chippewa boatmen. It is a wild and nerve-frazzling sport and the odds are in favor of the big trout who tear off thirty or forty yards of line at a rush and then will sulk at the base of a big rock and refuse to be stirred into action by the pumping of a stout fly rod aided by a fluent monologue of Ojibwayian profanity. Sometimes it takes two hours to land a really big rainbow under those circumstances.

The Soo affords great fishing. But it is a wild nightmare kind of fishing that is second only in strenuousness to angling for tuna off Catalina Island. Most of the trout, too, take a spinner and refuse a fly, and to the ninety-nine percent pure fly fisherman, there are no one hundred per-centers, that is a big drawback.

Of course the rainbow trout of the Soo will take a fly but it is rough handling them in that tremendous volume of water on the light tackle a fly fisherman loves. It is dan-gerous wading in the spots that can be waded too, for a misstep will take the angler over his head in the rapids. A canoe is a necessity to fish the very best water.

Altogether it is a rough, tough, mauling game, lacking in the meditative qualities of the Izaak Walton school of angling. What would make a fitting Valhalla for the good fisherman when he dies would be a regular trout river with plenty of rainbow trout in it jumping crazy for the fly.

There is such a one not forty miles from the Soo called the—well, called the river. It is about as wide as a river should be and a little deeper than a river ought to be and to get the proper picture you want to imagine in rapid suc-cession the following fade-ins:

A high pine-covered bluff that rises steep up out of the shadows. A short sand slope down to the river and a quick elbow turn with a little flood wood jammed in the bend and then a pool.

A pool where the moselle-colored water sweeps into a dark swirl and expanse that is blue-brown with depth and fifty feet across.

There is the setting.

The action is supplied by two figures that slog into the picture up the trail along the riverbank with loads on their backs that would tire a packhorse. These loads are pitched over the heads onto the patch of ferns by the edge of the deep pool. That is incorrect. Really the figures lurch a lit-tle forward and the tump line loosens and the pack slumps onto the ground. Men don't pitch loads at the end of an eight-mile hike.

One of the figures looks up and notes the bluff is flat-tened on top and that there is a good place to put a tent. The other is lying on his back and looking straight up in the air. The first reaches over and picks up a grasshopper that is stiff with the fall of the evening dew and tosses him into the pool.

The hopper floats spraddle-legged on the water of the pool an instant, an eddy catches him and then there is a yard-long flash of flame, and a trout as long as your forearm has shot into the air and the hopper has disappeared.

"Did you see that?" gasped the man who had tossed in the grasshopper.

It was a useless question, for the other, who a moment before would have served as a model for a study entitled "Utter Fatigue," was jerking his fly rod out of the case and holding a leader in his mouth.

We decided on a McGinty and a Royal Coachman for the flies and at the second cast there was a swirl like the explosion of a depth bomb, the line went taut and the rainbow shot two feet out of water. He tore down the pool and the line went out until the core of the reel showed. He jumped, and each time he shot into the air we lowered the tip and prayed. Finally he jumped and the line went slack and Jacques reeled in. We thought he was gone and then he jumped right under our faces. He had shot upstream toward us so fast that it looked as though he were off.

When I finally netted him and rushed him up the bank and could feel his huge strength in the tremendous muscular jerks he made when I held him flat against the bank, it was almost dark. He measured twenty-six inches and weighed nine pounds and seven ounces.

That is rainbow trout fishing.

The rainbow takes the fly more willingly than he does bait. The McGinty, a fly that looks like a yellowjacket, is the best. It should be tied on a number eight or ten hook.

The smaller flies get more strikes but are too small to hold the really big fish. The rainbow trout will live in the same streams with brook trout but they are found in different kinds of places. Brook trout will be forced into the shady holes under the bank and where alders hang over the banks, and the rainbow will dominate the clear pools and the fast shallows.

Magazine writers and magazine covers to the contrary,

the brook, or speckled, trout does not leap out of water after he has been hooked. Given plenty of line, he will fight a deep rushing fight. Of course if you hold the fish too tight he will be forced by the rush of the current to flop on top of the water.

But the rainbow always leaps on a slack or tight line. His leaps are not mere flops, either, but actual jumps out of and parallel with the water of from a foot to five feet. A five-foot jump by any fish sounds improbable, but it is true.

If you don't believe it, tie on to one in fast water and try and force him. Maybe if he is a five-pounder he will throw me down and only jump four feet eleven inches.

SEA TROUT FISHING

Sir Edward Grey

An eminent British statesman's love af-
fair with Scotland's sea-going trout.

All through May and June the keenest angler may well be content to stay by a good dry fly river, for he is having the best and most interesting fishing that this part of the season can give him. But after June is over, good though some days in July may be, I own that a certain feeling of restlessness comes over me. I struggle against it, for it seems a sort of disloyalty to the river and the country which have given so much pleasure, but it will assert itself, just as perhaps the migratory instinct works in the nature of birds, some of which leave their summer homes long before the warm days have come to an end, while there is still abundance of food and everything that they need. As the summer goes on it is felt more and more that the glory of the woods of the south of England is over, that they have subsided into a sombre monotony and silence, which will last till autumn. One feels too that the water meadows are a little too soft and that the air lacks freshness; and so, without consciously desiring a change, one begins to think of rocks and keener air. The even-flowing chalk stream, with its mills and dams and hatches, the river which is so clear and gentle, so docile and perfectly under control, seems just a little tame, till at last there rises up before one's mind the full-formed images of rough noisy streams and great brown pools clearing after a flood.

One stands in thought beside them, and is impatient to be really there.

It may be easy to provide the change of scene, if that is the only thing desired, but how can this change be combined with the best of fishing from the middle of July through August and into September? Some salmon rivers may, with the help of lucky floods, give good sport at this time, but the angler cannot get the best of salmon fishing now. It is only grilse and small salmon that he can expect to get at their best. The bigger fish, with which it really needs a big rod and strong salmon gut to cope, will not, as a rule, be fresh run or in fine condition. There is, however, one sort of angling that is at its best, and indeed is only good at all in the months of July, August, and September. These are the months in which the sea trout run up fresh from the sea, and it is in pursuit of them that the best sport is now to be had. It is not to large rivers that one generally goes in search of sea trout fishing, and the reason for this is to be found partly in the habits of sea trout, and partly in the arrangements made by mankind with respect to rivers and their rents. Large rivers, to which sea trout have free access, will also have numbers of salmon, and if they are let at all will be let at rents for which the presence of salmon is entirely responsible, and which are far in excess of what is charged or paid for the best sea trout fishing alone. Sea trout in a large salmon river are not of much more account than grouse in a deer forest, and are even looked upon as a nuisance when they are running and take a salmon fly freely, whilst the angler is expecting salmon. If one lived always upon a large river, and could fish all through the season, it would be better in the latter half of July and beginning of August to take only a small rod and fish especially for sea trout, but at this time of year the salmon and grilse are showing freely in the streams and pools where they lie, and the angler, who may only have a very limited amount of salmon fishing in the year, generally takes the chance of getting some of the salmon which he sees, and disregards the sea trout. It is difficult to fish contentedly for smaller fish and not to try for the bigger, when the latter are constantly showing themselves, and the result is that one sometimes wastes the opportunity of first-rate sport with sea trout in order to have a very indifferent day's salmon fishing. I remember one week in July, when sea trout were running on a first-rate salmon river in Scotland. They rested in numbers in a very long stream and pool where they could easily be reached by wading, but salmon and grilse were there too, and I fished with nothing but salmon flies and salmon gut and a seventeen feet rod. I was continually hooking sea trout of all weights from one pound to three pounds, and of course getting no fun with them on such tackle: if I had used a small rod, and been content to fish the sides of the stream and the stiller parts with sea trout flies, I should have had wonderful sport with sea trout, and probably have hooked an occasional small salmon or grilse also, even though it was impossible to cover the whole water properly with anything but a salmon rod. As it was, my total for five days was four salmon (none of them large) and six grilse, besides a number of fresh run sea trout, which were all wasted as far as sport was concerned. The memory of that week is one of wasted opportunities, which have never recurred. On the other hand, if I were by that pool again and the same conditions were present, I should remember that once in July a friend of mine landed fourteen fresh run salmon and grilse in one day from the stream there, and if I gave myself up to sea trout fishing I might be tormented by the thought that I was missing an opportunity of having such a day as he once had. Such are some of the perplexities of sea trout fishing in large rivers.

Large rivers, however, are not the most suitable for sea trout fishing. The sea trout is not content to stay for days and weeks in running water or strong streams, as the salmon is. What it really likes is to get to deep still water as soon as possible; and small rivers giving easy access to lochs, or having deep still reaches of their own, are the best places for sea trout fishing.

The streams and shorter pools of these rivers give the best sport of all, *when the fish are there,* but it must be remembered that sea trout pass quickly through the run-

ning water, and the best river fishing for sea trout is limited to the particular weeks of the season and the special
conditions of the river, in which sea trout run up from the
salt water. The season during which these fish run in the
greatest numbers is in July and August. During these
months they accumulate at the mouths of small rivers and
burns, going to and fro in the tidal water waiting for a
flood. With each flood or spate, as it is called, quantities of
the fish move up the river, and when the water is still
high, but falling, the angler has his great opportunity.

Let us suppose that he has been for some days on a good
sea trout river towards the end of July, that there has been
no rain for some weeks, and that he has wandered about
for a few days catching hardly anything, but knowing that
fish are showing freely at the mouth of the river and waiting to come up. At last there comes rain. First the dust is
laid; then the water begins to show upon the road; and
presently little white streams appear on the sides of the
hills. Still the rain becomes heavier and continues, and the
angler goes out in it late in the evening to watch the river
beginning to rise. He listens to the sound of rain upon the
roof at night, and with the increasing certainty of a really
good spate a sort of corresponding current of excitement
rises in him. If the morning is fine, small rivers will be
high but will soon be falling, and he goes to a favourite
part almost with the certainty of good sport. Wonderful indeed is the delight of standing by a pool which for weeks
has been too low, the stream at its head a weak trickle, its
deep part smooth and almost stagnant, the end of it shallow, clear, and hopeless, and of seeing it now full of agita-
tion, life, and rich colour. The stream which was so
desultory before, now sweeps right down and through it,
rough and noisy at the top, smooth and quiet in the deep
parts, but always a good current; and the whole pool seems
full of character. Anything may come in such a pool as
this, it may be a small sea trout or one of two, three, or
four pounds, or a grilse, or a small salmon. That is the first
charm of this sort of fishing, after fishing for trout in a
chalk stream; there is such great variety of size. The average weight of sea trout caught, including the small half-

pounders, may be little over one pound, but there is the chance, sometimes the probability, of hooking something of five or ten pounds or more, for grilse and small salmon are always met with in sea trout rivers; and even the sea trout itself gets to heavy weights, though fish of five pounds and upwards are not common. While the river is high and the stream strong the best places are in the smooth currents at the tail of deep pools and heavy water, and in gentler rippling streams at the head of long shallow flats, but the only certain guide to the best places on each river is experience, and if the angler has no one to instruct him he must learn by fishing all places which look as if they might hold fish. If he works hard he will soon find out good places for himself. It is especially delightful to have knowledge of the water of a river and the ways of the fish which come up it, when this knowledge has been gained by fishing alone. The angler always believes that he has discovered some special places, which are better known to himself than to any one else. This belief is very likely true, but it is also true of other anglers, for experiences differ, and each season even on a known river adds something to one's knowledge of it, partly because the bed of the river and its banks are altered from time to time by floods.

There is another uncertainty about sea trout besides the glorious one of size, and that is the uncertainty of where the fish are. They seem to run very much in shoals, and one mile of a river may be full of them when there are comparatively few above or below. Whenever there has been a spate which has made the fish move, the angler has to find out where they are, and if he does not get them at once in what he knows to be favourite places, he had better try other parts of the river at some distance. He should always remember, however, that the fish may be in the pools he has already tried and may come to the fly later, and that it is easy to waste a whole day in running about without giving any part of the river a thorough trial. There is a tendency in sea trout fishing to spend time in trying to make sure where the biggest fish are. It is well to be on one's guard against this, and to remain where one meets with the first success, or where fish are seen. When a river is high and coloured the fish do not, as a rule, show themselves much by splashing or jumping, but whenever and wherever sea trout do show themselves in this way, it is an invaluable help to the angler, whose first object is to fish where the fish are, and whose great difficulty often is to be sure that he is doing this. What a contrast this is after a Hampshire chalk stream, where one comes to have an idea of the number and size of the trout in each meadow, and how much it adds to the wildness and hard work of fishing! In sea trout fishing there is no waiting about for the fish to come on the rise, but constant fishing and walking and experiment, and on good days the day does not seem long enough to find out for certain where the best of the fish are.

The sea trout is a wild mysterious animal without a home, and its habits differ as much from those of brown trout as the habits of wild fowl or woodcocks do from those of partridges. Being such a vagrant it never has the chance of the persistent continuous education in the matter of angling and tackle, which some brown trout receive, and its standard in the matter of flies and gut and casting is not so high or refined. On the other hand, its appetite in fresh water is more capricious, it is hardly ever on the lookout for any special flies which can be selected, and the angler has to trust more to the mood of the sea trout and his own knowledge of the river after a spate than to any superior excellence of skill beyond the average, or extra fineness of tackle. When sea trout are in the mood they take as freely as brown trout ever do, but in fresh water they are liable to longer spells of indifference or obstinacy. I think that, as is the case with salmon, sea trout do not enter rivers till they have stored up enough fat to last them, if need be, till they have spawned, but either because they still retain the power of digestion, or because they are more active and alert, more easily interested in what comes before them, they certainly rise to the fly much better than salmon do. One which I caught with a fly in a river after a spate disgorged several of the common black slugs, and it is clear therefore that they sometimes bring an appetite with them into fresh water. But for all that, sea trout cannot either expect or need to find a stock of food in clean rocky or stony fresh water, and the angler must be prepared for their often behaving like creatures that are quite independent of feeding.

The rise of a sea trout is generally bold and even fierce. Sometimes it takes the fly with a silent boil, or even without any sign on the surface if the fly is deeply sunk. The typical rise, however, of a sea trout has some sound about it. There is a quick white splash in the dark water, and (if the line is tight) the fish hooks itself. So violent and rapid sometimes is the sea trout manner of seizing the fly that it is not safe to use very fine drawn gut, for tackle which may be quite strong enough to play and land a three or four pound fish in open water, cannot always be trusted to stand the jerk of the sudden rush with which even a two pound fish seizes the fly. A sea trout is not in the habit of feeding quietly upon flies floating at ease upon the surface. It may do this occasionally, but it is not used to this method of feeding as brown trout are, and it takes a fly moving under water, as if the fly were a thing trying to escape from it. There are days when almost every fish that rises seems to hook itself without needing effort or attention on the angler's part; and there are other days—generally in bright weather when the water is low,—when the fish rise short, because they are shy; they just touch the fly, and on these days I think the angler can do a good deal to improve his sport by striking quickly, by using fine gut, and by fishing delicately with a long line. There are yet other days when sea trout rise boldly and playfully, but fail to touch the fly at all; and indeed "fail" is the wrong word to use, for I think that on these days the fish do not intend to take the fly, and their rises are the results of high spirits and exuberant activity. And so the angler appears to have an excellent chance each time of hooking a fish, when the fish has perhaps never opened its mouth at all. Sometimes a sea trout that has risen and not been touched by the hook will rise again, but they are very uncertain in this respect, and I do not fish over one a second time with the same expectation of another rise, that I feel in the case of a salmon that has risen once and missed the fly. Of course one always feels wronged and aggrieved when a sea trout, which has not been pricked and has no excuse, refuses to give another chance, but there are days when fish after fish rises once, and only once, without touching the hook. On the whole, however, sea trout, when they do rise, may be said to take hold very well.

It was said just now that sea trout fishing was especially dependent upon the state of the water, and it is true that a falling river after a spate is the great opportunity, but the angler need not despair even when the water is at its lowest, if there have previously been floods to bring fish into the river, and if there are fairly deep pools and long stretches of deep still water. The fish collect in these places when the water is low, and if there is a breeze, which blows fairly up or down the stream and so makes a good ripple, a very good basket may be made. Even when there is no breeze and a bright sun, it is possible to have some sport with the small class of sea trout known as "herling" and by various other names. These smaller fish run later than most of the large ones, and are often met with in shoals. They average only between half a pound and three-quarters of a pound, but they fight with extraordinary activity and strength, and they sometimes rise when no other fish thinks of doing so. I was once by a small sea trout river on one very hot bright day in August. The streams were shrunken and weak, the still places were smooth as glass, and the water, as is the case in bare rocky parts of the Western Islands, was very little tinged with peat and exceptionally clear. The fish were in the river, but there was only depth enough for them in quite still water, and to fish in that seemed hopeless. I sat down and opened my box of flies. Ordinary sea trout flies seemed double their proper size on such a day and by such water. One could not think of trying them, and one shuddered at the thickness of undrawn gut, and yet there was the river, and the day, and the fish, and I was alone and seven miles from the lodge. Something had to be done. So I took out a well-tapered trout cast ending in fine drawn gut, and added about a yard of transparent stout gut to the thick end of it. On the fine end I put a plain black hackle fly of a size suitable for brown trout. A really heavy basket was of course out of the question, and I did not rise any large fish, though there were some to be seen at the bottom of the pools; but by using a small rod and this very fine tackle, I did succeed in getting about ten pounds' weight of the smaller fish, and though the largest was under one pound, I had many a good fight. The conditions made the fishing interesting, there was enough success to keep me at work, and if the result was not very remarkable, it was at any rate enough to give a feeling of having overcome difficulties, and saved what seemed at first a hopeless situation. It was very pretty fishing too, for one could see the gleam of the silver fish, even when they came short or took a fly under water. In similar conditions, but with a little breeze, I have found fresh run fish up to a pound and a half in weight rise freely. Fresh run sea trout are at all times exceedingly tender mouthed, and with small hooks one must expect to lose many of them even with the most careful handling.

Of all fish the sea trout fights the best in proportion to its size. Its strength when fresh run is greater than that of a brown trout of the same size, and being, as it often is, a stranger to the pool, or at best only a temporary visitor, it does not so often concentrate its efforts upon getting to some known refuge, but rushes wildly from place to place. The fight of a sea trout is thus stronger than that of a brown trout and, if possible, even more active and full of quick turns. There is no fish with which one has to be so much on one's guard against being surprised, either by sudden rushes or by jumps in the air, and as far as the actual playing of a fish is concerned, for sheer enjoyment and rapidity of sensation, I prefer a good fresh run sea trout of three or four pounds in a river on a single-handed rod and fine tackle to anything else.

For this sort of fishing in a small river, I like to use a single-handed rod, but one that is very strong. One not only has more sport with the fish hooked on a rod like this, but one fishes more delicately, and can use finer gut than is safe with a double-handed rod; and finer gut makes a considerable difference in the number of fish hooked, ex-

cept when the water is very much coloured. With a small
rod an angler, who has nerve and patience, will land even
salmon successfully on a casting line tapered to end with
the finest undrawn gut, provided always that the water is
free from obstructions, such as tree roots and weeds, and
that the angler can follow the fish either along the bank or
by wading.

Every now and then comes the great event of hooking a
grilse or salmon on a sea trout rod and fine tackle, and
then there is a long and most interesting contest, to which
the angler addresses himself with every nerve strung by
excitement. At first his business is to be very modest in
asserting himself, and to save his tackle by following the
fish as much as he can, rather than by letting out line,
which may get drowned in the current. But from the first
he selects some favourable piece of water below him, and
endeavours to conduct the fish towards it. Often enough, in
spite of all he can do, the contest drifts away from the desired place; for the fish may get there too soon and carry
the angler past it, in which case he must then select with
his eye some other place and make that the object of his
movements. The best place of all for the last stage of the
fight, when the angler feels that the time has come to con-
tend not only for the safety of his tackle but for victory, is a
quiet back-water with a shelving bank of gravel, which is
even, and free from very large stones. Any smooth shallow
place will do well enough, but a back-water sometimes
brings sudden confusion and helplessness upon a tired fish.
When a fresh grilse or salmon has been landed on sea trout
tackle and a single-handed rod, the angler must have
made good use of his resources of quickness, judgment, decision, patience and self-control, and should feel that come
what may afterwards the good fortune of that day's angling has been made safe.

Hitherto angling for sea trout in rivers only has been
discussed in this chapter, but probably more of these fish
are caught by anglers in lochs than in rivers. It is a pity
that this should have to be so, but, if a loch is accessible,
sea trout will not rest till they get to it, and there they are
content to remain, till they go up the small streams to

spawn. Loch fishing is for obvious reasons not so interesting as river fishing. There is not the variety and individuality of stream and pool and condition of water; whilst in most cases it is necessary to fish from a boat, drifting sideways with the wind, so that the angler is always moving involuntarily towards his own flies, which he is at the same time working towards himself. Most people very much prefer to fish from firm ground, where they can cast when they please, move as they please, and stop where they please to linger over a favourite place.

On some lochs, however, the sea trout lie near the sides, and can be reached either from the bank or by wading. There the angler can be independent, and may have very good sport, though the advantage of covering a large extent of water turns the scale in favour of a double-handed rod. Except on very rough days, fine tackle is important in loch fishing, and as in angling from the bank one cannot make sure of being able to follow the fish, it is necessary, not to have a heavier line, but to have more of it. I once hooked a grilse of nearly five pounds on trout tackle, and a single-handed rod, when I had only thirty yards of line on the reel, and when I was fishing from the bank of a loch on which there was no boat. Twice the grilse ran dangerously near to the limit of the line; twice as a last resource I slacked the line as much as I could, in the hope of making the fish think it was free and cease its efforts, and each time it seemed puzzled, and let me very quietly and cautiously recover some line. Whether a catastrophe was really saved by these tactics I cannot be sure, but they are worth trying in an emergency. That grilse, at any rate, was landed.

In lochs the fish are even more capricious in their moods than they are in rivers. One generally attributes these moods to the weather; there always seems to me to be something in the weather, on any given day, when the fish will not rise, which is the cause of my having no sport; and being of an excessively sanguine temperament—of which I hope never to be cured—I discover that evening some change, actual or impending, in the wind or the sky or the temperature, which I am satisfied will make the next day entirely different. I look forward full of happy expectation. Yet with all this study of weather, I have not been able to arrive at any theory which is satisfactory.

The best day I ever had with sea trout in a river was when the water was not very high, and there was a gloomy gale from the east in August. The best day I ever had on a loch was bright and hot, and with only a very slight breeze —not nearly enough in appearance for fishing. Till midday I had not had one rise, and had only seen two fish. Then the breeze improved just enough to make a small ripple, and quantities of daddy-long-legs came upon the water; the little black loch trout all under four ounces were very pleased with these straggling insects, and pursued and took them. I did not actually see a sea trout take one, but the large fish began to show by making boils on the surface, and my belief is that the daddy-long-legs were the cause; and wherever the sea trout showed, and I could reach them from the bank, they took my fly.

220

There is very interesting sea trout fishing to be had in Shetland, of which I once had some experience. It was on a property of some 12,000 acres, remote from all hotels, and so indented by small and large voes that the actual coast line was about thirty miles, all wild and rocky. There were innumerable lochs, but the overflow of most of them fell into the sea over some precipice, which no fish could ascend, and the sea trout lochs were practically only two in number. Two burns flowed from these lochs to the sea, and joined each other about a mile from their common mouth. Very little was known about the fish, as far as angling was concerned, and I found myself—for I was alone in the first days—with the delightful prospect of exploring the possibilities of salt and fresh water, remarkable both for extent and variety. When first I saw the burn it was very low, and the deeper part of it looked like a sulky black ditch. This burn had so little water that it seemed impossible any fish could have got up the rocky places at the mouth, but even then there were fresh run sea trout up to two pounds' weight in the black peaty holes, and they took a fly well. When a spate came in the last week in August, and in other spates during September, quantities of sea trout and grilse came up this burn, and we always found a number of fresh run fish in its pools willing to rise at all heights of water.

The lochs were less satisfactory. There was no boat upon them, the bottom was of soft peat, and the wading peculiar. After wading a few steps into the water, one's feet sank into the soft bottom, masses of bubbles came up with a wallowing sound, and one had an impression of standing upon a yielding surface, which would collapse suddenly and let one down into an abyss. There was no firm ground in the lochs whatever, but we became used to the alarming feel of the soft peat and to the bubbles, and in time lost our fear, though we observed a certain caution to the end. The most troublesome habit of the lochs was that of becoming perfectly thick after a night of wind and rain, and even in the rare and short intervals of quiet weather the water in them was always full of floating particles. I think the fish would have risen better in clearer water, but even as it was we found that some fish would take so long as the colour of the lochs remained black; when the colour became brown, fishing in them was hopeless.

The third and most interesting sort of fishing was in the voes in salt water. There was one voe some two miles in length, with two small burns about a quarter of a mile apart at the head of it. It looked a likely place upon the large map, and we walked over to it one Sunday afternoon to see and hear what we could. There were a few crofters near the sea at the place, and we were told by one of them that fish were seen jumping in the voe in September, and that some one was supposed to have fished there once and caught nothing. We thought this hopeful, for where fish are seen in Shetland they may be caught, and one day I walked over to experiment. I seldom spent a more wretched and hopeless morning. There was no sign of a sea trout, and to be wading amongst sea weed, throwing small flies in common salt water with a split cane rod, seemed perfectly foolish and mad. The burns were only large enough for minnows, and I could see that there was nothing in them. Discomfort was added to hopelessness, for my mackintosh had been forgotten, and some miles of rough peat hags and bogs were between me and the house: the morning had been fine, but about ten o'clock a series of cold, pitiless storms began, which lashed the voe with wind and heavy rain. This would not have been intolerable, if it had not been for the long waders, without which the deep water of the voe could not be reached; but to stand in heavy rain with waders nearly up to the arm-pits, and without an overcoat, is to turn oneself into a receptacle for collecting fresh water. Desolate hills rose immediately behind, and as each storm came frowning up over the top of them, I retired from the water and crouched behind an old boat on the shore till the fury was past. After some hours of flogging the sea, hooking only sea weed, and dodging the storms, there was no spirit left in me. Blank despair overwhelmed me, and I turned to go. My back was to the water, but I had got only a few paces from it when I heard a splash, and looking round, saw where a fish had jumped, the first sign of one seen that day. I went straight to the place and caught a sea trout almost at once, and in the few remaining hours of the day landed sixteen pounds' weight of fish with fly. It may not seem a very heavy basket, but it was something to carry over the moor in addition to heavy waders, and not to be despised as a contrast to the prospect of the morning. I had a delightful reaction from despair to good spirits, and the satisfaction which perhaps a successful prospector or pioneer feels in a new country. The largest fish that day was under three pounds, but I lost one or two good fish in sea weed, and saw some much larger.

We still had much to learn about that voe and the trout there. They moved with the tide, and we had to understand their habits and follow their movements. Sometimes the burns had been in flood, and brought down muddy fresh water which floated on the top of the sea water. A good wind soon carried this out to sea, but if the wind was blowing up instead of down the voe, it dammed back all the burn water at the head, and made fishing impossible. Much time was spent in learning these and other tricks or secrets of the place.

Some of the trout in the sea were brown trout. The largest we caught weighed four pounds and three-quarters, and several were over two pounds. They were perfectly distinct from the sea trout, and had yellow under-sides and some red spots, but their flesh was in colour and flavour that of sea trout. We saw several grilse and small salmon jumping in this voe, and in October they turned quite red without having been in fresh water at all, but we did not succeed in hooking any of them. I suppose that none of the large fish, neither salmon, sea trout, nor brown trout, attempted to enter the little burns till they were quite ready to spawn. They then could have gone only a little way up in a flood, and no doubt returned to the sea immediately after having spawned.

We were told that there were no true salmon in Shetland, but we certainly caught many fish from three pounds to six pounds, which were exactly like grilse, and would have been called grilse without hesitation anywhere else. They were quite distinct from the sea trout, though the latter overlapped the grilse in size, and our largest sea trout were heavier than our smallest grilse. Some of the large fish, which were jumping in the voes, were apparently salmon, and perhaps we might have hooked some of them, if we had used some large bait instead of flies, but we were always having some success with flies, expecting still more, and experimenting with flies of different kinds, and so the time passed away. In spite of the forked tail and other distinctions, I cannot say that I always find it quite easy to be sure whether a fish which I have landed is a large grilse or a small salmon; but the difference between sea trout and grilse seems to me clear enough, for the one is unmistakably a trout, and the other is not.

Migratory *salmonidae* are generally divided into three species—*salmo salar, salmo eriox,* and *salmo trutta.* Of *salmo eriox,* the bull trout, I have had no experience. It has the reputation of being a powerful fish, but a very bad riser, and in rivers such as the Coquet of being almost useless for angling purposes. As a kelt it takes a fly well enough in the spring. *Salmo trutta,* the salmon trout, is, I believe, the best sporting fish for its size in the world. There seem to me to be two distinct classes of *salmo trutta.* There is the mature fish, which ranges in weight from one

pound up to five pounds as a rule, and may grow exceptionally to much larger weights; and there is a smaller
fish, which enters the rivers rather later in vast quantities. This latter ranges in weight from four ounces to any
size up to one pound. It goes by various names on different
rivers, but is commonly supposed to be the grilse of *salmo
trutta,* and both in its appearance and in its rash unwary
nature, it has all the characteristics of being a young fish,
which is mature neither in mind nor body. In most rivers,
however, these fish of the smaller class seem to outnumber
the mature sea trout of all ages, which is not the case,
taking all the season through, as between grilse and
salmon.

Sometimes I think that sea trout fishing is the best of all
sport. It combines all the wildness of salmon fishing, with
the independence of trout fishing, and one may have all
the excitement of hooking large fish without using a heavy
rod and heavy tackle. There is less rule and less formality
about it than there is about salmon fishing, and there
seems more scope for the individuality of the angler. Perhaps this is partly because the sea trout season comes so
directly after a long period of work in the stale air of cities,
and coincides with the first burst into freedom and fresh
atmosphere. The difference is so great in August, after a
few days of exercise in the air of the North, that there
come times when the angler, who wanders alone after sea
trout down glens and over moors, has a sense of physical
energy and strength beyond all his experience in ordinary
life. Often after walking a mile or two on the way to the
river, at a brisk pace, there comes upon one a feeling of
"fitness," of being made of nothing but health and strength
so perfect, that life need have no other end but to enjoy
them. It is as though till that moment one had breathed
with only a part of one's lungs, and as though now for the
first time the whole lungs were filling with air. The pure
act of breathing at such times seems glorious. People talk
of being a child of nature, and moments such as these are
the times when it is possible to feel so; to know the full joy
of animal life—to desire nothing beyond. There are times
when I have stood still for joy of it all, on my way through

the wild freedom of a Highland moor, and felt the wind, and looked upon the mountains and water and light and sky, till I felt conscious only of the strength of a mighty current of life, which swept away all consciousness of self, and made me a part of all that I beheld.

THE BEST-LOVED TROUT STREAM OF THEM ALL

Corey Ford

Memories of America's most famous trout river, the Beaverkill, during its glory days of the twenties and thirties.

They've torn down the old covered bridge at Rockland, beneath whose porcupine-chewed timbers I caught a muskrat once on a dry fly, a No. 14 Light Cahill, as I recall. He was not a very large muskrat, but I had him hooked securely through an ear, and he put a permanent set in my 4-ounce Thomas rod before I managed to beach him on the side of the pool. The ancient structure is gone now, replaced by an efficient steel span; but the pool is still there, and the dark lovely run below it, and the succeeding miles of foaming swirls and fast eddies that have made the Beaverkill—for me, at least—the best-loved of them all.

I suppose it's the historic American trout stream. Generations of anglers have floundered through its rapids, and tripped over their waders in its cold deep holes, and hung up their backcasts in the hemlocks along its banks. Leading sportsmen from all over the world have come to whip its legendary pools. The record brook trout in New York State, 8½ pounds, was taken in one of its tributaries. It was here in the Catskills that the art of dry-fly tying was born in America, some sixty years ago, when Theodore Gordon created the famous Quill that bears his name. Many of our other popular patterns, the Hendrickson and the Fan-wing Royal and the Female Beaverkill, were designed to imitate the insects hatching along the Beaverkill's grassy banks.

I was born on the Beaverkill myself, in a manner of speaking. I learned to cast a dry fly over Barnhart's Pool, under the choleric instruction of Ted Townsend, the old master. I've fished many hundred streams since, but to this day, whenever I look down on a promising bit of water in Canada or Alaska, I find myself comparing it with Barnhart's, or Junction Pool, or Cairn's. They're all still there, the fine old pools with names that fall like music on the ear. Barrel Pool, and Hendrickson's, and Horse Brook Run, and School House Rocks, where at night the big browns still make flying fish of the dace in the riffles. Mountain Pool, and Wagon Wheel Pool, and Cemetery Pool, and Painter's Bend, where I saw Ted Townsend land a 5-pound brook by moonlight on a No. 18 Black Gnat. The Forks at Roscoe, and Ferdon's Eddy, and Desbrow's Pool, named after the dour undertaker who used to rise before dawn each morning and stake his claim in the center of his favorite stretch, fending off all intruders by casting his fly vigorously in their general direction. Once, when Desbrow was summoned home to conduct the obsequies for a prominent citizen who had thoughtlessly died in the middle of fishing season, I sneaked into his pool and managed to hook a 2-pound squaretail just as Dezzy returned panting to the stream. Before his apoplectic gaze I scooped up the trout in my net and held it aloft for him to see. The strands of the net gave way, the trout fell back into the current and was instantly whisked out of sight. I made my way to the bank without a word, and Dezzy stalked past me triumphantly and took his place in the middle of the pool. For all I know, he's still there.

The stream has changed since the good old days, of

course. The flood-control boys have shoved their bulldozers through the center of some of the finest pools to deepen the channel, and subsequent spring freshets have thrown up ugly gravel beds and partially filled the favorite holes. The generally lowered water tables in the East, dropping stead-ily since the early '30's, have killed off a large part of the nymph life, and the fly hatches today are sparse and un-predictable. They've built a public camp site below Lew-beach, with fifty-three permanent fireplaces, running water, and sanitary facilities—public toilets, no less— where Gene Wright and I used to roll up in our sleeping bags and wait for the early morning rise. They've put in a modern paved highway where the old winding road used to follow the river, and more and more anglers zip up from the city each year to dredge the holes with worms. Auto-mobile tires and empty beer cans and old boots litter the spawning beds. The last time I visited the Beaverkill, there was a diving board over my favorite pool, and a fam-ily of picnickers were tossing eggshells unconcernedly into the sacred waters.

2 2 8

The fishing isn't what it used to be, they tell you today. When I first fished the Beaverkill, over twenty-five years ago, they told me sadly: "The fishing nowadays isn't what it was." I suppose that when Hendrick Hudson sailed up to the Catskills, the Indians told him: "You should have dis-covered this place a hundred years ago. That's when the fishing was really good." It doesn't matter: a trout stream is more than the fish in it. A great trout stream like the Beaverkill is a legend, a fly book filled with memories, a part of the lives of all the devoted anglers, living or dead, who ever held a taut line in its current. A generation from now, I have no doubt they'll still be standing on the same rocks and hammering the same pools, and climbing back up the bank with the same empty creels and the same in-sistent alibis: The water was too high. The water was too low. It was too hot. It was too cold. It was too bright. It was too dark. The fishing isn't what it used to be. . . .

This wide placid river, flowing westward through New York State to join the East Branch of the Delaware near the Pennsylvania border, has led a tumultuous life. It was born in humble surroundings in the heart of the Catskills, just west of Slide Mountain. A mere pewling freshet, it left home at an early age and worked its determined way south, cascading down the mountainside on its slippery bottom, foraging across the boggy meadows, feeding hungrily on every spring hole and trickle. By the time it crossed into Sullivan County it had grown to be a brawling brook—it fought under the name of Little Beaverkill—which could take on any angler and throw him in its strong current. It wrestled its way south, in a series of swift falls, past the towns of Beaverkill and Rockland down to Roscoe. There it met the gentle Willowemoc, an attractive trout stream from the east, and their romance was consummated in a happy marriage of waters at Junction Pool. The Willowemoc gracefully surrendered its identity, and the Big Beaverkill, a broad and mature river now, settled down contentedly amid pastoral meadows to raise its prolific family of brook trout and browns and rainbows.

229

It is an ideal trout stream, with much of its watershed still protected by good forest cover, and underlaid by a rock formation favorable to water conservation. Its source is at 2,860 feet, and the average rate of fall is about 42 feet per mile, making its course just swift enough. There are no ponds, artificial or otherwise, and no falls or dams that would be a barrier to fish. In all but the lowest stretch, the stream temperature is suitable for browns and rainbows, and the upper mileage is cold enough to support square-tails all summer. The bottom is strewn with blocky boulders, which offer good shelter for trout; and an abundance of small feeder tributaries, such as Russell and Berry Brooks, provide natural nursery streams.

Probably the outstanding reason that the Beaverkill achieved its fame is the fantastic amount of insect life that flourishes along its course each May and June. I have never seen such hatches of flies along a trout stream, before or since. There was usually a smaller hatch in the morning, I remember, but the great hatches used to occur between 6 and 9 of an evening. Avid anglers would patrol the stream in shifts all afternoon, as far down as Cooks

Falls, waiting to spot the first telltale insects moving upstream. You could always tell when a hatch was about to
begin. A car would streak along the road, a breathless fisherman would race up the porch steps to awaken his slumbering partner and snatch a pair of waders from the hook
by the door. As the magic word spread, more and more
anglers would pour out of their lodgings, struggling into
fishing jackets and shouldering creels as they ran. Within
minutes the whole placid valley would be boiling with activity as excited fishermen braked their cars beside the
stream in a spurt of gravel, scrambled past each other
down the bank, and waded out into their chosen pools, rod
in hand, ready for the fateful moment.

You waited there in ominous silence. The stream flowed
past you quietly, with nary a rise to mar its smooth untroubled surface. The sun was setting, and the waning
lemon light glinted on the wings of a couple of large dun-
colored flies drifting lazily in the air. Another fly appeared,
and then several more; they seemed to come mysteriously
from nowhere. All at once the sky overhead was filled with
them. They beat upstream horizontally like snowflakes
driven by a gale, fluttering against your face, zigzagging
heavily down, down toward the water, flopping exhausted
at last onto the stream. Abruptly, as they lit, the quiet pool
exploded all around you with hungry trout. There seemed
to be a fish for every fly. A great brown rose before you; as
you cast to it, a big brookie turned at your feet: a couple of
monsters struck simultaneously at an insect just behind
you. The blizzard of flies continued to swirl past you, the
pool bubbled and seethed as though someone were tossing
handfuls of pebbles into the stream, the splashes of breaking trout mingled with the skirl of your reel and the song
of your tight line cutting across the current in the final
dusk.

I don't know to this day which insects made up the biggest hatches. Some say they were may flies; others insist
they were coffin flies; still others argue they were stones.
The controversy still rages among old-timers. Most of them
incline to the belief that they were stones, perhaps out of
deference to Art Tyler, of Livingston Manor, who claimed

he used an artificial stone to take that 10¼-pound 30-inch brown near Elk Brook on May 17, 1930. On the other hand, I remember a 4½-pound brown, in the icebox at Ferdon's, which was definitely taken on a Yellow May. I know. I was on the other end of the line.

My fishing partner in those days was Tom Wenning, now the drama editor of *Newsweek* Magazine, and the only man I have ever known who could fall into a stream clear over his head and come up again with his pipe still going. We always stayed at Ferdon's, a rambling friendly boarding-house on the bank of the Beaverkill, just above the famous pool that bears its name. Ferdon's catered to fishermen. There were nails along the clapboards of the front porch on which to rest your rod at night, and you could hang your waders over the railing to dry, and take off your wet pants in the living room and wring out your socks in the fire-place. Somehow, whenever I write a fishing story, I always seem to be describing Ferdon's: the smoke-filled upstairs bedroom with our freshly greased enameled line draped over the chandelier and our boots comfortably crossed on the white counterpane as we oiled our reels; the spacious icebox with its individual pans of trout, each marked with the owner's name; the dining room where we lingered over coffee to tell about the ones that got away: "Here I had him right up to the net, he'd have gone five pounds, maybe six, I wouldn't have been surprised if he went seven or even eight...."

It was at Ferdon's that I first came to know Ted Town-send, the fabled game warden of Westchester County, a violent, opinionated, profane, wonderful man, the most complete angler I have ever known. Ted was a true artist with the dry fly. His partner, Melly Rosch of White Plains, used to claim that Ted could place a Female Beaverkill on the water so naturally that a male Beaverkill, flying above it, would light alongside and attempt to mate it on the spot. Ted never admitted this, though on the other hand he never denied it; but I know for a fact that he could catch a trout when there wasn't one there. I've seen him do it. He would stand beside a deep run and float his fly down over it patiently, forty or fifty times, until some slumbering brown, peering up blearily at the succession of tidbits passing overhead, would conclude that the evening hatch had begun ahead of time and would rouse himself to strike at Ted's lure on the fifty-first cast.

Ted tied his own flies, of course, usually right on the bank. He would arrive at streamside with a long butterfly net in which he would capture the several insects hovering over the water. Then he would repair to a nearby rock, spread out the specimens beside him, and consider them thoughtfully for a while. Once he had made up his mind which succulent insect seemed to be the chef's special for that day, he would open a large sewing basket he always carried, take out a small vise, scissors, spools of varicolored silk thread, skeins of wool, peacock herl, tinsel and assorted feathers, and skillfully fashion a facsimile of the fly so accurate that it used to fool me, let alone the fish. Ted was always a stickler for color, insisting that a trout could detect the slightest difference in shades. In support of this argument, he liked to cite an experience he had a few years back, when he stopped at a stationery store in Liberty and, more or less out of kindness to the proprietor, purchased three very old and faded Royal Coachmen which had been standing in the window so long that the sun had bleached their red windings to a vague pink. That afternoon, when no other fisherman on the stream was able to raise so much as a chub, Ted's three odd-colored Coachmen did a rushing business until dark. "It isn't the fish who are color-blind," Ted used to roar, "it's the goddam fishermen."

In addition to his other accomplishments, Ted added a new refinement to the angling art. He employed a trout spotter. While Tom Wenning and Ted and I would sit on the bank of the stream, smoking and playing endless games of Ghost, his loyal partner Melly would cruise up and down the highway in an open car, peering at the various pools through his binocular. Whenever he detected a rise, he would race back upstream, honk the horn violently, and bellow down to us: "Hurry up! Quick! I saw one come up twice, down at Cook's Falls!" Ted would drive back with him and take the trout, lead it to the net, and then gently release it. I never knew anyone who loved the sport more. Ted has gone now to the Happy Fishing Grounds; but I am confident at this moment that he is using a golden harpstring for a leader, and casting a Fan-wing Royal tied with white feathers plucked from his wing.

Ted Townsend was part of a great tradition that began in this country in 1890, when Theodore Gordon, the leading American angling authority of his time, received a packet of dry flies from the great English angler, F. M. Halford. Each fly was carefully identified in Halford's own handwriting, with appropriate flourishes, and his accompanying letter stated: "I can quite imagine that in some parts of your country fish could be taken with dry fly where the more usual sunk fly would be of no avail. My difficulty however as to advising you of patterns likely to be successful is chiefly due to the fact that I have no knowledge of the streams or lakes nor of the genera and species of natural flies prevalent in them....Knowing your own rivers, you can select the patterns which seem likely, and dress them yourself."

Thus the dry fly winged across the Atlantic to the New Word, and settled on the Beaverkill to stay. One of Gordon's first improvisations on the Halford patterns was the Quill Gordon—long my own favorite trout fly—of which he wrote modestly: "The quill is a very troublesome fly on a/c of its hackle, but as a dry fly it is typical of certain ephemera and I have had some remarkable experiences with it." The letters and notes of Theodore Gordon have been collected and edited with loving care by John McDonald in a fine volume titled *The Complete Fly Fisherman*, published by Scribner's, an American classic comparable to Walton's *Compleat Angler;* and the historic packet of Halford flies are today in the possession of Gordon's early fishing companion and pupil, Roy Steenrod, State Game Protector of Liberty, N. Y. Each summer week Steenrod visits the New York State Conservation Department's Education Camp for boys near De Bruce, to instruct the teenage outdoorsmen on the traditions of American fly tying and the proper use of the rod. There could be no finer teacher.

Gordon's influence still lives in the thriving school of fly tying practicing in Sullivan County today: Roy Steenrod himself, the creator of the immortal Hendrickson and the somewhat less known but increasingly popular Murray's Favorite; Reub Cross of the Neversink, a disciple of Gordon's, one of the country's leading professional fly tyers; the Harry Darbees of Livingston Manor; and the W. C. Dettes of Roscoe, N. Y. When I first knew Walt Dette, he was a gangling youngster working in Sipple's Drugstore in Roscoe, and improving his time, between mixing chocolate ice-cream sodas and dispensing liver pills, by tying trout flies surreptitiously behind the counter. Each afternoon after hours I would go fishing with Walt and his pal Harry Darbee in the stream behind the town. I can still see Walt splashing across the rapids in dungarees and high leather boots—he always scorned waders, and would wallow through the water up to his waist in the most frigid weather—and casting one or another of his homemade flies accurately into the jaws of a rising trout. Today Walt and his attractive wife Winnie have risen to the top of their profession, fashioning some of the most perfect feathered lures produced anywhere, here or in England. Perhaps I am prejudiced: Walt named a trout fly after me once, the Corey Ford fly, a cream-colored pattern with a gray body and a long black tail. It was not a very good resemblance—my own body tends more or less to the conventional pink, and I seldom wear a long black tail except to formal weddings—but I was flattered, none the less. I have been waiting ever since for Walt to fashion a Corey Ford trout that will take the fly.

Some famous brethren of the angle have been members of the Beaverkill fraternity: John Taintor Foote, beloved author of *The Wedding Gift;* George M. La Branche, whose *The Dry Fly on Fast Water* has been for years a potent influence on fishermen in this country; Dan Holland, one of the nation's leading trout authorities and, I think, the finest fly caster I have ever known; Bill Schaldach, the noted outdoor artist and etcher; Sparse Grey Hackle, of course, who has fished the stream longer than anyone else can remember; John Alden Knight, inventor of the solunar

234

tables, which are devised to tell fishermen when the trout will bite. (Unfortunately Mr. Knight has never found out how to make sure the trout read his tables.)

The old gang still hangs out at Keener's, and the Beaverkill Club, and the Brooklyn Flyfishing Club though some of the familiar faces have begun to be missed of late. Pop Robbins, and Louis Rhead, and A. E. Hendrickson and his friend Stevenson; Jim Payne, and Bob Whyte, the Scottish bootmaker from New York who could yell louder than anyone else except Ted Townsend, and Jack Cauchois, the bucktail champ in fast water, and Herbert Pendleton, and Jack Mercer. The Foster brothers from Wilkes Barre, Art Neu and Ken Lockwood from New Jersey, Lou Petrie and Melly Rosch and Tom Foster and Hyney and Schirmer from White Plains....

They still take the occasional trophy trout. Clayton Seagears, genial director of Conservation Education for New York State, a veteran angler who knows and loves the Catskill waters, reports that the boys are bringing in big fish with about the same regularity as of old. Every year Niles Fairbairn, caretaker of the Conservation Education Camp at De Bruce, takes several over 5 pounds, though now he fishes only on moonless nights with a black fly tied on a No. 6 hook. Mike Lane of Liberty points with pride to a 6-pounder brown taken at the Lewbeach bridge pool on a squirrel-tail fly tied for him by Reub Cross. Seagears recalls that a Red Ibis, of all things, took a couple of other 6-pounders in the Cook's Falls pool, and a brown going over 6½ pounds fell to a dark wet fly at night in the run below the old Sprague school. The old familiar patterns are still the most popular—the Quill Gordon, the Hendrickson, the Cahills and the rest. The big lunkers still lurk beneath the overhanging rhododendron and laurel, and at night, standing with a flashlight on School House rocks, you can see Old Chisel Jaws rolling at the tail of the pool, just as he used to roll a quarter century ago.

Wisely the New York State Conservation Department, which rates the Beaverkill one of the best naturally productive trout streams in the state, is working hard to offset the ever-increasing rod pressure. Stocking has been increased substantially in recent seasons. Last year, for example, 15,300 7½-inch browns and fifty 10-inch browns, plus 1,000 5-inch rainbows, were planted in the Delaware County part of the Beaverkill, up to a point midway between Roscoe and Cook's Falls. In the Sullivan County part of the stream, 8,700 7-inch browns, 800 7½-inch, 400 8-inch and 100 12-inch fish were released, along with a lesser number of rainbow, and every public feeder stream was likewise heavily stocked. This year, with the new Catskill Fish Hatchery at De Bruce in full operation for the first time, more than 40,000 pounds of trout were shelled out for the Catskill region alone, probably a state record in public stocking.

Other signs are encouraging. Wanton deforestation is under control in the Beaverkill watershed. The acid wood in the Catskills has virtually all been cut out, and manufacturing operations greatly reduced, and there have been no fish kills reported for a long time from the acid-factory business. The Conservation Department's pollution unit is constantly checking, but it doesn't seem to see any red light right now. Still better news, the threatened Beaverkill reservoir project to supply more water for New York City—a nightmare that has haunted sportsmen for a long time—has evidently been abandoned. The New York City Department of Water Supply, Gas and Electricity has elected to tap supplies on the Delaware instead—for which information every Beaverkill angler, aware of what happened to the Neversink, can breathe a profound sigh of relief.

Last but not least, the amount of posted water has been greatly reduced, and the state now owns a total of over fourteen miles of perpetual public fishing rights, mostly on the big water downstream from Roscoe. The Beaverkill Club and the Brooklyn Flyfishing Club still own sections of the stream which are closed to nonmembers; but, since they control and stock these waters, regularly, the posted areas serve as valuable reservoirs of trout that benefit the entire stream. Besides, it's always more fun when there are a few closed sections of a stream into which an ama-

teur poacher can slip his fly now and then. Some of my
most enjoyable moments were had when I used to sneak
into the forbidden water of Russell Brook, presided over by
an obdurate character named G. I. Treyz. I wonder how
many times I have torn my waders scrambling over the
barbed wire in headlong retreat, pursued by Mr. Treyz's
irate cries.

Another favorite poaching preserve of mine, as I recall,
was the deep run just below a forbidding stone mansion on
the Little Beaverkill, known as Craigie Clair. There was
always something of a mystery about Craigie Clair. Rumor
had it that the sole occupant was a beautiful but demented
young girl, who used to let down her golden hair from an
upstairs window and lure unwary anglers into her granite
castle, for what probably amounted to nothing worse than
an afternoon's pleasant seduction. I fished past Craigie
Clair hopefully a number of times, but I never got lured.
Maybe I wasn't the type. A few years ago, I understand,
the estate was sold to Father Divine—Peace, It's Wonderful—as a piscatorial heaven for his anglers.

No, the fishing isn't what it used to be. The current is
faster, it seems to me, and the rocks are more slippery
when you step up on them. It's farther to the other side of
the stream these days, and they've added a couple of bends
in the river that I never noticed before. The bank is higher
when you try to climb back to your car. And the kind of
leaders they're putting out nowadays are so fine you have
to hold them farther and farther away from your eyes to
see them, and it's getting harder to make out these modern
flies on the water.

The fishermen may change; but the Beaverkill never
grows old, any more than a legend can age, or a song. New
fishermen will arrive each year to spot its rises, and wade
its rapids, and explore its deep swift runs for the first time.
There's a likely looking pool, now. Barnhart's, I hear it's
called. I wonder if anybody ever fished it before. Maybe I'm
the first ever to put my fly over that fast eddy behind the
rock. . . .

Look out, young man. Watch your backcast; the ghosts of
a hundred departed anglers are standing behind you. That

pool you are entering was once the favorite fishing hole of John Taintor Foote. Ted Townsend used to perch atop that very rock on which you are standing now. Perhaps Theodore Gordon dropped his first Quill over that same dark eddy where you have just cast your fly.

Good luck, young man, and good fishing. I hope you take that big old brown that lies below the boulder. I've been trying for him myself for twenty-five years.

HATCH OF HATCHES

Charles K. Fox

On countless streams, the diminutive "sulphurs" offer the year's most prolonged and productive dry-fly fishing.

There is a distinct similarity between cattle and casters in that each regards the grass as being greener on the other side of the fence. The following proves it in the case of a caster, one C. K. Fox. Involved was the combination of location, hatch and rise.

It was not by accident but because of accident that I was here, this being about the only place I could get to in order to fish at all. The nerve which runs down the back of the leg had been pinched in an accident, making driving and walking painful, the getting into and out of boots or waders a virtual two-man job, and contention with current, mud, and slippery rocks all but prohibitive. Driving time from home to this spot was a painfully long ten minutes; from parked car to pool, a hard two-minute walk, and from there casting distance was fifty feet and less. This particularly convenient place had been passed up before, the only reason being that greener pastures seemed to lie beyond.

It did not feel good to settle down on the wooden shot-gun-shell box, which had been brought along for that purpose; but it felt worse to stand. Upstream fifty feet was a beautiful, five-foot, natural waterfall in the big brook or the little river, nomenclature depending upon where you are from. In front was a flow of smooth water about two feet deep beside a high stone wall crowned with a dense growth of lilac. Fifty feet below was a low log dam with an interesting brushpile across the far corner. Actually the location was directly in back of a house in a small town, but I could see no one, or no house for that matter, from my low place under a canopy of high foliage; and no one would be seeing me. There wasn't even a dog around to protect his home against the crippled stranger armed with a little fly rod. The tumbling and splashing of water was a soul satisfying sound.

There had to be some trout in the deep picture pool featuring the falls and some more trout under the brushpile, and most certainly the surface feeders among them would know about the evening Sulphur hatch and would have developed a feeding pattern to capitalize upon it. Maybe their feeding stations would be nicely spaced within my range between the tail of the pool and the breast of the dam. That is what I hoped for in my fishing from one spot, a sort of fisherman's throne. Enthusiasm was mounting. It looked so fishy and buggy and the stream stretch was so beautiful that a feeling of guilt crept over me for overlooking its potential in the past.

240

The sun was setting in a red west when the first Sulphur dun appeared on the surface. The canary-colored wings were cocked skyward. There was a futile attempt to become airborn as the insect appeared to bounce on the water. For another yard it rode the surface; then again the wings were tested. This time the beautiful little fly could follow the dictates and intent of Nature and climb slowly and unsteadily away from the water and into the waiting arms of the overhead foliage. There it would undergo a strange metamorphose: the shedding of the skin and the sealing of the mouth. In an evening or two, and symbolically in the evening of its life, he or she would fly to the corridor over the water to perform the only remaining mission in life but its most important, procreation.

There followed other emerging sub-imagos, first breaking through the surface tension, the lift into the air, then the slow laborious flight into the foliage. Thus the evening hatch of duns was in progress. Now several could be seen at one time in the air and another just leaving the water.

Something else was stirring too. The imagos were leaving the leaves to mill about the high boughs of the trees, the tops of which are still bathed in sunlight. Now the flight in quest of mates on those cleared and strengthened wings was sure and fast. For every dun which left the water, there seemed to be 100 spinners milling above, the difference in numbers being because the duns emerge slowly over a period of time whereas the spinners return in mass.

Before my eyes a dun riding on the surface disappeared in a dimple. It was the first rise of the evening, a little fish in what I thought of as my stretch. Shortly there was another dimple, another slurp and another casualty in the aquatic insect world. I sat on the box and watched. The rod set up and ready to go, Sulphur imitation included, was propped up against a bush, but I did not reach for the equipment.

241

The spinners were pairing up and their quick irregular flight was bringing them closer to the water. The tempo increased in their excited nuptial dance. Exhausted males would drop helter skelter, some landing on the water, others on the land. Their normal passing, so unlike the normal death of the members of the animal kingdom, was one of ecstasy. The females carried on to deliver their precious cargoes of egg masses to the right place in the stream. Nature steered them to broken well-aerated water. In a general way their irregular flight was upstream. Any time a nymph becomes unattached it is carried along with the current, thus the upstream flight of the fertilized females insures population of the entire watershed, otherwise in the course of time a hatch would work its way out of a stream.

Now in the failing light, there were duns, dead males and spent female spinners on the water before me. Some drifting flies were traveling in every line of drift. And in every line of drift there was a feeding trout. The better fish were in the better places. This was obvious because of the variation in the rise forms and the sound of the rises. Within casting distance were approximately fifteen voraciously feeding fish, three of which appeared to be extremely good ones. The reaction of one Pennsylvania-German friend to this would have been: "The fly is up, the rise is on."

Nature was staging a fantastic display. By the time the greens darkened and black velvet patterns melted into the silvery background of flowing water, activity was at its zenith. It was the lush time of year, the period before the hot-weather burn, and the most comfortable time to be abroad of an evening. As I sat there in the half light not disposed to stir, I watched the flies in the air and the rings on the water. It was then that I realized that this is the best hatch of all for me, therefore it should be my favorite. You may call them "Little Yellow Drakes," "Pale Watery Duns" or "Little Light Cahills," I call them "Sulphurs." In the days before Charlie Wetzel and Preston Jennings had produced their books relating to the naturals and their imitations Bob McCafferty and I were attempting to identify and classify hatches. In order to understand each other, in our fishing talk back and forth, we had to give insects names, and appropriately these were the "Sulphurs."

Thus this chapter has to do with what to my way of thinking is the most important hatch, the greatest hatch, the most interesting hatch. Involved are: stage setting, the actors and the action. Let's start at the beginning.

In our trout world why do so many rave about dry-fly fishing? It is because everything about it is prolonged and much is visible. Things start before a fish is hooked and there are times when hooking requires considerable doing. One sees the hatch, then the rise forms, then he attempts to watch the hatch, then he delivers his offering, then he watches it drift into the window of the fish. Anticipation is prolonged, expectation is prolonged, execution is prolonged. If things are right, that is if the fly and the float are right as far as *the* trout is concerned, the fly disappears in a ring and when the angler tightens the line there is a living throbbing resistance. Electrifying impact is appropriate phraseology to describe the contact.

Here is a unique hatch because it prevails over a long period of time. This not only establishes a feeding pattern on the part of the fish, but it makes for selectivity. In lowland streams early stragglers mark their appearance in late April. Further north and in higher altitudes the date is deferred. On some streams the hatch is in full bloom by May 10.

Early Sulphurs have a blueish wing and in my judgment the most effective size of pattern is number 16. Duns appear on the water in the afternoon, and the fall of spinners starts before sundown. By Decoration Day though, the flies are a bit smaller and the wings of the dun are canary yellow. The time of emergence of the duns is after sundown and the fall of spinners takes place in the failing light. This situation continues for weeks on end, a real bonanza. A number 18 fly now does a better job than a 16. Whether these two which slightly differ in appearance and size are separate and distinct species or whether they are different stages of the same species is academic. Only an entomologist by careful microscopic examination can identify the various drakes (mayflies) and the work must be done with male spinners—not duns and not females—it is that highly specialized.

There are at least two species of the same size and color but I suspect more. *Epeorus vitrea* has two tails, whereas *Ephemerella dorothea* has three. Both become airborn quickly, the duns doing a minimum of drifting. The spinners furnish the bulk of the fishing.

Over the years two common and popular patterns have been employed to match these hatches, or if you prefer this hatch: Light Cahill and Pale Evening Dun. To this can be added two more standard patterns but not so well known: Tup's Indispensible (American version) and R. B. Fox (R. B. for Ray Bergman and Fox because the body material is light colored belly fur from a vixen). To this quartet of workables I want to add two more specials, and therein lies a tale worth telling.

George Harvey of Pennsylvania State University, or more appropriately of the Central Pennsylvania limestone streams, and I, engaged one winter in a little patter which went something like this:

    H. "I have finally come up with an improved sulphur imitation which works better than other patterns."

    F. "So have I."

    H. "The trout usually take this one with confidence and without hesitation."

    F. "Same with mine."

    H. "This pattern is the result of trial and error."

    F. "Mine too."

    H. "It has an off-color in it which to the human eye does not appear in the natural."

    F. "So does mine."

    H. "Funny thing, the odd color is bright orange."

    F. "Yes, bright orange."

    H. "You sound like Charlie McCarthy."

    F. "I'm serious."

    H. "Mine has two colors of hackle, a few turns of honey and a few turns of orange, intermingled; otherwise specs are same as Pale Evening Dun."

    F. "Here is where I get out of the rut. Mine has an orange gantron body, otherwise specs are same Pale Evening Dun."

For my sulphur fishing I would not be without either of these two. Sometimes I start out in the evening with one, sometimes the other. There are times when one does not seem to suit a particular fish but the other will, so before I give up I prefer to show a discriminating fish both. For old time sake once in a while I turn to a Pale Evening Dun, an R. B. Fox or a Tup's Indispensable. Often they will produce but it appears that the trout like the orange jobs a little better.

Vince Marinaro has two special patterns, one for the dun, the other for the spinner. His sub-imago imitation has upright wings cut from duck feathers dyed yellow and his thorax-style tie of hackle, that is hackle in the middle of the body; whereas he ties the imago with a body of ivory-colored porcupine quill, and wings, hackle points tied spent.

Imitation has been called the sincerest form of flattery. The best imitation for a given hatch is the one which delivers the highest success percentage. And so it goes with pattern, always an interesting phase of matching the hatch with the dry fly.

There are two reasons why the sulphur eaters are hyperselective—a polite way of saying they separate the men from the boys. This is a late hatch, for the yellows come last and by the time it comes along the suicide fish and the less discriminating fish have ended up in frying pans; and the stream is lower and clearer and the smaller pale fly is more difficult to imitate well than is the case with the bigger early season dark flies.

The stream flats are of particular interest because they carry so many of the better fish and rise forms can be seen so readily thereon, but flat water makes for examination and discrimination by both trout and angler, the trout because there is more time for scrutiny and for the angler because by rise forms he can spot the better fish.

How big are some of the surface feeders? The great Theodore Gordon answered that question in this way. "Fly fishing is more interesting where we know a few really big fish exist. They may be slow to rise, but give them a fair chance, they will take a fly occasionally." He also wrote, "In a low stage of water (trout) are very shy and secretive."

In reporting on the sulphurs and in writing about George Harvey and Theodore Gordon it should be pointed out that the latter fished in the home country of the former and he did so in sulphur time. The following was published in the old *Forest and Stream* magazine of March 14, 1903, under the name of Theodore Gordon and before the time of George Harvey:

> "Many years ago I was fishing a fine large limestone stream near Bellefonte, Pa., in company with a native of that town, who was a most expert angler and who cast in a particularly graceful manner. The scene of one afternoon's sport was a rather shallow mill dam constructed only a few years before; this dam

was full of brook trout of about a quarter of a pound each and they were rising steadily all over the water. We cast and cast, and compared the flies in our respective books. Finally in the envelope in the pocket of his book my friend found a small straw-colored fly closely approximating the fly at which the trout were rising. He put it on and in half an hour or a little over, caught 42 trout. He had only one fly of the kind, so I was forced to play audience, nothing I could offer being tempting to the fish."

There have been years when a rise to the sulphur produced the highlight of the season. Such happened to be the case for me in 1965. My eye was caught by a widening circle in the silvery smoothness and my ear by a slurp; obviously it was a big fish. The location lent itself to a long and dragless float, but should the fish be hooked, thirty feet downstream was a large man-made brushpile.

After a few drifts the fish sucked in the Harvey Sulphur and sank back apparently unperturbed by the connection. There was no bolt, no jump, just smug complacency. In about half a minute some violent jerking occurred as though the trout were corkscrewing. In spite of the protective light tip of the little rod this was too much for the 5X strand of nylon.

Several days later Dr. Dale Coman of Philadelphia, author of the salmon book dealing with Maine's Pleasant Stream, visited me. He had enjoyed an interesting day with big fish on a sinking black ant, but knowing him to be a dry fly man at heart I suggested at dusk, that he accompany me in an effort to add icing to the cake. Upon our arrival at the scene of my recent catastrophe we saw that the big fish was at it again—same place, same way, and the hatch was fine.

The good doctor looked over the situation. He tied his choice sulphur imitation to the leader. The line was lengthened and the distance measured by false casting. The fly dropped lightly to the surface five feet above the fish. It drifted without drag, a perfect delivery. That which was hoped for transpired—the fly disappeared in a little whirlpool and the hook point became imbedded. The fish simply settled back. After an apparent analysis of the situation it shook its head or twisted so violently that the leader could not take it. I knew exactly how the doctor felt and, too, what was going through his mind.

Subsequent evenings I watched for the big surface feeder but he did not show again but something else turned up. One evening what appeared to be two excellent fish put up along the grassy bank across the way about thirty feet apart. It was dusk and both were busy eating sulphurs.

Instead of working into casting position below the lower of the two and trying for him first, I elected to do something unorthodox. After cutting back from 5X to 4X and attaching the gantron sulphur, I literally sneaked into a casting position so that one fish was up and across and the other down and across.

More often than not, upon being hooked with a dry fly, these big stream-bred browns bolt upstream then jump, thus to increase chances for both it might be better to go after the upper one first in the attempt to avoid disturbance of the other. The stalk had been successful, for both fish continued to feed well.

Things worked fine. The upper fish took the fly, bolted upstream, jumped, then fought to hold that position. In due time it was landed without disturbing the lower trout. The fly was cleaned and dried by blowing on it, then pitched to fish number two with a quartering downstream kick-back cast. Confidently the trout took the imitation. And so it was that I took two eighteen inchers on back to back casts to highlight a season.

That troubled month, longer ago than it seems and longer ago than I like to think it was, I experienced some great fishing to rising trout from the shotgun-shell box along Cedar Run. Evening after evening and week after week sulphurs emerged and sulphurs returned, and evening after evening the trout rose. I know because I was there. None of these handsome fish were taken away from their beautiful place and some of them were caught and returned more than once.

By virtue of the duration of the sulphur hatch, its density, its consistency, its distribution; and by virtue of the activity it generates; and by virtue of the angling challenge it creates, here is the backbone for dusk fishing on many a stream for many a week. What a great fountainhead for rising trout are these wonderful Sulphurs at the bewitching hour which marks the completion of another day.

THE RIVER POOLS DOWNSTREAM

R. Palmer Baker, Jr.

Trouters may say they're fully satisfied by the intimacy of small-brook fishing, but the roll of a monster trout brings out the beast in them.

I n the summer months, the forest shade and cold currents of the headwater brooks can tempt the most sophisticated of anglers. The level of his favorite brook drops until there seems hardly enough for the smallest trout. Yet this is the season when the few comparatively big fish of the year are caught. In the dark woods and ravines above the farmhouse the little headwater pools are still cold with spring water. After the stream has run in spate from a summer rain, a few native fish of ten or twelve inches will move up to these pools from the warmer waters of the stream below.

One can be very content with this kind of fishing for a while. It suits the easy summer days. After supper, the angler takes his rod from the pegs on the farmhouse porch, slips a fly box into his hip pocket, and crosses the meadow to the woods upstream. There, kneeling in the shadow at the side of a clear run, he sees the refracted image of a nine-inch trout as it swims up from the cover of a tree root and takes its feeding station. A hatch of very small flies can be seen coming down with the current. They are non-descript, gray in color. The angler's fly, an Adams, is too large, but the color is close, and he decides to take a chance. Using only two rods' length of line and leader, and after easing a little downstream so that the horizontal back cast will not be seen by the trout, the angler is lucky and drops the fly in the water just above and to the side of the trout.

This time the trout turns and takes the fly quickly and surely. The fisherman gives himself the pleasure of allowing the fish to run a moment before he beaches it and returns it to the water. He walks contentedly downstream and comes out of the woods into the dusky meadow.

Then something happens to break this summer spell. It may be a turn in the weather. One afternoon as I fished a pasture brook in Vermont, the sky darkened and a wet wind came down the valley from the east. Suddenly I thought of the cold days of early spring, casting for big fish with the streamer fly, and I wanted to leave these upland valleys and narrow waters.

What I remembered was a rainy morning during the first week of May. A friend and I were fishing along the New York line, drifting weighted nymphs under the flooded stream banks. Only a few stocked trout had rewarded our efforts when, all at once, the cannibal browns came up from the depths and began to feed.

A hundred feet below the point where we were fishing the stream had flooded back through an alder thicket and covered the edges of a low-lying meadow with a foot or two of water. As I examined this location, a minnow jumped twice along the inshore edge of the thicket. Hurriedly I broke the nymph from my leader and tied on a streamer fly, a blue-green Supervisor. After approaching closer, I cast the fly to the point where the minnow had jumped. The result was immediate. A big trout struck the fly, jumped, and then took the line with him through the alders. He jumped once again on the other side, the blue-green Supervisor clear to view on the side of his jaw, and then, of course, he was gone.

One fish like this can make a season, but twice again during the next half hour I had a similar chance and lost it. Meanwhile, my companion landed a great sixteen-incher, the brown and white bucktail fly firmly embedded in its cannibal jaw.

Memory of this kind of fishing is bound to strain the angler's attachment to little trout and the upland streams. Only the actual sight of a cannibal brown can break it more cleanly.

In the eastern Adirondacks I know a spring brook which flows through a village—close to red brick houses and the main street, lined with sugar maples—to join the local river on its outskirts. The river fish spawn here in the fall, so the entire stretch is posted and protected. In the center of the village, at an intersection, there is a pool where many of the big fish stay all summer and fatten on the hamburger which is thrown to them by enthusiasts like my daughter.

Most of the fish in the pool are brown trout. If caught, they would scarcely be worth eating. They do not have the beauty of their little brothers and cousins. The biggest of them lie under the bridge in darkness, often ignoring the hamburger which is thrown to them. Yet as one leans over the railing of the bridge and perceives the dark shapes moving there in the shadowed water, the power and sagacity of these fish are so apparent that they always stir the imagination. As the smaller trout in the pool begin to splash and feed greedily on the surface, one of these big browns, these monsters, moves out from the bridge with a surge, rolls heavily to take one piece of hamburger, then another, and in a moment drops back to his hold. My daughter jumps with excitement and wonder, and I appreciate again why the charms of the little brooks and little trout are not enough to bind the angler. I am determined to set up my biggest rod again, get into waders, and fish the river pools downstream.

THE SPAWNING RUN

William Humphrey

The classic short novel about some very fishy goings-on at a Welsh salmon-fishing hotel.

dorset, may 12

The Itchen, the Test, the Frome: the fabled chalk streams of south England, where Dame Juliana Berners and Isaak Walton fished—here I am in the middle of them, it's spring, the season has opened, and I'd might as well be in the Sahara. Even the Piddle, known also as the Puddle—the brook running through the farm here—holds good trout. I have seen them hanging in the shallows above the millrace, resting from their run, reaccustoming themselves to fresh water—for these will be sea-run trout, gamest of them all, returning to spawn: broad in the shoulder, deep in the belly, spotted like the gravel of the stream bed so that at first you don't see them, only their rippling shadows on the bed. The personal property, every one of them, of Mr. "Porky" Mitchell, the meat-pie king. Eighty-five hundred pounds sterling he paid for the fishing in three miles of the stream for ten years. So Tom Mears, my landlord, tells me. I stroll over daily to watch these trout. They congregate below the signpost which reads STRICTLY PRIVATE FISHING, just downstream from the stone bridge with the weatherworn cast-iron plaque threatening transportation to Virginia to anyone found defacing it. Mr. Mitchell's water bailiff watches me.

dorset, may 13

The Anglo-Saxons are anglers. Here on Sundays queues of them with cane poles and minnow pails line the banks of the quarter-mile of public water. In and out among their lines one of Her Majesty the Queen's swans and her cygnets glide. The serenity is seldom disturbed by anybody's catching anything.

Nowhere is the class division more sharply drawn than in the national pastime. "Fishing in Britain," says the pamphlet sent me by The British Travel and Holiday Association, "falls into three classes: game, sea, and coarse." Read: upper, middle, and lower. Trout taken from the public water here must be returned; they are the property of Mr. Mitchell that have strayed. Only coarse fish may be kept by the coarse.

Discussed fishing with my new friends at The Pure Drop.

"Pike season don't begin for another two months, but there's some fair fishing round and about for roach, dace, tench," I'm told.

I remember reading those names of English fish in Walton, but what they are I don't know. They sound "coarse."

"I'm talking about trout," I say.

I get the look I've seen them give those who frequent the Saloon Bar, where the same beer costs tuppence ha'penny a pint more than it does here in the Public Bar. Bill Turner, speaking for them all, says, "Trout, is it? Ah well, I wouldn't know, not being a toff meself."

dorset, may 15

While watching the fish in the millrace today, I glimpsed something go through that looked like a torpedo.

Immoderate people, the British, especially in their pastimes, their reputation to the contrary notwithstanding. Take my new friend Dr., which is to say Mr., M.

M. is an authority, perhaps *the* authority, on the long-term effects of prisoner-of-war-camp diet on the male urinary system. On this important and insufficiently heeded aspect of war, M. has testified as an expert at war-crimes trials and in many veterans' disability-pension case hearings. This, however, is a study which M. has taken up only in the last few years, and which he pursues only out of fishing season. He is retired from practice.

He retired and came home from Africa to London three years ago, then moved down here, where he has the fishing on Thursdays and Fridays on a half-mile beat on the Frome, and Mondays, Tuesdays, and Wednesdays on a three-quarter-mile beat on the Piddle, sublet from Mitchell, the meat-pie king. Saturdays he plays the football pools.

2 5 4

I met M. in the farmyard yesterday afternoon when my wife and I came in from our bike ride over the heath. He was wearing waders and was busy rigging up a bamboo fly rod. I watched him do it. He jointed the rod, first greasing the male ferrule by rubbing it on the wing of his nose, attached the reel, drew the already greased line through the guides, attached a leader (a "cast" they call it here) with a deftly tied central draught knot, opened a fly book, and selected a fly. Holding it between thumb and forefinger he said—his first words to me—"What fly is that?"

I took it from him. I had tied the pattern. "I don't know what you may call it here; we would call that a Gold-ribbed Hare's Ear where I'm from. It's a number 14," I said.

He reached into the trunk of his car (the "boot" they say here) and took out another rod. He jointed this rod, put on a reel, threaded the line through the guides, and handed it to me.

"You'll do," he said. "Come along."

We went past the old gristmill and under the railroad trestle and across the meadow to where his beat of the river begins. A slow, flat, winding, and narrow stream the

Piddle is, never more than ten or twelve feet wide, though just as deep, and choked with water weeds that twine snakily in the current. Along its banks not a tree or a bush to interfere with casting.

We fished for an hour, or rather I fished: M. sat on the bank, smoking his pipe and watching. I do not like to be watched while I fish. In fact, I cannot fish if I'm watched. Cannot even cast my fly properly. And I felt bad that he was giving up his sport, especially knowing how costly it was. He refused to fish, however. "I do it every day," he said. "I want to see you catch something." I caught nothing.

After an hour he announced that it was time for tiffin. I tried to decline half his tea, but when he said that if I did not share it with him he would eat none of it either, I said I would share it with him. So I had half of one of Mr. Mitchell's pork pies, half a cucumber sandwich, half a banana sandwich, and a cup of tea. Afterward I accepted a fill for my pipe from his tobacco pouch. While we smoked, M. told me about himself.

Upon finishing his residency in tropical medicine, he got married, went on a fishing honeymoon to Ireland, returned to London, where he set his wife up in a flat in South Kensington, and shipped out to Nairobi. There he spent the next twenty-five years, returning home on three months' leave every year to fish, and to see his wife. Once in that time he came back for an entire year. He had come into a legacy of £3000, which he spent on salmon fishing in Scotland. Best year of his life. If he should ever win a pot in the football pools, it's what he would do again. His period of service in Nairobi concluded, he came home three years ago, gave up the flat in London and brought his wife (their grown son was now out in Ottawa) down here and bought his fishing. On this beat here he had killed six so far, this early in the season, the biggest one thirty-two pounds.

"A thirty-two-pound trout!" I exclaimed.

"No, no. Not trout. Salmon."

"Salmon! In this little trickle of a stream?"

Now I know what that shape was that passed through the millrace yesterday, its dorsal fin out of water like a periscope.

This evening, telling Tom Mears about my day, I learned why M. did not fish while I was fishing. Here in England when one buys a beat on a piece of water, or subleases as M. does from the meat-pie king, one not only buys a specified number of days of the week, or half-days, one also buys a specified number of rods. What M. has is one rod for his days on his beat. Should he bring along a guest, he may not fish himself. I won't be taking up his invitation to go with him another time. In fact, I must give up hope of fishing in Britain. It's too complicated.

dorset, may 17

So much for yesterday's resolution! I was at my desk this morning when I heard Tom call up from below, "Bill? Come down! Something here I think you'll want to see."

On the bricks of the back court, at the feet of a man in waders, lay the biggest fish I have ever seen. Silver, sleek, shaped like the fuselage of a jet plane. Its jaws were bared in a ferocious snarl. I had never seen one, but I recognized it.

"Yes, that's a right nice cock salmon. Should run to about forty pounds, maybe forty-five," said the man in waders.

I stretched myself out on the bricks beside the fish. We were just about a match.

And from there I lay looking up at Mr. Porky Mitchell with envy and class hatred.

dorset, may 19

"Scotland," said Tom. "There's the place for you. Up there they've got fishing hotels where you can buy rights by the day or by the week."

"Too far. Too expensive."

"Wales, then. Be there by afternoon."

Wales.... The Severn. The Wye. The Usk.... In the county town of Dorchester—Thomas Hardy's Casterbridge—where I went today to get myself outfitted with fishing tackle, I parked my car in the municipal lot.

"Enjoying your holiday over here, are you, sir?" asked

the attendant as he copied onto my ticket the number of my Virginia license plate.

"Very much, thank you."

"First visit to Dorchester? Perhaps I can tell you some of the sights to see."

"Very kind of you. As a matter of fact, I've been here before."

"What! Here to Dorchester?"

"Why, yes."

"What would ever bring you back a second time?"

"Well, what has brought me back several times is my interest in your great man, Hardy."

"Mr. Hardy, is it? I knew him well. I was his driver."

"His driver! Were you really? You fascinate me!"

"Do I then? Well, so I was! Yes, Mr. Hardy had one of the very earliest automobiles in Dorchester. A fine big Daimler it was, the kind they don't make anymore. I used to run him up to London every month. We did it always in under three hours. Loved speed, he did."

"Loved speed? Now I should never have expected that!" (He used to get about the town on a tricycle.)

"'George, faster!' he would say. 'George' (that's me) 'faster!' Ah, he was a fine man, and when he died he remembered me in his testament. I keep a photo of him here in the hut."

"Do you! Well, that is wonderful! You must cherish a very tender memory of him."

"I do. I do. Be glad to show it to you, if you'd care to see it."

"I'd love to see it!"

The photograph—framed—bore only a faint resemblance to Hardy. I said, "This doesn't look much like other portraits of him I have seen."

"Oh, you're wrong there, sir. I knew him well and that's caught him, all right. A speaking likeness, that. Yes, yes. Built some of the very finest houses in this town, did Mr. Hardy."

I knew that Hardy had spent a long apprenticeship as an architect, but it seemed hardly the thing to remember him for. "What's more important," I said, "he wrote some of the best novels and some of the most beautiful poems in the language."

"That will be the brother," said the parking-lot attendant. "It's Mr. *Henry* Hardy we're speaking of, the building contractor. Ah, he was a fine man, and it's a pleasure to talk to you about him."

My tackle consists of my rod: a two-handed ten-foot second-hand Farlow which looks as if it has caught a great many fish; line: oiled silk, torpedo-head taper, FBG; two hundred feet of backing, thirty-pound test; reel; hobnailed hip boots; two dozen gaudy big double-hooked salmon flies; gaff; two books on the salmon, his habits, and how to catch him. Or rather, no. One does not catch a salmon. One kills a salmon. The distinction resembles that preserved in English between the verbs "to murder" and "to assassinate": ordinary citizens are murdered, leaders are assassinated. So with the King of Fish. He is not caught, like your perch or your pike or your lowly pickerel. He is killed.

Mr. Porky Mitchell's peculiar word is now explained: salmon, male and female, are called cocks and hens, I learn from my books. The salmon appears to be a very odd fish.

ross-on-wye, may 21

In the spring a salmon's fancy also turns to thoughts of love. Not a young salmon's but an old salmon's. And not lightly. With the single-mindedness of a sailor returning home after a four-year cruise without shore leave.

The salmon is anadromous. That is to say, he leads a double life, one of them in freshwater, the other in saltwater. His freshwater life may be said to be his private, or love life; his saltwater life his ordinary, or workaday life. The salmon reverses the common order of human affairs: a lot is known about his private life but nothing at all about the rest. We get the chance to study him only when the salmon is making love. For when the salmon, aged two, and called at that stage a parr, leaves his native river and goes to sea (to be a smolt until he returns to spawn, whereupon he becomes a grilse), nobody, not even Professor

Jones, D. Sc., Ph.D., Senior Lecturer in Zoology, University of Liverpool, whose book *The Salmon* I am reading, knows where he goes or how he lives, whether in the sea he shoals together with his kind or goes his separate way, why some stay there longer than others or why some return home in the spring and others not until the autumn. He disappears into the unfished regions, or the unfished depths, or both, of the ocean, and is not seen again until—it may be as little as one year or as much as four years later—impelled by the spawning urge, he reenters the coastal waters and the estuaries and up the rivers to his native stream like some missing person returning after an absence of years from home.

Nothing of what the salmon does in the sea is known, only what he does not do: namely, reproduce himself. He cannot. For his mating and for the incubation of his off-spring, fast-flowing freshwater is required. And he can't, or won't, or at least would a lot rather not spawn in any but the same stream in which he himself was spawned. This may be far inland, perhaps deep in the mountains of Wales, and he, when he begins to feel the urge, may be in the Baltic Sea—in tagging experiments salmon have been tracked as far as sixteen hundred miles from their native streams. No matter—home he heads, and, what is even more remarkable, he knows how to find his way back. He does it, they think, by smell.

By 1653, when Walton published *The Compleat Angler*, tagging experiments had already shown that salmon, if they can, return to their native rivers to spawn. Walton writes,

> Much of this has been observed by tying a *Rib-band* or some known *tape* or *thred* in the tail of some young *Salmons*, which have been taken in Weirs as they swimm'd toward the salt water, and then by taking a part of them again with the known mark at the same place at their return from the Sea...and the like experiment hath been tryed upon young *Swallowes*, who have after six moneths absence,

2 5 9

been observed to return to the same chimney,
there make their nests and habitations for the
Summer following: which has inclined many to
think, that every *Salmon* usually returns to
the same river in which it was bred, as young
Pigeons taken out of the same *Dove-cote,* have
also been observed to do.

Since Walton's time, much thought and many inge-
nious experiments have sought answers to the questions,
why and how the salmon does this. Memory? Instinct?
The "conclusion" of these, up to now, is Professor Jones's
hypothesis that each river has its characteristic odor, and
that throughout the period of his wanderings in the sea
the salmon retains a memory of, one may say a nostalgia
for, this odor. Neither Professor Jones nor anybody else
knows how the salmon finds and follows the trail of this
scent through hundreds and hundreds of miles of salt
seawater. This smell Professor Jones supposes to be a
complex one, composed of many things, chemical and
physical, owing to the different substances dissolved in
the water, and it is this complexity which makes the
scent of each river unique and unmistakable to its
salmon offspring. One is asked to imagine the salmon
working his way home past tributaries where the scent is
almost but not quite the one he is seeking, like the hero
of Proust's *Remembrance of Things Past* almost succeeding but repeatedly just failing to recapture the sense of
happiness that came to him momentarily with the taste
of the *petite madeleine* dipped in tea, until finally the
flavor reminds of when he last tasted it and his mind is
flooded with recollections of his childhood vacations at
his Aunt Léonie's house in Combray.

Salmon do have a very fine sense of smell. Migrant
salmon on their way upstream have been seen to shy and
scatter when a bear put its paw in the water above them.
Also when a very dilute solution of the odor of the human
skin was put in the water above them. And they do not
respond this way when the odor introduced into the water
is not one they associate with one or another of their natu-

ral enemies. So their sense of smell is not only sharp, it is highly discriminating as well.

Say that he is *my* salmon, the one I am hoping to catch —kill, that is—a native of the parts I am headed for, a salmon of the River Teme, in mid-Wales. Through the sea he will have swum at speeds—this too established by tagging experiments—of up to sixty-two miles per day. He will have come, as I have just done, up the Bristol Channel. Off Cardiff he will have gotten his first whiff of fresh water; there the River Taff empties into the Channel, and there he will have rested for some days or even weeks, not from exhaustion, but because too sudden a change from salt water to fresh brings on a shock that can be fatal to him. Then past the Usk on his left, the Bristol Avon on his right, both redolent of the scent he is seeking, but neither just quite the thing itself. At Aust Ferry instead of the Wye he will have known to take the Severn, and to keep on it, ignoring hundreds of tributaries large and small, until just below Worcester, coming in from the left, is that waft which to him is like none other in the world.

The average salmon lives seven years. Thus a year in a salmon's life equals ten years in a man's life. Suppose a man left home at twenty and was gone for forty years, wandering as far as sixteen hundred miles away, and then at sixty he walked back without a map and with nobody along the way to ask directions of, no signposts to guide him, no landmarks: this would be about comparable to the salmon's feat in finding his way back to his native river to spawn. Add obstacles in his path in the form of falls as much as twelve feet high, not to be bypassed, to have to leap.

The salmon is named for his salient characteristic. *Salmo,* from the Latin, means "the leaper," and comes (as does the word salient, by the way) from the verb *salire,* to leap. People came and watched and wondered at the salmon leaping in Walton's time, and they still do. "Next, I shall tell you," Walton writes,

> that though they make very hard shift to get
> out of the fresh Rivers into the Sea, yet they

will make harder shift to get out of the salt
into the fresh Rivers, to spawn or possesse the
pleasures that they have formerly found in
them, to which end they will force themselves
through *Flood-gates,* or over *Weires,* or *hedges,*
or *stops* in the water, even beyond common belief. *Gesner* speaks of such places, as are known
to be above eight feet high above the water.
And our *Cambden* mentions (in his *Brittan-
nia*), the like wonder to be in *Pembrokeshire,*
where the river *Tivy* falls into the Sea, and
that the fall is so downright, and so high, that
the people stand and wonder at the strength
and slight that they see the *Salmon* use to get
out of the Sea into the said River; and the
manner and height of the place is so notable,
that it is known far by the name of *Salmon-
leap.*

262
——— At a pool in Ross-shire, according to Professor Jones,
salmon have been seen making a leap of eleven feet four
inches vertical, and he calculates that to do this the fish
must have been moving at a vertical speed of twenty miles
an hour as they left the water at the foot of the falls. We
saw nothing so spectacular as that; but we joined a small
crowd of people gathered on the bank of a river this afternoon and watched salmon leaping a falls about six feet
high, and their determination and their strength and their
grace, their hardihood even, as they hurled themselves at
what seemed an insurmountable obstacle, some of them
repeatedly falling back as time after time they just failed
to clear the top, drew cheers from all of us who saw it.

It may live as long as nine months more while spawning,
but the moment it re-enters freshwater the salmon has
eaten its last bite.

wales, may 22

Salmon fishing, Professor Jones—himself no angler, he
tells us—observes, is a sport for the well-to-do. While my

wife went inside to check us into the hotel I insinuated my
VW between two new Bentleys parked in the court. An
incensed peacock was pecking at himself in the hubcap of
one of the Bentleys with brainless persistency. Each peck
drew from his beak a dash of his spittle. When he had obli-
terated with his spittle the rival in that hubcap he spread
his tail proudly and went strutting to attack another Bentley hubcap, passing up those of my VW with lordly dis-
dain.

This hotel of ours, patronized by Bentley owners, with
peacocks to decorate its stately lawns, winding, as the bro-
chure puts it, among the lovely valley of the Teme, surrounded by thirty-five acres of parkland and enchanting
gardens, is a nineteenth-century reproduction of a four-
teenth-century Italian villa, with loggias and campanili,
called The Redd. That is not a Welsh word, nor, as one
might think after driving, as we did today, through Fforest
Fawr, a quaint old spelling of red. One who is up on his
salmon lore, as I am fast becoming, knows that a redd is a
salmon's nest.

2 6 3

"They won't be biting tomorrow," said my wife on her
return.

"What?"

"The fish. Won't be biting tomorrow."

"How do you come to know that?"

"Learned it the first thing. Old gentleman just inside the
door was banging a barometer on the wall. Seeing me he
burst into a broad frown and said, 'They won't be biting
tomorrow.' So that's the outlook, my friend."

"Fellow guest?"

"A sample. Others coming out of the woodwork. This is
going to be fun."

"Fishing," said mine host, Mr. Osborne, "is with artificial fly, strictly."

It may be that he says the same thing in the same tone
to his British guests as well, but I thought I detected a
pointedness in the way he said it to me. Turning inside out
the pockets of my chinos, "Haven't got a worm on me," I
said. Mr. Osborne was not amused. Maybe not convinced.

We stood on the flagged terrace overlooking the valley a hundred and fifty feet below, the top of a great pine tree level with our eyes. Below us spread a meadow of vivid green, its pile as regular as wall-to-wall carpeting, grazed by a herd of red Hereford cattle. At four o'clock in the afternoon the river was shadowed by the mountain rising directly behind it. Small pastures and hangers of dark trees dotted the mountainside, and scattered small gray stone farmhouses, low to the ground.

"Still time to have a try at it if you'd like," said Mr. Osborne. "On the house. Go down and have a look at the big pool just there. That was Major Butler's beat today, but he's come in already, having killed a twenty-seven-pound cock. There's more where that one came from."

I went down through the enchanting garden. The rhododendrons, laid out in a maze and growing twelve feet tall, were in full bloom and murmurous with bees. The garden path ended at a five-barred gate. Attached to its right-hand post and swinging at a right angle to the bars was a low hinged gate at the top of the long flight of wooden steps leading down to the water. A woman in a tweed suit and wearing a felt hat stood at this gate, her back to me, watching something below so intently that I had to hem and then hem again and finally to say, "Excuse me, please." She turned then, slowly, not startled, for it was plain that she had heard all my little signals, and gave me a smoldering look. I am writing this before going to bed, but it is not because of what came later that I say it: her look was smoldering. She was deep in reverie. And yet she was quite aware of me. Aware of and quite indifferent to me, even disdainful of me, and, far from embarrassed and trying to hide the mood I had surprised her in, she seemed to flaunt it before me. I have seen such a look in women's eyes before, both hot and haughty—newlyweds often have it: *I have been aroused, yes, but I've got my man, I'm not for you.* Now, however, I am perhaps letting myself be influenced by what came later.

Halfway down the steps I met a man coming up. We brushed in passing, so narrow was the way. But I did not see his face nor think to return his "Good afternoon" to me until it was too late, still burning as I was from the woman's look.

Above the pool the water was fast and broken, but at the pool it broadened and deepened and flattened out. Above the still surface of the pool hovered a mist of mayflies performing their nuptial flight, rising and dipping like swallows at evening, the females dropping to the surface for an instant to deposit their eggs, others, their mating and with it their brief lives over, falling spent to the water on outspread wings. The faint, barely audible sound, as of a bubble bursting, which a dimpling trout makes as it sucks in a fly, was multiplied so many times it sounded as though the pool were at a slow boil. Then as I watched, trout, mostly small, began to leap for the hovering flies, rising straight out into the air and straining upright on their tails on the surface of the water like trained puppies begging. Then I heard a wallop and a heavy splash and out of the corner of my eye saw spray and then saw rings rippling outward in widening circles that rapidly covered the entire pool from bank to bank. I took the steps up three at a time and, flinging open the gate, nearly hit in the back the man I had met coming down. He was talking to the woman. Neither of them took notice of me.

On the way downstairs in the hotel, rod, gaff, fly book in hand, I met my wife.

"How does it look?" she asked.

"Scary. There's one old sockdolager in there that if I should hook him is liable to pull me in and chomp off a leg."

"I'll come along and protect you," she said.

"Come on then! Because they're not going to be biting tomorrow."

We went back down the path toward the gate. Nearing it, I saw something that made me take my wife's elbow and steer her aside and hustle her down an alley of rhododendrons until we got where I felt I could safely speak. I said, "Go quietly out there and look down that way and come back and tell me if you see what I think I just saw."

When she finally tore herself away and came back to me, my wife said, "If I hadn't seen it for myself—"

"I still don't," I said.

But another look convinced me.

"Right up there against that gate," I said to my wife. "In public. In broad daylight."

"Not fifty yards from the hotel," said my wife. "All rooms booked."

"Standing up," I said. "Fully clothed."

"I don't believe it either," said my wife. "I'd better take another look to convince myself."

"You've looked your fill already," I said.

"Do you suppose," said she, "that they're married?"

"To each other, do you mean?"

"Can we get back to the house that way around the bushes?"

"We're not going back to the house."

"What are we going to do, watch?"

"Wait."

So, me thinking of all those fish on the rise and especially of the one that had made that mighty wallop, those tidal waves, we waited. I timed them quite generously, I thought, then I went and peeked around the rhododendrons. They were at it still. I rejoined my wife, who was beginning to find my role in this highly comical. That hatch of flies would soon end and with it the evening rise. Why was I being so discreet for two such flagrant fornicators? Taking my wife by the hand I strode boldly out and down the path. The man's back was to us, hers was braced against the five-barred gate. He was hunched low, of necessity, and over his shoulder her face was visible, her head thrown back and her eyes closed. At the stage of his work, or rather his pleasure, to which he had arrived, or was arriving, he was oblivious to our approach. I observed in passing that he was gray-haired and getting bald on the crown, and also that rings glinted on the fingers with which she clasped him to her, one of them a gold wedding band. I opened the gate narrowly—there was not room to open it wider—and my wife passed through. At that moment the lady opened her eyes and looked over her partner's shoulder and, seeing me, smiled like a cat being stroked and then let her eyes close again. I squeezed through the gate and down the stairs to the river, where I caught nothing.

Before dinner, to the bar (club license, membership open to guests upon payment of nominal subscription, good for length of stay) for a drink and curious for a closer look at our country copulatives of the afternoon. Passing the various tables and overhearing the conversations was like walking down an English street and hearing every house's telly tuned in on the same channel. Remarks sometimes rather muffled coming through thick military-style mustaches. "Jock Scott. Twenty-pound gut. Let it go past his snout, then lunged at it. Straight upstream taking the line clean down to the backing. Thought for a moment I'd foul-hooked him." Most of the gentlemen had dressed for dinner, the ladies all wore dinner gowns. Men in their sixties, women in their forties.

We never did see our siren of the garden gate again, nor did we recognize her partner (whose face neither of us had ever seen) until, on our way in to dinner en masse, my wife nudged me, nodded and whispered, "There. There's our man. I'd know that back anywhere." She had certainly spotted him. He could have been thus identified for arrest. But though unmistakable from the rear, Holloway, as he is known to all, or "poor Holloway," or "poor old Holloway," seen from the front, even allowing for his advantage of ten years over the rest, he being not much beyond fifty, looked as unlikely as any of them to be the Priapus we had seen perform earlier in the day. He was low-built, balding, and gray, as I noted earlier, getting paunchy, and, except for the ruddy tip of his nose, pallid in complexion. Nor did he look to me as if he quite belonged to those well-to-do whom Professor Jones says salmon fishing is the sport of. The guests at this place all know one another, being regulars who return year after year with the fish, and Holloway is treated by all as an old companion and equal. But I sensed that he was not. Between them and him I sensed a subtle but essential difference. Like the difference between one of Fortnum & Mason's old customers and one of its old salesclerks.

Wondering what sort of place this was where such a thing could happen as we had seen in the garden this afternoon, I played with the notion, whether he might not be on the payroll, like the tennis and riding instructor—an unadvertised attraction, of course: the salmon for the gentlemen, he for the salmon widows—until, as we were rising from our tables after dinner to leave, I saw him do a thing which, while it confirmed my suspicion that he was not to the sporting classes born (and one does not belong unless born to them), strongly suggested that he was not a member of the staff: he took from his blazer pocket a ball-point pen and on the label of his wine bottle drew a line to mark the level of his consumption.

I forgot to note that he was unaccompanied and dined at a table for one. He was the only gentleman who dined alone, though some ladies did. These, I'm told, are widows —some of them quite youngish widows—who since the death of their angler husbands return regularly to The Redd for their holidays out of loyalty to their memories.

Even in Britain, where it is much more plentiful than it is in most countries, fresh salmon sells at the fishmonger's for fifteen shillings upward a pound. To quote Professor Jones, "The days are long past when apprentices in Britain petitioned against being given salmon to eat more than twice a week. The eating of salmon in Britain is now a luxury." And that fifteen-shilling salmon on sale at the fishmonger's is commercially caught salmon, from the coastal trawlers' nets. What a pound of salmon costs the sportsman who, like Mr. Porky Mitchell, has leased a beat on a river, or one who has traveled to Wales or Scotland and put up at some place like The Redd, and who may go for years without even hooking a fish, it is not possible to calculate: it must come close to the cost of those humming-birds' tongues served at the feasts of the Roman emperors.

So when our fellow guest, Major Butler, instead of having that twenty-seven-pound cock he killed today boxed in ice and shipped home, as he might have done, had it served with his compliments to his fellow guests for dinner this evening, I thought this was a very generous gesture on his part until I tasted it. Salmon in Britain is poached ("in

great numbers," runs the joke) in milk. The taste is de-
scribable. Poached milk.

At the table next to ours, with his lady, sat the old gentleman my wife met first, the one banging the barometer
in the hall and predicting "they won't bite tomorrow," and
after dinner we four drank coffee together in the lounge.
Each spring for forty-two years, with time out for wars,
Admiral Blakey has left the deep salt sea with the salmon
and followed them up the Teme to The Redd, though for
the last three of those years, on doctor's orders, he has not
fished. This he tells me with quiet pride. But his wife: her
smile looks forty-two years old. A Navy widow for most of
the year, then on her holidays a salmon widow for forty-
two years. I am reminded of the latest bit of lore I have
learned from Professor Jones: "Those female salmon which
for lack of opportunity or other reasons do not spawn, and
which ultimately reabsorb their genital products (which
fill their entire body cavity), are called *baggots*, or
rawners." I know I shall never cast fly over water again
without seeing in memory Mrs. Blakey's baggotty smile,
and feeling a twinge of complicity.

It was Holloway who led the general male exodus to bed
following the nine-o'clock news on the telly. They had had
a strenuous day on their beats (Holloway had had on his, I
could vouch), and must be up and out early for another one
tomorrow, besides, "We're not as young as we were, are we,
Tom?"—one of those remarks which you know the first
time you hear it you're going to be hearing again, often.
Many of them needed to be awakened in their armchairs
and sent off to bed by their wives. Not Holloway, the first
to retire, who has none. Watching him go, the Admiral
shook his head so many times I decided he too had been
behind a rhododendron watching this afternoon's tryst at
the garden gate.

"Poor old Holloway," the Admiral at length sighed and
said. It was then that I learned the name. "Poor bugger.
You've got to admire perseverance like that."

I evinced interest.

"Fishes here. Fishes below here. Fishes above here," said
the Admiral, sighing and shaking his head. "Fishes the

Usk. The Severn. The Wye. Twenty years he's been fishing
and never has caught a fish yet. Now that takes character.
That is what I call sportsmanship. I mean to say, we're
here to fish not to catch fish and all that—still, twenty
years! I've been a keen angler in my time, but I do not
believe I could have carried on with no more encourage-
ment than that. Ah, but you should see the poor fellow on
his beat! Can't handle his rod. Never knows where his fly
will light, or if it will—he's got it caught in the trees more
than he's got it in the water. Slips and falls while he's wading at least once a week and comes in half-drowned. Comes
down with the grippe—that Teme water's cold this time of
year—and we—the women, that is—have to take turns
nursing him. I don't know how many times he's hooked
himself on his back cast and had to be taken to the surgeon
to have the fly cut out. Nasty thing, a three-ought Jock
Scott in the earlobe. And yet the man carries on and keeps
coming back for more. Never complains. Actually seems to
enjoy himself here. Always cheerful. Always hopeful. Jolly
good sport about it, too. Takes any amount of ribbing and
takes it with a smile. Not many like that. It wants pluck."

"Never married?" I asked.

"Oh, no. No, no. Confirmed bachelor."

Though his days on the stream are over and he will
never cast a Jock Scott again, the Admiral retires, at his
wife's reminder, at half past nine. I last see him giving the
barometer a final bang, then going slowly up the stairs
shaking his head. Shortly afterward the bar comes alive
for the night and Holloway is down again in time for the
first round, the only unattached man. And while the veteran brothers of the angle alone upstairs in their beds
sleep the simple sleep of Father Isaak Walton, poor old
Holloway reigns over their wives like a pasha in his
harem, or like a cock salmon among the hens on the
spaw. . . .

The scream of a woman being murdered was what made
me break off. I thought at the time it was the scream of a
woman being murdered. Now five minutes later I don't
know what to think. For I was alone when I dashed into
the hallway in my pajamas, except for Holloway, also in

his, who, in tiptoeing from the door of his bedroom to that
of another one not his, gave me a wink in passing from
which I inferred he was not going to the aid of a lady having her throat slowly slit.

wales, may 23

The woman screamed all night long at irregular intervals
of from a quarter to half an hour, stopping only at day-
break. She was not being murdered, then, only tortured.
Yet at breakfast this morning none of the other men (we
anglers breakfast while our wives are still in bed) indicated by word or look that he had heard anything un-
toward in the night. They can't have slept through it.
Impossible. Is this something known and accepted by all
the regulars, one of those things one doesn't speak about?
Would it not be in bad taste of me to mention what everyone else overlooks? Can poor Mr. Osborne, like Jane Eyre's
Mr. Rochester, have a lunatic earlier wife attached to the
wall by a chain somewhere in an outlying wing who howls
by night? If so, I wouldn't want to be the one to draw attention to it.

I felt conspicuous enough already, dressed as I would
dress to go fishing back home, in old blue jeans, a blue
work shirt I once wore to paint a red barn, and my Brooklyn Dodgers baseball cap, while my fellow guests wore
Harris Tweed jackets, drill-cord riding breeches, tweed
hats from Lock's, and neckties.

After breakfast—eggs with salmon—we drew lots for
our beats on the river. It had begun to rain in the night so
we all set off in rain gear—I in my plastic mac—over our
waders and hip boots, and with our pipes turned down. I
speak not only for myself when I say that our turned-down
pipes, with rain dripping from them, perfectly symbolized
our spirits. A north wind was blowing, and "when the wind
is in the north, then the fisherman goeth not forth"; Admiral Blakey, with forty-two years of barometer-banging behind him, had foretold that they wouldn't be biting today;
and the rain was coming down in spouts. Some of us might
have turned back, but for the presence of Holloway in our

midst. That shamed us for our faintheartedness. Gaff in hand, like a bishop's crook, he set an example for anglers everywhere to follow. If he, with his dismal record, could carry on undismayed, we could, we must.

The rain had washed all the hubcaps clean and bright and the peacock found himself surrounded this morning by fresh rivals.

One fishes for salmon in waters one may oneself safely drink, waters of the clearest crystal—when not in spate, that is. For the salmon is the most fastidious of fish and does not tolerate the least pollution. His sensitivity to human wastes and to the wastes of manufacture kills him or else drives him away in disgust.

The Teme is a spring river. That is to say, its salmon return to spawn in the spring. Other rivers are fall rivers; their salmon return in the fall. But all salmon spawn in the fall, including those that come back into the rivers in the spring. And while they wait, some of them for up to nine months, they fast.

Can it really be true that salmon, such voracious eaters in the ocean, once they re-enter freshwater, fast? Fast absolutely? Fast to the death? All salmon? All salmon fast, absolutely, and all but a few of them fast to the death. Not much is certain about this little-known though much-studied fish, but that much is. Never a trace of food has been found in the dissected insides of one, not even those known to have been in the river for periods of up to nine months. People have always found this hard to credit, and it was once widely believed that none was ever caught with food in its stomach because they vomited on being hooked. Not so. They quit eating.

Then why will they—sometimes—strike at a fisherman's fly? Or a shrimp (prawn, they say here)? Or a fly tied to imitate a prawn? Or a minnow? Or a spinner made to imitate a minnow? Or a gob of worms on a hook? Why, indeed? To this, the oldest and most intriguing question about the salmon, you will not find the answer even in Professor Jones's book (about which I am beginning to feel as the little girl felt about the one she was assigned to review, and reviewed so pithily, to wit: This book tells me more about penguins than I care to know). Professor Jones speculates that it may be done out of irritability, and anyone who has ever seen a salmon (I am thinking now of the male salmon) taken from the spawning bed can easily see why he should think so. The salmon at this stage looks irritable. In fact, he looks downright ferocious, deformed by his single-minded obsession with sex.

What does the salmon live on? Love; that's the obvious answer. But he's not living, he's dying. This is going to be the death of him. He's eating himself alive: all that stored-up deep-sea fat, and not just fat, muscle, too. As he lies in the pool doing nothing, not even eating, from March until September, his idle mind on evil thoughts, his disused alimentary organs shrink and shrivel and practically disappear to make room for the gonads that swell and swell and swell until that is all he—or she—is inside. Meanwhile the silver sheen he came in with from the sea turns dull, and his meat turns red and kipper. The male grows a growth, called a kype, on the tip of his underjaw, forcing it away from the upper one, which also develops a hook, giving to his expression a rapacious snarl.

When the time comes for the salmon to spawn—when the female is "running ripe"—after a brief courtship in the quiet of the pools, they move upstream into the swift water. It is there that the eggs must be laid because they require for their incubation constant percolation of the water through the gravel surrounding them in their redd.

It is as impossible for a salmon as it is for you or me to tell whether another salmon is a male or a female just by looking. For much of their lives they don't care. When the time comes to care the salmon have a way of telling who's who, or rather, who's what. A salmon sidles up to another salmon and quivers. If the other fish quivers in response then it's a male like himself, but if it turns over on its side and begins flapping its tail on the river bottom, then it's a match.

When she is ready to spawn the female salmon begins "cutting." That is, flapping her tail against the river bottom so hard she digs a hole in the gravel. With her anal fin she keeps feeling the hole until she is satisfied with the

2 7 3

depth of it. It must be about a foot deep to suit her. When she is satisfied with it she crouches over the hole. Thereupon the male salmon joins her. He draws alongside her without touching. He begins to quiver eagerly. She gapes. He gapes.

For lunch today my wife was served *croquettes de saumon*. I had one of my old friend Mitchell's meat pies in a box put up for me by the hotel. For me, Admiral Blakey's glum prediction proved accurate and I returned fishless and as wet as a fish myself. But for two of my fellow guests, I heard with an envious heart, a game smile, and a sinking appetite, the day yielded salmon of large size. Again all night long every few minutes that woman screamed, and again we were the only ones to notice it. Only long familiarity with it can explain the self-composure of our fellow guests. That, or the well-known British self-discipline. As for me, I don't think I could ever get used to it. It curdles my American blood. The first time it happened I bolted from bed and into the hall again. I was still there listening for it to come again when poor old Holloway emerged from his room and went tiptoeing past in his pajamas. He gave me his wink, and, in my amazement, I believe I may have returned it.

The mating of salmon, concluded:

It is concluded, all but. That was it. A union without contact between the partners, a crouch, a quiver, a mutual gape. It not only doesn't look like much fun, from the human point of view; when you remember what a long way they've come, past what snares and ambushes, over almost insuperable obstacles, how they have gone hungry and grown disfigured, and knowing as you do that it will prove fatal, it seems pitifully unworthy of the trouble. A cheat. There is worse to come.

Friends, if you have tears prepare to shed them now. I know I nearly did when I got to the chapter in Professor Jones's book in which in cold ichthyological prose he relates the betrayal, the ignominy which now overtakes this grand fish.

For the sake of this moment the salmon has swum maybe fifteen hundred miles through nobody knows what perils of the deep. He has—and he is one of the few that have—eluded the trawlers' nets and the fishmonger's cold slate slab, or, more ignoble end still, the cannery. He will not have come this far without having felt the barb and fought free of some of the many Jock Scotts and Black Doses and Silver Doctors dangled temptingly before him. He has leaped twelve-foot-high falls. He has survived gill maggots, fin worms, leeches, boils, white rot, white spot, gill catarrh, fungus, carp lice, sea lice. For this he has fasted, for this he will die. Now he is about to achieve fulfillment of his desire. The female has finished her cutting. With her anal fin she has felt out the redd and found it satisfactory. He now hangs alongside her, quivering eagerly. She crouches. She gapes. He gapes. She sheds some of her eggs, about nine hundred of them. Now begins for him the release of some of that pent-up milt which in two ripe testes fills his entire body. And from out of nowhere, more often than not, some impudent little Holloway of a parr darts in and discharges his tuppence worth! This little delinquent may be no more than four inches long. *He* has swum no seas. *He* has leapt no falls. *He* has foiled no Englishman armed with two-handed rod of split bamboo. He has been nowhere, done nothing, cheeky little imp. Yet this little love thief, this mischievous minnow scarcely out of his caviarhood, has just cuckolded a cock salmon some two hundred times his size, right under his nose, so to speak, and has cheated him of his paternity as well; for puny as they are, they are potent, these precocious parr.

But then the old cock was once a parr himself and played the same trick on his elders and betters in his youth.

After shedding her eggs the female salmon moves a little ways upstream and begins cutting another redd. She is killing two birds with one stone. For the gravel raised in the cutting of this new redd is carried downstream by the current and covers the eggs she has just deposited.

Back at the hotel, today for lunch there were *timbales de saumon*.

wales, may 27

The mystery of the woman who screams in the night is solved. My wife finally mustered the courage to speak of it to one of the other ladies. It's the peahen. It's the mating season for them, too, and peahens, it seems, do that at this time. My God, said my wife, what does her mate do to her to make her scream like that? Or not do to her to make her scream like that, said the other lady, vain, self-infatuated creature; had you thought, my dear, of that?

And so life for a salmon begins not in but under a river, where, along with eight or nine hundred of his brother and sister caviar, his mother has buried him. That will have been in the fall. Next spring he hatches out, though remaining inside the redd.

At first the infant salmon is nothing more than a drop of egg yolk with a tail and a pair of bug eyes. This little tadpole is called an alevin.

If he is not found and eaten by another salmon or a trout or washed away in a spate of the river or stepped on by a cow or a wading angler, the alevin, after about a month, by which time his egg sac has been consumed, comes out of the redd into the river a proper little fish, a fingerling or a fry, at which change his actuarial table dips even more sharply. For now he is the prey not only of his cannibal kin and of his cousins the trout, but also of pike, perch, chub, eels, ducks, swans, herons, and cormorants, and of droughts, for the fingerling is even more sensitive than he will be when he grows up to any rise in the water's temperature.

When the young salmon grows to be longer than a man's finger then it is no longer a fingerling. It is then a parr—here in Wales, a sil; in other localities (I am indebted to Professor Jones for this list of delightful names): a pink, a samlet, a peal, a branlin, a skegger (so Walton called them), a locksper, a skirling, a laspring, and a samson.

It's about this time that a salmon finds out whether it's a he or a she. If a she, there is nothing to do but be patient and wait; if a he, then the fun has begun, at the old cocks' expense.

The salmon remains a parr for two years, spending the

whole of the time in his native pool or near it, growing to be about four or five inches long and to weigh about as many ounces. Then the salmon goes to sea, a smolt now. After just one year there it may be a foot and a half long and weigh three pounds or more. If it stays there four years it will come back four or five feet long and weighing forty or forty-five pounds. The salmon is a grilse when it returns to spawn, a kelt after having done so.

Thus one salmon in his time plays many parts, his acts being seven ages: egg, alevin, fingerling or fry, parr, smolt, grilse (cock or hen), and, last scene of all, which ends this strange eventful history, kelthood and mere oblivion, sans teeth, sans eyes, sans taste, sans everything.

Unless it be a hen and she turns out an old maid, and then she has another: baggott, or rawner.

Lunch today: *quenelles de saumon.*

wales, may 28

Every time I'm just about to doze off to sleep the peahen screams. What can he be doing to her?

In the evening, after dinner, before trooping off to bed, we anglers attend to our tackle.

Rather than disjoint our rods at the end of the day only to have to joint them again early on the morrow, we stand them jointed in a rack inside the ground-floor gentlemen's loo (as it's called here), to the right just inside the front door, opposite the barometer. There too we leave our gaffs and our rain gear, our muddy boots and waders, and there after dinner we go to get our reels and unwind our wet lines to hang them out to dry overnight. The open but covered loggia provides an ideal place for this, and we stretch them between brass hooks in the walls. Then those—and I am one of them—who favor knotted tapered leaders (or casts) over the knotless ones which are sold by the tackle shops, convinced that they sink better—and a leader must sink, for otherwise it casts a shadow, and nothing frightens a fish like a shadow—those, I say, who think as I think, sit snipping from their spools lengths of monofilament nylon of graduated gauges and joining them together with good blood knots pulled tight. Meanwhile others of us tie flies out of feathers and fur and tinsel. This done, we hone the barbs of our hooks, which from striking against gravel and stones in the stream all day have become blunted. Many a good fish has gotten away thanks to a blunt hook, and it is Admiral Blakey's judgment that the logbook (more on this later), in which not once in twenty years does Holloway's name appear, might tell a different story if instead of making a bloody fool of himself among the ladies after dinner he spent his time sharpening his hooks. Then we oil our reels and we patch any holes or rips in our waders and boots and then we yawn and we recall the strenuous day we have had on the beat and tell one another that we must be up and out early for another one tomorrow and we remind ourselves that we are not as young as we once were and we excuse ourselves to the ladies and then we go up to bed.

Today for lunch there was *soufflé de saumon*. There is a gap of a day in my diary.

I came in wet and fishless late yesterday afternoon, to find in my bed, where she had spent the day, going without lunch, my own salmon widow. The mood of the place and the season was upon her. On my approaching near and giving a quiver, she responded by showing a readiness to spawn. Indeed, she was running ripe; as for me, I grew a kype on the spot. We passed up supper, fasting instead, and came down late this morning, feeling and looking rather kelt.

If a wink can be said to be broad, Holloway's was to me at cocktail time this evening.

Is it a leftover bit of old sympathetic magic—drink your enemy's blood, eat his flesh, and thereby acquire the power to think as he thinks before he thinks it—that lies behind this unbroken diet of salmon?

Three years have gone by since Admiral Blakey last felt the thrill of a taut line, and for the last couple of years before that his catch was small as the limit of the reach of his arm was exceeded by his progressive farsightedness, and the growing smallness of fishhooks' eyes forced the old angler to set forth in the morning with his Jock Scott tied on his leader for him and to have to abandon his sport and trudge home if through misadventure he lost it and could find no younger brother of the fraternity along the stream bank to tie on another one for him.

Now that his angling is ended, the Admiral's evenings, like the Admiral's days, are spent in catching, or rather re-catching fish, in memory. Admiral Blakey's memory for fish is naturally retentive, and this is in contrast to his memory for any and everything else. His wife must prompt him whenever he tries to recall any of their children's Christian names, but he can and, what is worse, does tell you the weight of, down to the odd ounces, and the weather, wind, and water conditions attendant upon the killing of every fish he ever killed in his life. And you can be man or woman indifferently for the Admiral to tell you this; he no more knows the sex of his listener than a salmon past quivering knows who, that is to say what, he is communicating with. The man's talk, like the menu of this hotel, is always the same. He has caught a lot of fish in his time, and has more stories to tell about them—and the ones that got away—than a hen salmon has eggs.

The Blakeys have four children. He had a little trouble recalling exactly how many there were of them, but she reminded him with such positiveness I could not but think the number corresponded to the number of their conjugal embraces, lifetime. Despite myself, under the influence of this place I tried to imagine one of those embraces. The most I could conjure up was something with about as much intimacy of contact as that between the cock salmon and the hen. I pictured the two of them lying side by side without touching, and after a while gaping together.

I could never in the course of our acquaintance—short, to be sure, though it got to seem very long before it ended —form any image of the admiral in Admiral Blakey. Here was a man who had risen to a post of supreme command in a profession fabled in story and song, and it all seemed to have passed over him without leaving a trace, supplanted by the sport he had pursued. He never reminisced about his naval adventures, his imagery was not drawn from ships or the sea, his talk was as un-nautical as a cotton farmer's. He had but his one topic, and had I had the rights

of those bygone apprentices, I should certainly have petitioned against being served it more than twice a week.
True, I had my chance to study Admiral Blakey only while
at The Redd during spawning season; of what he is like
during the rest, which is the greater part, of the year, I
know no more than any of us knows of the salmon's life in
the sea. He may get it all out of his system during his one
month here and on leaving have no more interest left in
angling than a kelt has in sex, for all I know about it. If
this be so, however, I fear it may leave the old gentleman
quite spent, with no topic for talk at all, and to this fear I
am prompted by the unbroken silence which at table, as
well as at all other times, reigns between him and his wife.

The Admiral's memory for fish, as I said, is naturally good.
But in telling my wife that the wind was south-southwest at
seven miles an hour, the barometer at 29.44 inches and
rising, the water low and clear, that he was using a 2/0
Durham Ranger on a ten-pound gut when at 4:42 p.m., June
10, 1929, after a fight lasting twenty-one minutes, he killed
a hen salmon measuring thirty-four and one half inches and
weighing thirty-two pounds six and three-quarter ounces,
the Admiral is assisted in the details by a promptbook here
in the hotel. This document, in eighty-nine volumes, one for
each year going back to 1881, is a record of every fish ever
caught here by the hotel's every guest, with all attendant
circumstances. This is the book in which, guest though he
has been for twenty of those years, poor old Holloway's name
never once appears, and neither will poor old Humphrey's, it
begins to seem pretty certain. These volumes provide the
Admiral his reading matter. He spends the day poring over
them and chuckling to himself, and he is only too happy to
share his pleasure with any lady who happens along. In the
current one, kept not in the bookcase along with the rest but
out on a table in the salon, I had seen, despite all my contriv-
ances not to see them, my more fortunate—more skillful,
should I not say?—fellow anglers taking turns making their
entries for the day while digesting their salmon in the evening.

This evening I was perusing the volume for 1934, mar-
veling again at the British national sense of honor that

would entrust the keeping of a fishing log to the fisherman themselves, when my wife got off the Admiral's hook and he joined me.

"Nineteen thirty-four!" said the Admiral, and over his watery eyes spread the mist of happy recollection which the mention of any one of the last forty-two years excluding the very last five can produce. "The eighteenth of June, 1934! There's a day I shall always remember, and yet you won't find it noted in the book there. I'd drawn number six as my beat that day. A rainy day it was, barometer at thirty inches and steady, the wind out of the west at nine miles an hour, gusting up to fourteen. My rod was a Leonard, thirteen feet long, mounted with a 6/0 Hardy reel. My line was a King Eider silk, backed with three hundred feet of thirty-pound backing. My cast tapered from .060 inches in the butt to .022 in the tippet. I was fishing a 2/0 Silver Wilkinson, having observed in the river quantities of chub minnows which that pattern in that size most closely imitated. It was precisely twelve noon by the clock in nearby Llanblfchfpstdwwy Church tower when I got a strike that very nearly tore the rod from my grip. This fish behaved in a most uncommon manner from the start. As you know, Humphrey, once hooked, a salmon can be generally relied upon to run in the direction in which he invariably faces owing to rheotaxis, also known as rheotropism, namely, upstream. This fish never once made an upstream run; he went steadily, and at a steady speed approximating that of the current, downriver. Within moments he had taken my line and three-quarters of my backing. I put all the pressure on him I dared, giving him the butt of the rod and straining the gut to just under breaking point. There was no turning or raising him. Straight downriver hugging the bed he went as though determined to get back into the sea. I could regain not an inch of my line and I dared not let him have an inch more than he had already. There was but one tactic to adopt: wade with him downstream keeping pressure on him constantly until he should tire. We were, as I said, near Llanblfchfpstdwwy Church, on beat six, and the time was precisely twelve noon. At half past two we passed the ruins of Cwffd-nant-Bwlch Abbey, and I still had regained none of my line. This of course had taken us through beats seven, eight, and nine, where in succession my good friends the Reverend Smythe-Prestwick, may he rest in peace, Colonel Watson, and Mr. Finchley, had very obligingly withdrawn their lines and themselves from the water to allow my fish and me to pass through. Though my rod was bowed into a hoop, the fish swam on untiringly. I began to think perhaps I had foul-hooked him. We went by and through the villages of Mmfcwmmr, Upper Llndwrtfynydd-ar-y-bryn, Lower Llndwrtfynydd-ar-y-bryn, and Bwlch-ddû, and were passing The 23rd Royal Welch Fusiliers—that's a pub—some five miles from our point of contact, when at last I felt him begin to weaken. I now began to reel in steadily, and within another half-mile I got my first sight of him. Or, rather, them. For to my astonishment and delight, I discovered that I had got on not one but two large fish, one to each of the fly's two hooks. A most uncommon occurrence even in the life of a very experienced angler, and so I resolved to have them mounted, side by side and cheek by jowl, sharing the fly. At last I brought them to gaff, and at seven thirty-four p.m. I lifted from the water the biggest pair of waders I believe I ever saw in my life. I said to myself at the time that the man who came out of them would scale sixteen stone. And I was proved right when two days later my good friend Colonel Watson, fishing beat number two, hooked him on a 4/0 Black Dose."

At dinner this evening, or rather at dinner's end, Holloway, after marking the label of his wine bottle, came over to the Blakeys' table.

"Well, Admiral," he said, with a wink at me over the old angler's head. "Well, Mrs. Blakey. It's been lovely seeing you both again. Lovely. I shall look forward to seeing you both again next year. Good-bye."

"Good-bye," said the Admiral.

"Good-bye," said Mrs. Blakey.

"He's going, then, is he?" said the Admiral, shaking his head sympathetically at Holloway's departing back.

"No, dear. We are."
"Oh, yes. To be sure. So we are."

wales, june 1

Fishing demands faith. Faith like St. Peter's when the Lord bade him cast his hook into the water and catch a fish for money to pay tribute to Caesar. To catch a fish you have got to have faith that the water you are fishing in has got fish in it, and that you are going to catch one of them. You still may not catch anything; but you certainly won't if you don't fish your best, and you won't do this without faith to inspire you to do it. You won't approach the water carefully. You won't study the water carefully. You won't cast carefully. You won't fish out your cast: to do this, patience is required, and patience is grounded on faith. You won't fish each stretch of the water thoroughly before giving up on it and moving to the next stretch. The satisfactions of a day's fishing are deep; and just as deep on a day when you don't catch a fish; but unless you keep faith that you are going to catch a fish that day, then fishing seems a waste—a waste of time, money, effort, and, most depressing, a waste of spirit. Faith and faith alone can guard the fisherman against a demon of which he is particularly the prey, the demon of self-irony, from acquiescence in the opinion of the ignorant that he is making a fool of himself. Few things can make a man feel more fully a man than fishing, if he has got faith; nothing can make a man feel more fully a fool if he has not got faith.

After nine days of fishing the Teme without once getting a nibble I had lost my faith. Not my faith that there were fish in the river. They were there, all right. With my own eyes I had seen, and with my own knife and fork had eaten, a miraculous draught of Teme fishes. The fish were there; I had lost my faith that I was going to catch one of them, and my cup of self-irony ranneth over. I cast and I cast and I cast again with that big heavy rod, I beat those waters until my wrists swelled and stiffened and ached me all night long while that peahen screamed, and I marveled

283

how Holloway could make shift to keep on at this drudgery even as a camouflage to the pleasures that he returns here to possesse *(sic)* himself of.

Then this afternoon, defeated, deflated, and dejected, heedless in my approach, clomping along the bank in my heavy, hobnailed boots and casting my shadow I cared not where—the first shadow I had been able to cast since coming into Wales—I came to a bend in the river where the undercutting of the bank by the current made a pool and into this pool I did not cast my Green Highlander, I dismissed it there, with leave to go where it would on its own; I didn't care if I never saw it again.

The big fly lighted at the head of the pool near the opposite bank and quickly sank. Absently I watched the line swing out into the current. I saw it stop. I was hooked on a snag. In my mood this was all I needed and, lowering my rod I grasped the line to break the fly off, disjoint my rod, and go home. But I was using a heavy leader, one bigger in the tippet than any leader I had ever used in my trout fishing back home was in the butt, and it would not break. I gave another angry yank, whereupon my line began to move. I thought I had dislodged the snag from the riverbed and was still hooked to it, until I reflected that an object dislodged from the riverbed would move downstream with the current, not upstream. I had had a strike and had struck back without even knowing it and had hooked the biggest fish of my life.

I reeled in the slack line and raised my rod. He was still on. His run was short. He had gone to the bottom to sulk and I could not budge him. When I put the butt of the rod to him and saw the rod bow and heard the line tighten and felt his size and strength, a sense of my unworthiness came over me and I was smitten with guilt and contrition.

I didn't deserve to land this fish. Fishing without faith, I had done nothing as it ought to be done. He had hooked himself—I just happened to be holding the other end of the line. I pictured him lying there on the riverbed in all his unseen silvery majesty. How mysterious and marvelous a creature he was! I thought how far he had come to get here and of the obstacles he had braved and bested. While keeping pressure on him with my rod held high, I thought of the towering falls he had leapt, driven by the overmastering urge to breed and perpetuate his kind. And here was I about to kill him before he could achieve the hard-won consummation of his desire. It was the king of fish I was about to assassinate. I felt like a cur.

How often in books published by the most reputable houses, with editors who verify their authors' every assertion, had I read with soul dilated of one of that great-hearted breed of dry-fly ascetics who, every time he caught Old Methuselah, the venerable yard-long brown trout of Potts' Pool, put him back—until under cover of darkness one night a clod armed with nightcrawlers and a clothesline unblushingly yanked Old Methuselah out and brained him with a car jack and the magic of Potts' Pool departed forever. I said to my soul now, I won't gaff him. A fish as noble as this deserved a better end than poached in milk or jellied in aspic and garnished with blobs of mayonnaise. I could see myself already, this evening at the hotel, smiling a wistful smile when my fat and fish-fed fellow guests commiserated with me on my day after penning their entries in the logbook. For when I had fought the fish into submission, when I had mastered his valiant spirit with my own even more valiant one, when he turned over and lay floating belly-up at my feet, I would carefully extract the hook and hold him right-side-up and facing into the current until he got his breath back, and then I would bid him go, finned friend, go, my brother, and do not slink in shame, go in pride and intact, gallant old warrior, go, and eschew Green Highlanders.

I would like hell.

I sometimes return a little fish to the water, but I leave it to those knights of the outdoors who contribute articles to the sporting magazines, and who catch so many more of them than I ever will, to put back big ones.

I raised my rod so high it quivered; still the fish clung stubbornly to his spot. Every once in a while the fish would give a little shake of his head, transmitted to me through the taut line, as if to test whether he still had me hooked. I held on. He would let minutes pass, then would wallow and shake his head as if he were enjoying this. It was like having a bull by the ring in his nose and being afraid to let go of it. At one point, resting one of my wrists by holding the end of the rod between my legs, I had a moment of wild wonder at myself, at the question I had just asked myself: did I really want to catch a fish this big? Heretical thought for a fisherman; yet I could not relate this to fishing as I knew it. I was used to exulting when I netted a fourteen-inch trout weighing a pound and a quarter. Now my hopes had been overfulfilled. Truth was, I was scared of the sea monster that I had—or that had me—on the line and couldn't get off.

After fifteen minutes my fish began to move. The drag on my reel was set to just under the breaking strength of my leader, yet he stripped line from the reel with a speed that made the ratchet buzz like a doorbell. I was not wading but was on the bank; now I began to run along the bank—I should say, I was dragged along it. When he had gone a hundred and fifty yards upstream—with me giving him precious line at one point so I could negotiate a fence stile, then sprinting, in hobnailed hip boots, to regain it—he braked, shook his head, then turned and sped downstream a hundred and fifty yards, taking me back over the fence stile. I still had not seen him, and the slant of my line in the water told me I was not going to see him for some time to come. He was deep, hugging the river bottom.

For forty-five minutes he kept this up—I clambered over that fence stile six times from both directions—growing an inch longer and a pound heavier in my mind—my wrists, too—each minute. When he quit it was not gradually, it was all at once, as if he had fought with every ounce of his strength and all his determination up to the very end. I stepped into the shallow water at the edge, and, gaining line, began reeling him toward me. Ten feet from where I stood his dorsal fin broke water. It was three feet back from where my line entered the water; three feet back from it the tip of his tail broke the surface. My mouth was dry with desire. I gaffed him. Or rather, I made a pass at him with the gaff, nicked him, he turned, lunged, and was gone. The line snapped back and wound itself around the rod like a vine. My leader had parted at one of the blood knots I had so tightly tied. There was something detestable in the very shape—curly, coiled, kinky—of the end I was left holding. Imagine a pig the size of a penny and he would have a tail just like that.

I smiled wistfully, all right, that evening at the hotel when the others, penning their entries in the logbook, commiserated with me on my day.

ross-on-wye, june 2

At lunch today—*mousse de saumon*—Holloway drained his bottle of wine. He is moving on further upstream for his annual stay at another fisherman's hotel to try his rotten luck there. Poor old Holloway! You've got to admire perseverance like that. We also were leaving this afternoon, also leaving behind in the logbook no record of our stay. But, with the wind east-southeast and the barometer at twenty-nine inches and falling, using a Green Highlander on a 2/0 hook, I had had one get away that would easily have gone to thirty-five—what am I saying?—forty-five pounds! Up to the end Holloway was still trying. He will be making the spawning run up the Teme and stopping at The Redd again next spring, his twenty-first. The last I saw of Holloway he was teaching a willing pupil, young Mrs. Bradley, whose old husband drew a rather distant beat on the river this morning, a lesson in the gentle art of angling. Which, as Walton's Piscator instances in support of his contention that ours is an art of high esteem, was how Anthony and Cleopatra also whiled away their leisure moments.

And the poor salmon, on whom love seems so hard—do all of them die after spawning? Nine-tenths of them do; of those that survive it, nine-tenths are hens. Professor Jones offers no explanation of why so many more of the males die than the females. At the risk of anthropomorphizing, I would suggest it's from shame at being so often and so openly cuckolded by those pesky parr; except that there is no evidence to indicate that the cock salmon know anything more about what is going on right under their own tails than the anglers did who came to angle for them at The Redd. The widowed hens return, the way we have just come today, to the sea, and there grow fat and sleek and silvery again and then return to spawn another time. Some durable old girls make it back twice more. A few old rips make it back three more times.